Mopping Up !

The War,
Through the Eyes of Bobbie Burns,
Regimental Mascot

by

Lieutenant Jack Munroe
Princess Patricia's Canadian Light Infantry
1914-1918

CEF BOOKS
2007

© Preface, Biography, Editor's Notes, N.M. Christie

Library and Archives Canada Cataloguing in Publication
Munroe, Jack, 1873-1942
   Mopping up! / Jack Munroe.

(Special Limited Edition Reprint series ; 7)
First ed. published: New York: H.K. Fly Co., c1918
ISBN 978 -1-896979-56-4

1. Munroe, Jack, 1873-1942. 2. World War, 1914-1918–Personal narratives, Canadian. 3. Canada. Canadian Army. Princess Patricia's Canadian Light Infantry – Biography. I. Title. II. Series.

D640.M88 2006   940.4'8171   C2006-905762-1

Published by: CEF BOOKS
                    P.O. Box 40083, Ottawa, Ontario
                    CANADA, KIV 0W8.
                    1-613-823-7000, www.cefbooks.ca

Titles in the Special Edition Reprint series (*Available 2007):

1*) Scouting Thrills by Captain George B. McKean,VC, MC, MM;
14th Battalion, C.E.F. (Original 1919)

2*) The 116th Battalion in France, 1914-18 by The Adjutant. (Orig 1921)

3*) The 2nd Canadian Mounted Rifles in France and Flanders, 1914-18 by G. Chalmers Johnston. (Original c.1922)

4*) Private Timothy Fergus Clancy by Will Bird, MM. (Original 1930)

5*) Not Mentioned in Despatches; A Memoir, 1914-1917 by Fred W. Bagnall, 14th Battalion, C.E.F. (Original 1933)

6*) Prisoner 5 - 1 - 11; The Memoir of a P.O.W. By Harry Laird, 4th Canadian Mounted Rifles, C.E.F. (Original 1919)

7*) Mopping Up! by Lieutenant Jack Monroe. P.P.C.L.I. (Original 1918)

8*) Shrieks and Crashes; a Memoir of 1917 by Wilfred B. Kerr, C.F.A

9*) Arms and The Maple Leaf; a Memoir of 1918 by W.B. Kerr, C.F.A.

10) I, That's Me; The story of an Escaper by Major Peter Anderson, DSO & Bar., 3rd Battalion, C.E.F. (Original c.1930)

The Editor would like to thank Linda Horton of Manotick, Ontario.
Cover design by Sean Horton, Manotick, Ontario.

Introduction to the 2007 Edition

Jack Munroe was already a Canadian hero prior to the outbreak of the Great War in 1914. His boxing matches against the world's heavyweight best, including the reigning champ of the time, James. J. Jeffries and the legendary Jack Johnson, had made him an international celebrity. Munroe was also a renowned miner, and had filed many successful claims in Northern Ontario. To add to his reputation he played a dominant role in saving Golden City in Northern Ontario from the great fire of 1911. His fame had spread so widely that his enlistment in 1914 prompted a Canadian author, Jesse Edgar Middleton, to write *The Ballad of Jack Munroe*.

Mopping Up! is Jack Munroe's memoir of the Great War. Although it is creatively told as "Through the Eyes of Bobbie Burns, Regimental Mascot," it is foremost an accurate portrayal of the life of a Canadian soldier, an original member of the Princess Patricia's Canadian Light Infantry, 1914-1915. It is clear by the names and locations mentioned that Munroe has told a very detailed account of the first ten months of the war.

Bobbie Burns was Munroe's faithful companion, a collie whose devotion to his master would make any dog-owner envious. Stories of losing the little dog in Northern Ontario and how, after 10 days and 200 miles, Bobbie found his way home, back to Jack, or how the dog always knew when Jack was returning from one of his prospecting journeys and be waiting for him at the train station, are very touching. The devotion between the two is powerful, and has the feel of a children's movie. *Mopping Up!*, although very charming, is also very sad. Munroe tells of death in the trenches and recounts in detail how many of his good friends died. His accurate recounting of the death of Colonel Farquahar ensures that his story is the real thing and not a child's novel. In the end Jack Munroe paid for his patriotism with almost everything he had. His two good friends were killed, his mighty right arm disabled; and by the end of 1915 this Canadian hero was finished. Only the ever-faithful Bobbie remained of his former life.

The history which unfolds in this book is the story of the raising of the Princess Patricia's Canadian Light Infantry in 1914 and their first actions near Ypres in 1915. A few comments are in order to explain the birth of this famous Regiment.

The Princess Patricia's Canadian Light Infantry, 1914-1918.

The Patricias were the only privately raised Canadian Regiment in the First World War. When War was declared in 1914 there was a huge outpouring of patriotism, which caused thousands of men to enlist. Everybody wanted to get into "It", and there was fear that the war would be over before they could. Hamilton Gault, a wealthy Montrealer, decided he would skip the formal recruiting process, and through his political connections offered a Regiment of infantry directly to the Governor-General, The Duke of Connaught. He promised to put up $100,000 to raise and equip the Regiment, and as an added selling point, he offered to name it after the Duke's daughter, Princess Patricia. His offer was accepted and within months more than 1,000 recruits had collected at Ottawa's Landsdowne Park.

Many of the recruits were former British soldiers. Of the 1,098 original Patricias 1,049 had previous military service. The officers-in-charge were Francis Farquhar and Herbert Buller, both from the Duke's personal staff. Jack Munroe enlisted as a Private, #1769 in "No. 4" Company, with his friends Rob and Fred. The original Pats were 90% British-born with the remainder coming from 11 other countries. Canadian-born enlistments accounted for less than 10% of the complement.

In August 1914 the PPCLI entrained for Levis, Quebec, and in September, sailed to England. After training in England for two months the military experience of their men was recognized and on December 20th, 1914 they crossed the Channel to France to join the 80th Brigade of the 27th Imperial Division. They were the first Canadian unit to see action on the Western front.

Over the next four years the Patricias fought in every major engagement, including Ypres, the Somme, Vimy and Passchendaele. By the end of the war 5,106 men had passed through their ranks, and 1,272 Patricias had been killed and 2,806 wounded.

Mopping Up! is a unique story of the First World War. It is a melancholy account of the early days of battle, of the patriotism and the grim realities of war. The relationship between Jack and Bobbie enhances the initial innocence of the great adventure. It is interesting to note that Eric Knight, author of the children's classic, *Lassie Come Home*, served with the Patricias in 1918. You have to wonder if Knight got his inspiration for Lassie from Bobbie Burns, Regimental Mascot.

Norm Christie
Ottawa, Ontario,
March 2007.

The Ballad of Jack Munroe

Oh, this is the tale of Jack Munroe,
  With arm of iron and fist of brass,
Who fought a Champion long ago!
  (The glittering years! How swift they pass!)
And his back was broad and his eyes were bright
And his soul was square and his spirit light.

He trampled far over the mossy rocks,
  The rocks which bloom into cobalt rose,
Where the geese go past in their arrow flocks,
  Where the spruce sings soft as the Norther blows,
Where the Polar Torches illume the sky
And the mystic lakes of the forest lie.

He came one day to the mining town
  Across the lake in his bark canoe.
He filed his claims and they wrote them down
  And plotted them all, and put them through.
Then they spoke to him, by the veriest chance,
Of the bloody war on the plains of France.

"A war?" he said, with a questing eye.
  "Is England in it?" They answered, "Yes."
Then Jack Munroe raised his head on high
  And answered: "It's up to me I guess.
I have a sister. She gets my coin.
Make out my will. I'm a-goin' to join."

And thus it was that Jack Munroe
  Brought deeds and papers, a goodly store,
To the claim Recorder the miners know
  And saw them behind a good steel door,
And signed his will, and remarked: "So long!
I was always stuck on the bugle's song."

For he said: "It's Duty, and nothing else,"
  And his lips were tight and his smile was grim,
And what are the odds if I don't come back?
"So put me down for the Private's Mess.
  The King is calling, and I'm for him.
And what are the odds if I don't come back?
They named me after the Union Jack."

And so he signed with the "Princess Pats."
  You saw the beautiful regiment start
With the saucy swing and the rakish hats
  And the love of a Girl in every heart.
And this is the stories the miners tell
Of a fighting-man who set out for Hell.

Jesse Edgar Middleton, 1918
(1872 - 1960)

*Lieutenant Jack Munroe and Bobbie Burns, Mascot of the
Princess Pats.*

TABLE OF CONTENTS

To the memory of those

"PRINCESS PATS"

**and their Comrades of all Nations,
Cemented in the Red Bond
for World Freedom,
who have**

"GONE WEST"

INTRODUCING BOBBIE BURNS

Upon a day in April, 1905, Mexico City, as I recall it, was hotter than any other community on the North American continent ever dared to be. Out of the molten glare streaming from heavens of brass I seeped into the rotunda of the Hotel Plaza, an ancient stone pile which somehow brought one's thoughts back to the days of the original Spanish Fathers.

There, immersed in swimming heat, I beheld a fellow-being tortured with more of discomfort than my own.

He was not a human being. Life, on four furry legs, fawned up at me with lolling tongue. A beautiful coat he wore, this collie puppy of a year or thereabouts; a coat of dark sable hue and with white collar, a glorious ruff around his throat. But it was a coat which belonged not in the infernal heat of the tropics, but in northern snows.

Sprawling upon the floor, he rose as I approached him. He looked up in my face and whined. His eyes were filmy with heat; his throat was gasping; in the pathetic dumb language of the dog, man's best friend, he strove to acquaint me with his need – and I understood him.

Let who will believe in chance. I believe in destiny. As surely as I believe that God ordained that the insolent militarists of Germany should set "Der Tag" too soon, and thus invite their ultimate destruction at the hands of an outraged civilization, so I believe the day was appointed for the meeting with me of my beloved dumb comrade. I believe that he was destined to come to me and remain with me till death parts us; that it is appointed on some future day we shall range together some fair field of the beyond.

With the first look of appeal in his wistful eyes, with the responsive understanding in my own, there was forged between us the link unbreakable. With Bobbie Burns and I there is no wondering whether there can be "love at first sight." We know.

So, reading his need, I procured him a drink of water. The poor, parched, suffocating puppy lapped it greedily. With every draught the wonderful, dark, liquid eyes – eyes that even in his infancy were deep with amazing wisdom – eloquently attested the instant emotion of love, enduring love, which somehow my coming had inspired in him.

Was it because of a kindred racial sympathy? Because his forebears and mine had alike fared amid the "banks and braes o' Bonnie Doon"?

I do not know. I know only that, as Fate decreed, I came, I saw, and my comrade concurred in my unspoken immediate wish for possession of him. I know only, as was proved by his subsequent actions, that with my literally walking into his life, his keen canine mind then and there settled the question of his future. I was his – and he was mine forever.

Acquainted thoroughly with the Scotch collie, I knew, of course, that of all the tribes of dogs, he was emphatically the "one man dog." But this was to be at once impressed upon my mind with more force than I expected.

As I gave his head what I considered a parting pat, I regretfully dismissed my acquisitive thought regarding him. It was too much to expect that the owner, whoever he might be, would consider parting with so fine a pup. So, "Goodbye, boy," said I, and walked out of the rotunda into the blazing heat.

At the corner below the hotel something following at my heels attracted my attention. I looked backward and downward.

It was the collie pup.

"I appreciate the compliment, you know," I told him, with a grave attempt to impress upon him the ethics of the situation, "but it won't do. Probably the heat has confused you. You see, you don't belong to me."

He stood, panting in the heat, and smiled up at me steadily. His brush waved in dissent of my denial. As plainly as if he had spoken the words, he was telling me:

"I may not belong to you – yet. But – Master – you belong to me!"

What can you do against such determination?

But the collie took the entire initiative. And to reach my side he sought not to leave another man, but a woman.

At the risk of offending my feminine readers I must admit that, in the morning of his eventful life, the collie was so ungallant.

A week had passed since he first espied me. The second day, while he had remained as securely attached to my heels as the leather thereof, I found who owned him. (Theoretically.)

She was a woman living in the Plaza. She had been a nurse in the family of President Madero, of Mexico. The President had received the collie, in the early days of puppyhood, from a friend in Cleveland, Ohio. Later he had presented the dog to the nurse.

Notwithstanding my growing love for the dog, I made, of course, many attempts to induce him to remain with his owner. The outcome of my efforts is best described by recording a brief conversation between the nurse and myself on the seventh day after the pup had seen me and decided forthwith to switch orbits.

"He has eyes only for you!" she declared, as we stood in the rotunda with the collie gazing up at us inquiringly – and I am confident that he understood every word. "Take him; he is yours!"

"Ah, but, *señorita*," I demurred, with a show of reluctant incredulity, though my heart leaped with hypocritical joy. "I could not think of it! You mean that you will *part* with him?"

"*Sí, señor*. With happiness. He has no look for me now. Why should I cling to him? *Adios*, faithless one!"

With a careless gesture of farewell toward the collie, whose only acknowledgment was to wag his tail and beam at me, she started to leave us, a tall graceful figure in her garb of the sisterhood of mercy which is worn by the nurses of Mexico.

I detained her. "I wish to pay you for him, of course. And to thank you."

"To thank me is sufficient, *señor*." She was again turning away.

"One moment, *señorita*, if you please," I interposed. "What is the puppy's name?"

She responded with a sequence of syllables, in liquid Spanish, and hurried out, leaving me staring perplexedly at the collie. I had caught only the first three syllables. Decidedly, he must be re-christened. My taste was for less syllables.

While gazing at him as he stood wide-eyed, wistful and expectant, his tufted ears pointing forward giving him the look of intense alertness that is a hall-mark of his royal tribe, an inspiration winged to me.

"You fairly smack of the heather," I told him. "Scotland has raised braw men and braw dogs. Your name is Bobbie Burns."

That was thirteen years ago.

Many more than enough to prove Bobbie Burns a thoroughbred by nature as well as in breeding. His years have proved that "blood will tell"; that the collie I subsequently discovered to be directly descended from the great Douglas Blush, of Scotland, famous bench winner of the 90's and a mother of many famous sons, and from a father internationally famous, was a four-footed gentleman, fitted by destiny for the unique career which has been his.

From the day that he followed me out of the hotel rotunda – at last my property as I was his – the way of the four winds claimed us. Always the mirage of the morrow – the age-old lure of rolling stones – beckoned us; nor did I extract more pleasure from the cycles of restless change than did he.

He was my traveling pal, my chum, my comrade. From coast to coast, gray Atlantic to blue Pacific; from the Arctic Sea to the bow of the Southern Gulf; from the drowsing East to the Western Front. So he fared with me. And now, back among the deep still lakes and shaggy mountains and primordial rocks of the Ontario region he loves better than all else in the world's weldings of loveliness and grandeur, he enjoys the present and muses with dignity upon the past. Muses deeply, with the wisdom of the matured dog who has put away the irresponsibility of the pup. Muses in the Northland wherein he will end his honorable days; known to all, beloved of all folk who dwell in the mining towns and the spreading timberlands which hedge them in dense circles which it will take decades of woodsmen's ringing axes to thin.

Whither I went he went also; my people were his people; my gods his gods. Humblest – and proudest – of friends, he asked only to be with me. Whisked hither and yon to every city in America and Canada, he has ridden in baggage cars or under the car seats. He has gone down to the sea with me in ships. He has heeled in my tracks through tropical jungles or across frozen reaches. And finally came the great adventure, when he followed me through the trenches with the same nonchalance that he exhibited in peaceful days in trailing me through Yonge Street in Toronto, Broadway in New York, the Strand in London.

Came the call to arms on August 12th, 1914, eight days after Great Britain declared war on Germany, when he set out with me on this new and strangest of exploits, that I knew must have occasioned him bewilderment, though it was not in his cool and steady nature to betray that feeling. Thence, through a series of marvelous adventures, till June 16th, 1915, when a German "sniper" winged me in the open at Armentières, France.

For a year and a half, the first few months between life and death, I was in the Netley hospital, and by special and unprecedented permission Bobbie Burns remained with me. In January, 1917, we sailed back to Canada; the northern region which, in all his wanderings, his steadfast mind had charted as home. No human being could have more surely registered delight at the return, and home we now are, and having grown older and therefore tired of wandering, his only desire is that we shall remain at home.

So the present days of the sometime mascot of the famous Canadian regiment, "The Princess Patricias," are peaceful. During the days of storm now over, no dog ever enjoyed so much of attention, or more generously responded to sentiments of simple friendliness. During the dark days overseas, but of darkness relieved by the lurid fire of patriotism – our mascot's noble head was caressed by the hands of kings and queens, of dukes and duchesses, of princes and the most beautiful of princesses. Many generals, presidents, premiers, lords and statesmen by the score; ambassadors, plenipotentiaries and diplomats of assorted varieties, have bent to pat that long, lean head lighted by the dark, soft, wonderful eyes of infinite appeal, of infinite courage, of infinite faith. And, reverting to the army with its clash of drama and its shadows of tragedy, commandants, colonels and other officers by the hundreds, from the ends of the earth, have paid him the "man to man" tribute; while as for the men o' the line, – God bless them! – the men o' the line he loved more than all others because his master was among them; his friendships among them were legion.

All of this attention of volume unprecedented even among all the previous members of his famous tribe, Bobbie Burns accepted with the calmest dignity, the quietest of appreciation. Throughout it his poise was undisturbed. Of royal blood himself, his was the spirit of democracy that is intertwined with the truest of royalty in this world that is becoming enlightened.

In the quality of sagacity – a consideration far in advance of the possession of "show points" – Bobbie Burns is remarkable, even in this famed race of dogs. His inherent wisdom borders on human accomplishment, and definitely surpasses it in some ways. It includes an uncanny "*loup garou*" knowledge, or foresight. I have no doubt that, as a puppy, sifted through the annual "grist mill" in operation at all kennel clubs, and sent as a gift of friendship to the President of the Southern Republic – the man who was afterward shot to death by his countrymen – Bobbie Burns' prophetic vision may have looked forward to the day when he should meet me and we should range the remainder of life's journey together.

I have said that in some respects his knowledge transcends that vouchsafed the human mind. The true dog lover will nod his head in affirmation of this statement. But, for the benefit of those readers who know less of the four-footed noblemen and the fearless rangers of the dog world, I will append a striking illustration or two of the truth of my contention. They are incidents which have amazed even myself, who have known my comrade so well.

Upon an occasion some years ago, in the northern Ontario country, in which we live and which we love, I was away on business for some days. Nobody at home knew on what date I would return. Yet Bobbie Burns knew the day, the hour, the minute when I would come. With a certitude of intention and movement that caused subsequent wonderment among those at home, he set out one morning at a steady trot for the distant station, which he had not visited since I had left. He was at the station a few minutes in advance of the locomotive and he greeted me as I stepped down from the train. The oddest part of the entire circumstance was that the train was an hour and a half late, and he timed his departure from home so as to exactly reach it, accompanying the action by the signs of impatience which always marked his anticipation of my return when I had been on a journey without him.

He had no calendars to guide him; no timetables to inform him; nothing to tell him that on that particular day the train was late. But something told him that I was thinking of him, and would appear just when and where I did.

Sometimes I wonder if bright dogs do not pity us men for our mental limitations!

I will give another illustration, one fully as amazing.

Once I was prospecting in the Ontario mining region and started for home, catching the train at a lonely station. I supposed that Bobbie was under the seat, taking it for granted that he had preceded me into the car as he had always done. But I found that somehow he had contrived to miss the train.

It was the loneliest of regions. In the case of most dogs, I should have settled in my mind that we had parted company once and for all, but I could not believe that I had seen the last of Bobbie. Nor had I.

The train brought me home to Porcupine. Remember that never before had Bobbie visited that rugged region with me. Yet, ten days after he missed the train, he trotted into Porcupine, and home. He upreared and flung his forepaws upon my shoulders, the happiest, wriggling, homecoming prodigal son of a collie in Canada, or in all the world. Meanwhile I had burned the wires in efforts to locate him, but he would not wait to be found.

In that ten days of weary traveling he had covered two hundred miles of as rough, unbroken country as there is in the world. It was a wilderness without roads or trails; a veritable black jungle unlighted by sun, moon or stars. He swam wide brown lakes and the rapids of swiftly coursing rivers. Hauling himself out dripping upon the banks he had to nose his way through the thickest of tangles. He had to avoid a legion of ferocious wild beasts for which he would have been no match. Yet he arrived home unharmed, surprisingly well and strong, though somewhat thin and not a little weary.

How, without compass or word of mouth to guide him, did he accomplish this master feat in woods-craft, that would have taxed the resource of the best equipped among "superior" men? He could pay no attention to the skies for his direction, since cloudy weather and the destiny of the forest forbade that. But *something* guided him; that mystic something beyond the reach of man, who helpless, as Bobbie was apparently helpless, must have wandered in circles till he died. It was something simple to Bobbie, as sure as fate and as accurate as the clock of time

The means by which Bobbie accomplished this end is beyond the present knowledge of man, though he may discover it in time. What led Bobbie through the wilds to his home was the spirit of the homing pigeon which guides the bird thousands of miles to its destination to its mate; to its love. So it was with Bobbie. The same spirit inevitably guided him to the magnet of his desire.

This mysterious knowledge, denied to man, guides Bobbie in the pages which follow. Through its sway he is enabled to tell his story of the departed heroic friends who are no more of this world. The friends who were kind and good to him, and who he believes know, in the life beyond this life, what he records of their strivings, their sorrows, their victory in death. And those who still live after the travail of battle, they, too, will know in perusing these pages, that Bobbie understood them and the end they sought.

From what I have instanced of the uncanny knowledge of the collie, I esteem it no far stretch of the imagination to assume that, though in France he was relegated to the rear trenches, his vision compassed the scenes at the front, where the future of the nations, the issue between democracy and autocracy, was waged. He divined their sorrows, their pleasures, their losses, their triumphs. His spirit was attuned to the message of the living – and the message of the dead. Through his strange knowledge, that is denied man, mysteries of the infinite were plain to him. This elusive something peopled his intelligence with images of truth.

The spirits of those who had died for truth he saw in the air about him, a sight denied human eyes. Even as a dog refuses to leave his master's grave till death releases his spirit to join the man's, waiting beyond. His sympathies, of depth and breadth incalculable, described their parting messages and now he gives them to the world. He translates truths dim to men, but plain to a dog of royal blood.

The occult essence of knowledge has abridged the gap which theoretically obtains between the divining of the dog, man's first and best friend, and his power to express it.

In his dumb way Bobbie Burns thus tells his story, culminating in the tragic experiences of the Western Front. He has told it to me in a thousand mediums, and by the faith of his dark eyes I know that in the Scheme it has been vouchsafed him as a compensation for his dumbness, for his inability to express in speech the truth so clear to him, to see *beyond.*

The aura of the spirit, invisible to man, is perceptible to honest, loyal, noble dogs. This aura, these varicolored rays of the soul emanating from human bodies, this mystic composite, reveals to the dog whether the nature of the man, met by chance, is good or evil. I have seen this inevitably tested many times. The dog *knows.* Note how sure is his vision; his loving friendliness to men of worth; his detestation of the unworthy, however craftily they may seek to hide their real nature; a detestation shown by supreme indifference or disdain, or perhaps by low growls.

From the depths of my varied experience I here record that I do not care much for a man's opinion of a dog. I am mostly interested *in the dog's opinion of the man.*

We of the pioneer north country, the democracy of Ontario, *love dogs.* And dogs love us.

Follows the story of "The Princess Pats" in the world's war for liberties, by Bobbie Burns as he would tell it had he "the gift of tongues."

Jack Munroe,
Cobalt, Ontario, Canada,
February, 1918.

Chapter I

"YOU SHALL GO!"

I suppose my eyes were getting a little green with jealousy as I watched the other collie, Rex, being fondled by Fred. I would have wriggled along, to try to divert Fred's attention, but the canoe was too cranky for such an experiment. Besides, had not big Pendragon, my master, my chief, told me to remain quiet?

So quiet I remained, though my black nose twitched and my brush waved slowly and my eyes grew greener watching Rex whom I love, but hate to see fondled. I like to get all the fondling myself.

Pendragon and Rob were paddling swiftly across Nighthawk Lake. Of all the lakes and streams about which I have paddled and sniffed in this glorious Northland I love Nighthawk Lake the best.

This lake lies a hundred miles north of Cobalt and two hundred miles south of Hudson Bay. It is cradled in wooded hills and bleak plateaus studded with rocks of the Lower Huronian age and the Cambrian era.

The day was beautiful, a rare day seen only in late summer – and in Northern Ontario. The sky was a deep blue sea of peace across which white dream ships were sailing. The dipping paddles cut rippling waters as brown as the dun mantle of late autumn. Out from the wooded shore crept ragged, straggling, sinister shadows.

Into these shadows we swept, and Rex and I, lying flat in the bottom of the canoe, twitched with eagerness to be among our beloved thickets, exploring virile smells of forest and fern.

Fred, who was in the center of the canoe, stood upright as Rob hallooed a welcome call that was flung back in weird echoes from the hills.

"Hey, boys! There's a good spot to land and have tea and a brush-up before taking the train for home."

Home!

The word sounded sweet to Rex and me. For a month now we had been away with the men, inspecting prospective mines, camping where we chanced to be.

With Rob's mention of "home," recalling it to us after a month's absence, two pairs of tufted ears came forward. Mine and Rex's. Did

The Call

you ever notice how *alert* we collies look when we prick up our ears?

I whined a little and Rex answered it. That is how we told each other how anxious we were to reach home once more and see all the chickens and pigeons and rabbits. Especially the rabbits. I have always loved to watch over them and keep away those other dogs who would have harmed them. Why, those other ignorant dogs do not know the difference between wild rabbits and tame ones! Rex and I are never so happy as when sleeping among our tame rabbits.

The canoe grounded and we gained the shore. Rob volunteered to go for the mail at the Connaught Station, a half-mile through the woods, while the other two men made tea.

Rex and I were busy, too. Rex had chased a saucy squirrel up a tree, and was disputing with him. Being somewhat older and more dignified than Rex, I watched over the food and equipment piled upon the shore. My squirrel days were over – or almost over.

Presently, while the camp-fire was burning lustily, Fred stripped off his clothes and plunged into the lake, swimming about with much splashing and shoutings such as men make in the woods when they are feeling well. Pendragon was by the fire, putting tea in the pot.

Occasionally he and Fred called cheerily to each other, and each encouraged Rex in the useless quest for the squirrel. Once Fred stood up in the water and playfully shied a pebble at the squirrel. He made no attempt to hit that impudent little ball of gray fluff, of course, but aimed only to encourage Rex in further barking.

All was peace and the gaiety we knew so well, with the shadow of no sorrow or care upon the horizon, but in the midst of it, I was silent and depressed, lying quietly by the pile of duffle I had elected to guard.

"What's the matter with Bobbie Burns?" called Fred suddenly, glancing at me curiously. "Sick a little, maybe, or just resting?"

I was not sick, and I was not resting. On the contrary I was very restless inside. Why, I could not have told, save that I found my mind dwelling – or rather, waiting – for something I knew was coming.

I had felt like this before; something like this. Sometimes it had been a portent of joy, sometimes of grief. But I had never known anything so *heavy* as this, so overwhelming.

I felt, somehow, as if I – all of us – approached a crisis. I felt it coming, whatever it was, some strange, terrible, awful Thing. And as this impression grew, such a prophetic sadness enveloped my spirit as it had never known.

What was this Thing? I did not know as yet. But somehow I found myself sighing as I lay, and watching the woodland path upon which

Rob had departed for the mail.

Suddenly, far up the trail, my keen ear caught the faint crackle of shrubbery, the soft thud of footsteps running. Now I knew that I had been expecting that sound, which was the reason that I had been the first to hear it.

I raised my muzzle, sniffling. My ears pricked forward. The sounds came nearer. I found my body tensing in an ache of suspense.

Came an increase of the threshing in the brush and a loud voice hailing. The two men – my master by the fire and Fred in the water – turned their faces toward the sound. Rex turned from the squirrel to listen, too.

Came the call again, nearer:

"Boys! Oh, boys!"

The prickling along my spine increased. I knew now in a measure what it meant; I had felt it before. It was the tingle of excitement, or expectation that had always meant for my master and for me the call to change, the transfer to new horizons in our restless journeyings through the world. But mixed with it now was this new element, that horror which I could not understand.

Also, I had recognized the voice, at the first call. It was Rob's.

For weeks we had been in the forest, cut off from the great outside world of people. In this time we had seen no men, white or red. I knew that it was some word from the cities and towns which now speeded Rob towards us, shouting as he came.

Now this thrill of expectancy possessed not me alone, but all of us.

Out from the trail into the open space, where our fire was burning, bounded Rob, waving a newspaper. It was the Cobalt *Daily Nugget*, the journal of the miners of all the North.

While he raced toward Pendragon at the fire; as Fred scrambled naked and dripping to the shore and ran to meet them both; Rob, who was red-faced, perspiring, breathless, cried out the news for which we were waiting: "*War! War, War!*"

"What do you mean?" cried Fred, while Pendragon reached for the paper.

"Britain's orders to the fleet!" excitedly exclaimed Rob again. "Capture or destroy the enemy!"

"You're joking!" gasped Fred, from whose hair, face and body rivulets of water were running. "What enemy? What has happened?"

Then my Pendy opened the paper and began to read aloud the big black headlines:

"All Cables to Germany Cut" ... "Enemy's Ships Cut Off" ... "French

Capture Many German Prisoners" ... "Germany's Ultimatum to Belgium" ... "Russia Continues Steady Advance in the Carpathians."

He stopped reading. All three looked at one another. "So it's Germany!" Fred muttered.

"Here! Two more papers!" said Rob, and thrust them toward his two pals. I noticed his hand was trembling with excitement.

They all settled down, Fred all dripping as he was, and silently began to read. I padded around, wondering what it was all about. What was this "war" of which they spoke?

I was in a fine state of concern as I saw the bacon beginning to burn, and the tea boiling over, and nobody paying any attention to the dinner.

What could this thing be that was making these big man pals of mine forget their appetites, whetted by many miles of forest ranging?

The bread toasting over the fire burned up. The teapot boiled dry. The bacon burned and sizzled, and finally took fire in the pan and was consumed in pungent ashes. Still nobody noticed. The fire burned low. Now it had wholly burned away.

I never saw such changes come over the face of my world in so short a time.

The three men read on in silence, occasionally exchanging papers. Rex and I watched their faces. Both of us were subdued and wondering. For in their faces were looks of quiet grimness we knew. We had seen the expression in moments that called for reprimanding or of punishment of dogs or of men, or perhaps while shooting dangerous rapids when life is in the balance.

They finished their reading together and stared at one another. Perhaps the reading had not taken them as long as it seemed to me. But it had been long enough for Fred's wet skin to become dry.

"Boys," said my Pendragon, " it seems to be up to us, 'Soldiers three.' What?"

For a moment they talked with one another only with their eyes. But because I know the speech of men's eyes, I knew that they all felt alike about this thing, whatever it was; this thing that I could feel ripping and tearing at the peace of the forest.

Then, with a common impulse, they reached out their hands to one another – all three of them in a strong clasp, and said together, as if one voice were speaking:

"We're on!"

I was to learn that in that moment one voice *had* spoken.

It was the voice of Canada.

Just one other word was said, Rob spoke it as he sprang up: "Train!"

They picked up the duffle at random and stuffed it into the canoe; the food and the tent and the bags of ore samples. But they left many things upon the beach, which greatly disturbed my sense of order.

Grabbing paddles, they leaped into the canoe and dug furiously into the brown water. The canoe streaked toward the station. Rex and I loped along the beach after it.

We all reached the station platform just as the train thundered in. Many men were about; more than I had ever seen at that lonely station. All were talking of war. What was this war, I wondered again, which possessed such evil power of turning desirable things topsy-turvy?

Usually what men we met, after returning from a sojourn in the wilds, were merry. But now everybody was so serious! There was a difference in the very atmosphere that was depressing.

As usual, Rex and I scrambled up the steps of the train in advance of our friends and crawled under the seats which they took. Shortly the train rambled on its way. How I hate the noise and bad smells of stuffy trains! I was glad indeed when Pendragon whistled us to jump off at the old home station of Porcupine. We romped and bounded off in great glee.

The dear old home things were awaiting me. The barn was still there, after the month in the forest ledges, and the chicks and bunnies were glad to see me. Rex and I noticed that in our absence many strange dogs had impudently made themselves familiar about the place, but we soon made them turn tail, my Pendragon's home was – and is – ours!

For a few hours the shadow that had settled over my spirit, during the moment that the "soldiers three" had gazed at one another and clasped hands, lifted, and I was blithe. I imagined that whatever it was that had threatened our peace – the life I had come to love – had fled, and that we would go on as we had been doing. For I had grown to middle age in my years of wandering, and when that period comes to a dog or to a man, a season of repose and of reflection is pleasant before the call comes to the next field of effort.

But soon I realized that my Pendy did not intend to go on in the peaceful paths of many unbroken happy months in the Northland. His strange, silent, thoughtful demeanor told me this. There was another adventure to come – one that I somehow sensed would be full of weariness, of pain, of more sorrow than my Pendy and I had seen in our previous farings through the fields of life. But whatever it was, we would breast it together, as we had always done. I was resigned.

No sooner had I made this resolution, however, than my soul was assailed with the cruelest fear it had ever known or will ever know. For the first time since I had met, loved and followed my master he was planning to go away on a long journey – without me.

Still and grim, my master, my king, my god, went about the premises, seemingly oblivious to me as I humbly heeled, striving for the attention now mysteriously denied me. Something big and terrible and divine was occupying his thoughts; something, I knew, that was of more importance than I, and with that I had no quarrel. But I yearned – so much! – for just a little place in his thoughts, the thoughts which had formerly yielded me place so commanding.

He went about town and I followed him, scarcely heeded by him. He went to a building and left papers that I heard called mining claims. Then, too, there was some talk about a will and testament.

Came a night when he sat out under the stars, near the house. He was gazing toward the east. Yet somehow I knew that he was looking past the forests. Yes, and even past the wide waters that rolled beyond them.

What did he see? I did not know; yet somehow, through the strange sympathy between us, I knew that his thoughts were of something monstrous and dark, the thing, of formless menace, affrighted me and filled me with loneliness. For I knew he thought of seeking and finding it – without me.

There had been a day in the south when my will had demanded that he should take me to himself. But now, humbled with the heavy wisdom of the years, I no longer demanded.

I laid my head against his knee in pleading.

The melancholy that only the collie knows oppressed me. My eyes, my wistful face, must have expressed all the pathos of my inner weeping.

Up into the face of my lord I looked, my heart near to bursting with agony. I knew he meant to go – somewhere – without me. With the only language I knew – the moan of the spirit – I was begging to be remembered, to be taken with him.

He felt the pressure of my head against his knee. Rather absently he looked down at me.

His big hand caressed my head. Still I looked up at him in the moonlight; looked with all my soul. I sought to impart my longing to go with him wherever he might go; over whatever hill or through whatever valley; to share life or death with him.

N ow my heart gave a suffocating throb of suspense.

Hungrily I watched that responsive something I had been seeking, now kindled in his face.

I knew that at last his thoughts had definitely returned to me – and that he understood me.

Tensed, waiting, suffering with suspense, I looked up at him while his hand stroked my head.

"So *that's* it!" he said, his tone a little wondering. "You want to go across with me. Eh, Bobbie?"

Like a tremendous flood, hope surged within me. I stood stock-still, trembling, my ears thrusting forward.

His face was grave as his eyes gazed into mine under the starlight. "Boy," he said, "you don't know how awful is this thing you want."

I only trembled the more; willed the harder – and appealed. What did I care how awful it might be? If he could go, why not I?

He sighed – and decided. "Well, I hardly know how I am to take a dog over there. But I can't resist you. I never could. Bobbie, old fellow, you shall go!"

Editor's Notes to Chapter I:

1) Throughout the book Jack Munroe is referred to as Pendragon. Rob and Fred are not positively identified, but knowing their occupation, and that they served in No. 4 Company, you can speculate on their identity.

Chapter II

BOBBIE BURNS, MASCOT

To hear that I was going seemed to surprise all my friends in Porcupine. Evidently they had supposed that no dogs would be allowed to go to war.

So I was immediately in receipt of more attention than ever, which did not displease me at all.

I spent my time trotting about the community, bidding everybody and everything good-bye.

It seemed, indeed, that this was no ordinary trip I was going on, and there was much talk of this mysterious war. And they were expressing the hope that no harm would come to the men of the region who were going, nor to me.

In a few days came the leavetaking. I went for a last word with Rex, who was tied up.

While we were snuggling in each other's necks, after the manner of dogs, I told Rex how sorry I was to go alone. Rex could not understand. There were a dozen men in the little group at the station, waiting for the train which should bear us southward. Hundreds of friends had accompanied our group there. I was patted and stroked on all sides.

However, I wondered what mysterious reason there was for all this fuss over what seemed to me an ordinary trip. We were taking no tents, no blankets, no canoe. The men of the group carried only light grips. Yet I had heard we were to be away for a long time! What did it all mean? I was being taken along, and that was all I cared for. Sufficient unto the morrow was the next day.

The train rolled into the station and I clawed up the steps ahead of my Pendy. Be sure that I never missed a train but once! That one time cost me a long journey through the wilds, for many anxious days and black nights, before I found my master.

As the train started I heard the people outside cheering, and they were still cheering as long as I could hear them. Then, as I lay curled under a car seat, there was only the clackety-click of the train and the hum of talk throughout the car. All of the talk concerned this war, a non-understandable subject over which I had puzzled my brain till I had given it up. I had decided I must wait to find what war was.

Many other men, it seemed, were going where our Procupine group intended going. At every succeeding station along the line were other wild crowds cheering. Yet, as it had been at Porcupine, mingled with the cheering there was sadness, and some there were who took leave of the little groups in silence, and with tears running down their faces. It was surely a most perplexing jumble, and I could make nothing of it!

Other men kept boarding the train, and the cheering continued as the train left each station. I soon grew tired of this and wished that my Pendy would give up whatever idea he had, and go back home with me. I would have liked to meet Rex just then, and have said: "Cheer up! You have not missed so much after all. Here I am returned, and glad to be!"

All day long we traveled in that stuffy train. At noon Pendragon got me some water, and as I lapped it thirstily I felt my spirits reviving.

At last we reached a station called North Bay, which seemed to be quite a busy community. At the usual signal I crawled from under the seat and left the train with the others. Never had I seen such a throng in the station in the Northland. It reminded me of the crowded platforms in San Francisco, or Chicago, or New York where I had been in previous years.

I gathered from the talk that hundreds of men were waiting for the same train that we were. Men and women, and some children, were scampering here and there, chattering of that same subject, the war. They told of terrible fighting and loss of life.

"I tell you, it's up to us Canucks to give the Germans a taste of their own medicine!" one man shouted. I shuddered at this. Pendragon had given me medicine more than once, and how I hated the taste of it! Those poor Germans were in for a disagreeable time, I reflected. But then, I had always felt better after being given medicine, and doubtless it would be the same way with the Germans.

The men were asking when the train for Ottawa would leave, and a man with brass buttons and with a pleasing voice replied that it would leave at about ten o'clock that night.

We strolled about the village. I met many dogs – good-natured ones and simple ones – and we played along the road. I like dogs of this description; there are so few playful dogs round about Porcupine. There they are more like the Indian "husky" kind, with sly and treacherous views toward everyone, and always waiting to overwhelm and devour anything and everyone not too strong to resist them.

We met many friends and acquaintances here and there through the village, and all wished us luck and a safe return.

We wandered back to the station just as the train arrived.

Shortly the train sped on its way. My alert brain soon discovered that we were spinning along in a different direction than before.

Pendy grinned at me in the morning as I crawled from under the seat, a little ashamed to have been so lazy.

"What's the matter, Bobbie?" he asked me. "Been dreaming? Well, stir yourself, old chap. Ottawa and breakfast!"

I barked joyously as I followed him out.

After about a mile of walking, and some inquiries, we soon found ourselves in large, well-kept, open grounds, with nice short grass growing all about and spacious buildings. I found this enclosure was called the Exhibition Grounds. And directly I was startled and dismayed for a while, the result of a sight such as I had never imagined.

All about were men – thousands of them, it seemed to me – and in a strange brown dress, looking all alike. There was a grimness, a severity, about this garb that gave me a sense of strangeness. More than that; it frightened me. They looked to me, in this first sight of them, like creatures from a world other than the realms I had always known.

I had lost sight of Pendragon, and a group of the brown men suddenly espied me, and beckoned to me, whistling and calling. Instead of coming confidently to them, as I usually did with men, I sidled away, trying feebly to wag my tail, so they would not wish to harm me. They look so fierce and strange!

As I tried to leave them they came toward me the faster, at which I started to run away from them. I ran right into the arms of one of them, that I had not seen, but whom I found the other men called "Joe."

How I have wished since that I had chanced to hear Joe's full name, so I could give it to you! For he is the man who gave me the other name, that at first sounded so strange to me.

However, I was much frightened at first, and cowered down as he caught me, and looked up at him. He had on a trim brown cap, like the others, and a buttoned brown jacket and full trousers to the knee, and the calves of his legs were all wound around, down to his russet shoes, with lapped brown cloth that they called puttees.

He held me with big hands while I trembled. He spoke to me:

"Why, old fellow! You're a lovely son of a pup, aren't you?"

The admiring tone, and the voice of kindness, sounded natural. They were what I was used to. I looked deep into his face. His eyes were nice, too; they were like Rob's or Fred's.

"Hey, boys!" he called again. "Come here and meet the new pal, the Mascot of the Princess Pats, God bless us! Mascot, meet the boys!"

They crowded around me, a brown cloud of them; exclaiming,

laughing, fondling me who had just been christened with my second name. A name I grew to love almost as much as my first.

Under their petting, however, the face of my world regained its wonted cordiality. After all, these strange beings called soldiers were my friends as truly as the men I had known in the peace world! I was much relieved and very happy. I wriggled so hard, in the attempt to show contrition for having misjudged them through their fierce appearance, that I suppose I looked like a salmon-colored accordion in action.

The word traveled through the grounds that the Princess Pats had a new and beautiful mascot, and for some time I held a regular levee. I was grabbed by one, then another and still another, till it seemed the whole world was handling me.

They all left after a time – it seemed that they were called away for something – and I found opportunity to look about me and to reflect. So this was what the army was like! Well, I was already fond of it. This colored clothing – "khaki" I heard it called – which had at first oppressed me, I now found quite cheerful in tone, since it was inhabited by such fine fellows, who received me as a comrade.

If this was war, why, I had as soon be at war always. But I could not understand the sympathy and the good-fellowship in it. I could not reconcile it with the sinister premonition I had felt as Rob came running through the forest with his news of war. Anything black or sinister? Why, this now seemed a joke! To be sure, it was a little rough. I had been petted so much and so hard that my skin was sore. But there was no hate in this, but only exuberant love, for which I entertained no rancor.

Never, I was sure, had anyone encountered such a nice bunch of men before, and I the only dog there, too!

I could see nothing in this war business to warrant tears or sympathy. Certainly everybody seemed to be enjoying himself, and not one of them more than I. We all had much good food and good water, fine baths in the canal in the mornings, a daily grand march out to the country, and much company and a variety of quietude and noise. Could anybody enjoy more harmonious and enjoyable existence?

Speaking of noise and harmony reminds me of the Princess Pats' famous bagpipe band. I regarded the outpourings of that organization with the most amazing contrast of emotions. It depended upon when I heard it.

I cannot explain the difference, but when the boys were marching, and I trotted along with them to the music of that band, it seemed harmony to me. But when the band just stood quietly in the grounds and played, it seemed to me just noise. How I hated those strains in that moment! Such whinings and howlings as those bagpipes then made! They could never be matched in any throat of my breed!

This brings me to the recording of what was a passing anxiety of mine.

In touch with the soldiers, loving them all and the new life, I became concerned with the fear that perhaps my Pendragon was not going to remain with them, after all. For, though all the others wore these soldier clothes of brown, and though Fred and Bob who had come with him also wore them – Pendy was still in the clothes in which he had come from Porcupine.

Could it be, I wondered, that he had decided to go back to Porcupine, and take me? I hoped not; I had grown to like this soldier life so well.

But one morning he appeared in khaki, like the others, and I was overjoyed. I ran to him, and smelled him, and they looked him over with my head on one side. Then I upreared with my forepaws on his breast and smiled at him. It seemed to me that his khaki suit was the finest I had ever seen him wear.

From the jokes of Fred and Rob, who were with him, I found he had been obliged to wait for his uniform. There had been no suit in stock large enough for him.

After this, reassured that we were to stay in this lovely war, I felt very happy and important as I trotted away toward the gate of the grounds.

Editor's Notes to Chapter II:

1) Landsdowne Park is still there, and an obscure plaque marks the momentous event of the raising of the PPCLI. It is sad that such an historic event is marked by such a minuscule memorial. It states:
A proud Regiment was born here in August 1914. Princess Patricia's Canadian Light Infantry.

Chapter III

" A SACK OF POTATOES "

Life was certainly a merry song at the Exhibition Grounds for a few days. Many people came to see us and called us "The P.P.C.L.I's," which did not take as long to say as The Princess Patricia's Canadian Light Infantry. And "mascot" took even less time to say, which may have been the reason everybody said it.

I grew to like that name "Mascot." It held a certain ring I liked, as did everybody else. Colonels, majors, captains, lieutenants, and many kinds of sergeants; yes, and noted people of every description, even titled royalty, went to much trouble to speak to me.

My friends, the soldiers, were always showing how many tricks I could do. I was proud to display my cleverness, as I am sure I can do as many tricks as any other dog can do. For instance – to bring the men's boots, their slippers or caps, and return them to where they were; that is something not many dogs can do the way I do it. I also close the door, and bring my own comb and put it back where I got it from. I sit up; I stand like a person; I walk around on two legs; *et cetera.*

The boys were delighted with my tricks, and to satisfy them they had to be done over and over. I got a little tired of them, and soon grew careless and didn't mind whether I did them correctly or not. But they seemed to appreciate them just as much whether they were done or *half* done.

In this matter of my tricks, I have never been so ready with them since those days. Pendragon has said since that I received too much attention, that I was spoiled. But I don't think it was so much that. Every day we grow older, you know. And when a dog is old, the smart tricks of his youth rather bore him. I have heard that it is the same with men.

Food and water were offered me every minute in the day by someone. After a while I would refuse to eat except when the others were eating. I wanted to be like everyone else, and sleep and eat when they did; to be one of and with them. It grew so, while I tried to be like them as much as I could, that I thought perhaps I was beginning to look like them. I was their "Mascot" – and their Mascot I shall remain in memory, though the majority lie under mounds "over there."

In a few days all the men from Porcupine, with whom I had come, were dressed in this brown stuff called khaki. By now I loved all the men garbed in it. They smelled the same and were just as fine as when in the garb of peace I had known all my life. But when I grew used to the khaki, it seemed no other color would do.

I would follow one of them the same as another, and recognized each and everyone of them. No matter where I encountered them, I knew them by the camp scent and welcomed them. The boys thought my facility very strange, but they failed to appreciate the subtlety of my sensitive nose. In this organ of mine, every twitch has its meaning.

We left Ottawa August 29th. Never shall I forget the excitement of that day.

It was a gloriously beautiful morning. The city was early astir.

The members of our bagpipe band tuned up at daybreak. How I hated that fiendish noise!

At last the regiment was lined up to be inspected by Colonel Farquhar. This took some time and was quite fatiguing. We had to stand at attention in the heat of the sun, obeying many boisterous and pedantic commands by the various newly made majors, lieutenants and N.C.O.'s.

Finally we were lined up and marched away at a fast pace. We were to take a special train at the station for Montreal, and there board a transport for France.

We marched between solid walls of people, banked on either side of the streets. It must have been two miles to the station. It was a long, tiresome, noisy tramp. In it I found only this comfort; that everybody noticed me. All seemed to have heard of the Mascot of the Princess Pats.

Moreover, my new friends had decked me for the occasion. The regimental colors of navy-blue and maroon, were tied in beautiful bows of ribbon about my neck and body.

It was a hot and stuffy day, but in the deafening cheering, the playing of many bands and the confusion on all sides, we forgot our discomfort. At last we reached the station.

There – but it is difficult for me to describe the mad capers of the huge masses of people that pushed and scrambled about and around us. Their moods were so strangely various. Many of the faces were sad and long and tear-stained. Others were crinkled with smiles or laughter. Some wore blank expressions of curiosity. Still others were singing and cheering. But the strangest folk to me were those who laughed and cried at the same time!

They would cry awhile and then laugh; short, silly, little laughs, and then they would cry and suddenly burst out in a mad "Hooray!" And it went on in this way till we boarded the train.

There was nothing to laugh at, and certainly nothing to cry over, so far as I could see. There seemed to be nothing to eat and nothing to drink, and I was hot, hungry and thirsty. However, I reflected that my soldier friends were probably the same, and if they could endure it, I could.

I was leaving Ottawa with regret, which I knew was shared by my comrades. Everybody had been so kind to us! The fond memories of all survivors of the P.P.C.L.I.'s will always revert to the August of 1914, in Ottawa.

The train started amid great excitement. The men and women who had been waiting for this moment yelled and waved their hands. Hats, handkerchiefs, umbrellas, coats; anything and everything were hysterically thrown high in air. All seemed mad, either with joy or grief; perhaps both.

We left Ottawa and the train went speeding along through the peaceful Canadian countryside. It was the next step in a fascinating adventure. In four hours we stopped again at a crowded station.

Such was the throng that we could hardly get out of the train. The noises were even louder, if possible, than those I had heard at the Ottawa station.

There was much commotion and uncertainty as the boys "numbered off." Few knew their places, and those who did, it seemed to me, had to be told many times before taking their proper positions. The orders, "Form Fours," and "Quick March," found that many of the less experienced men were where they ought not to have been.

At last order was obtained and we passed out through the iron gates and upon the street. I was taken along behind the others. I would rather have been in front, but had not the initiative. A leash, held in firm but gentle hands, decided where and how I should dog-trot at all times.

We marched perhaps a mile through cheering thousands. The vocal noise was aided and abetted by the blare of bands.

We finally arrived at a pier in front of a very large boat.

Right here I got the scare of my life. For awhile it looked as if I were to be left alone and friendless in a strange city.

My soldiers three, Pendragon and Rob and Fred, were standing together with me, when up to them on the pier came the Officer Commanding. He cast a look at me.

"What's this?" he asked curtly.

"He's the Mascot of the Princess Pats, sir," proudly replied Rob, while he saluted.

"He'll have to be left here," answered the O.C. "Why – why, sir?" gasped Fred, his face the picture of dismay.

"It would be no use taking him aboard. They wouldn't let you land him in England, or in France, either." And the O.C. walked away, leaving my soldiers three staring at one another, and I at them.

Fred was the first to recover from the general chagrin. A glow of inspiration lighted his eyes. He grabbed Pendragon by the shoulder and leaned forward.

"England and France are problems to be settled later, Jack," he said. "The first is right now, and I think I have the answer. What do you think of this plan?" And with a quick glance around, he whispered it behind his hand.

Pendragon nodded and beckoned for me to heel him. He walked toward a pile of gunny sacks, such as are used to put potatoes in, a short distance away. "Now, Bobbie," said my Pendy gravely, "listen to me! You are to keep perfectly quiet."

At which he picked me up by the scruff of the neck, dropped me in the sack and slung me over his shoulder.

My feelings at such undignified treatment may be imagined. A collie of the most royal blood of the Scottish Highlands crumpled in catch-as-catch-can fashion into a potato bag.

Amazement, wrath, chagrin, struggled in my mind as I reposed in a heap at the bottom of that sack. I was twisted and doubled till I was chewing my own brush. Just one consideration prevented me from howling my resentment at this unwonted handling. I remembered the warning words of Pendragon; and I had never disobeyed a word of his.

Meanwhile, with these conflicting thoughts racing through my mind, my Pendragon was tramping somewhere with me in the bag over his shoulder. From their voices I knew that Rob and Fred were with him.

From the upward trend, I soon knew we were proceeding up an inclined plane, which I afterward learned was called a gang-plank. Then we halted suddenly.

"What have you got there?" asked a gruff voice. Pendragon's voice answered him.

"Extra kit, sir!"

"Carry on!" replied the gruff voice. So Pendy and Rob and Fred, with myself as the "extra kit," passed into the transport, no longer molested.

Here you have the full story of an incident which the lips of thousands of soldiers have retailed in great glee, one mouth to the other. How the Mascot of the Princess Pats was lugged aboard the transport at Montreal as "an extra kit," befooling wary officials, but feeling not a bit "cocky" about it, but instead like a bally rot of potatoes! I feel indignant yet, every time I think of it!

My soldiers three walked along till I felt the sack lowered from Pendragon's shoulder to the floor. The top of it was opened and I emerged.

We were in a small stateroom. "Go under that bed, Bobbie, and keep quiet!" I was ordered. Obediently I complied, and remained there for several hours, without noise, till I felt the boat start to move amid the shrieking of whistles from other boats and the city.

Then I was taken out and brought to another part of the transport and tied to a large box.

I remained tied to this box all night. There was the fussing and fuming and stamping of many horses on the upper deck with me; they seemed very much frightened at the strangeness of their surroundings. Perhaps war was not so lovely, after all! I could not understand why we had not remained in Ottawa!

Came daylight, when I was almost exhausted. One of my friends came to me with something to eat and drink. My spirits revived; it is surprising what a difference some interior refreshment will make in a fellow's feelings!

I knew we were still near shore, as I could scent the land, on both sides of the boat. Home, sweet home, ran my thought; would I ever be home in the Northland again?

Perhaps this thing was not the roseate vision I had pictured while in Ottawa, I reflected, but I would stick it! I would never desert my friends. Besides, I had the utmost faith that all would come out right in the end.

During the day I was untied and allowed to run about the deck, and then I felt much better. I rambled about with the boys, one after another, trying my best to be one of them, their comrade, as always.

At last I heard rumors of our landing, and I was glad. The transport almost stopped, and we prepared to disembark, but that welcome privilege did not come as soon as we expected. We spent two nights on that old boat, waiting for orders.

At last came the day we left the boat, about ten o'clock of a beautiful September morning. I heard them saying we were going ashore for only a few days, and would then continue on the water journey.

I hoped we would be ashore longer than "a few days." I was so tired of that boat.

Chapter IV

FIRST VICTORY !

In great glee I followed Pendy, Rob and Fred, who were together, down the gang-plank. The whole battalion was leaving the boat. The smell of the land in my nostrils was sweet.

We proceeded to an open space, a sort of field nearby. Here, in a very few moments, occurred the first victory of the Princess Pats in the world's war. No cables carried the news of it around the globe, but the tongues of men have since done so.

I accompanied my soldiers to the field. It chanced that I was not on the leash. In the brief interval before my comrades came to attention I became conscious of that strange feeling which always warns me when something out of the ordinary is about to occur.

The space to which we had repaired was only a short distance from the pier. The men were all in line and standing at attention, waiting for the orders of Colonel-Farquhar. And with my sensitiveness, you may well believe that I was quiet and tensed with the others.

At which moment of all moments, a"lowbrow" of the canine tribe elected to jump me.

Not by word nor by look had I given that brute provocation!

I never saw him till he was leaping at me. I was standing at the extreme right of the front line, not far from Pendy. My thoughts were fixed on the coming order of the Colonel, who was sitting on a noble horse in front of the regiment.

Suddenly, in the midst of this premonitory calm, the tail of my eye caught a sight which at once explained my *"loup garou"* feeling as I left the boat.

From the side opposite the men – I had not noticed the enemy's presence at all – a big, brown, unwieldy body was hurtling in air, charging at me.

The single flash of my eye, turned that way even as I acted, was sufficient, even in this instant of surprise, to measure my unexpected foe and to enable me properly to protect myself.

He was a fierce, lumbering, coarse-haired dog of all sorts, which is to say a mongrel. From the scars on his heavy face and fat body I caught that he had indulged in many fights; though, being a mongrel, it may be that his ambition transcended his performances. At any rate, he was twice my size – and twice as slow. His clumsiness was pitiful!

He had made this leap at me. As he landed he brought his forepaws down hard, thinking to crush my back under his weight, and his jaws snapped together, aimed at my neck.

But my back was not there to be crushed. All his snapping jaws got of my neck was a mouthful of fur, which was still gagging him at the end of the combat.

As I swerved, I threw all my weight against his body, in an instinctive trick that is as old as the collie tribe, and toppled him neatly on his back. He now presented a ludicrous picture, all four paws waving up at me in token of surrender, a sudden look on his surprised face which I was to remember later on the Western Front, when I should hear captured Germans crying: "Merci, Kamerad!" among their downflung arms.

There was a "yellow streak" in that mongrel. Already, with the first reverse, he was begging for quarter.

But at this moment there was no mercy in my heart. There are folk who may pet a collie for a lifetime, and know only the loving side of him. But when chance called out the elementals, such people would realize him a many-sided dog.

Just now I was raging; with that cold, calm, cruel rage that is so much more deadly than hot unreasoning anger of blindness that is apt to defeat the very purpose of the wrath.

It was a rage of calculation. I knew just what I would do and how I would do it. It was a raging against the injustice of this unprovoked attack against me who had not harmed him; the blazing resolution that he would never try it again.

While I swiftly overtoppled him, holding him struggling while his forepaws vainly beat against my deep, shaggy breast and his mutterings pleaded for mercy from a fellow-being he had sought to destroy, I did not make a sound. I was reserving my force for an end more useful.

Even as he began the drumbeat with his paws, my long lean jaws darted swift as flame to his exposed soft neck. My teeth clicked home, deep in his throat. He howled in agony; I drove them in the deeper, and reveled in the hot taste of his blood.

Around me I was conscious of a tremendous uproar. All the fierce, exultant, fighting blood of my Scottish clans, the primal law of force, the birth-right of cunning and of might, welled within me. I was conscious of only one thought; it had been his life or mine – and now it would be his!

Now, with him completely in my power; assured of my vengeance for the wrong he had attempted, over the clear film of my thinking grew a red haze as my grip strengthened. Twice I shook my shaggy head, gaining a more deadly hold. Now, as if I had visioned them in dreams, gleamed about me the faces of men; strained and tensed and eager and exultant; men who had caught the subtle essence of the swift and unexpected drama; men whose imaginations caught the imperious demand of this law of life; the blow for the blow. As I worried that fat neck, sounded the bellows of satisfaction and encouragement about me.

At a still sharper howl from the prostrate mongrel a mighty grasp clutched me by the neck; a man's grasp; while a stentorian voice roared above the tumult an order I had no choice but to obey. For the hand and the voice were those of Pendragon.

"Bobbie! Let go!"

I suppose that no *gourmand* ever exchanged his prodigal menus for the bread and water of jail fare with more regret than I let go of the fat and gory neck of that miserable, overgrown, cowardly bully of a mongrel!

With one last shuddering, snarling, resigned sigh, however, I did it.

He hurried away, unfollowed by regrets, on four shaky legs and with the blood streaming from his neck. And I found myself, with some surprise at this swift return to complete sanity at the summons from Pendy, the recipient of a popular ovation.

It seemed that the incident "had broken up the meeting," as one of the boys said afterward. At the clashing of my rival and myself the regimental ranks had broken and men had come running to see. No dog fight ever had a more appreciative gallery, nor one in which partisanship was more one-sided. For every blessed man jack of that khaki crew was for the Mascot.

Though I was bloody-jawed, they seized me, and hugged me, and manhandled me, and cheered me, and roared for me with cries like these :

"First victory for the Princess Pats!" ... "Did you see Fritzie get the run?" ... "Give me a hug at him; don't be a damned hog!" ... "Hi! throw him here!" ... "Jack, what the bloody hell did you want to stop it for? Since when didn't *you* approve of a fight?" ... "Took him a half-minute, too; and him half the size! It was over before it begun!" ... "Come here, old leather-belly, an' leave me crack your ribs!" ... "He's all pep and all pepper; he was raised on both!" ... "Well, God bless his dog soul, *he's* a soldier, too!"

So they passed me around, shouting and laughing, as if I were the inflated leather in a basketball game, while every splendid fellow among them forgot all about where he was, or why he was there, in the joy of congratulating me!

And even while I was being passed along in this renewed adulation which I loved, and tossed bodily from hand to hand, my brain – always busy – whelmed with wonder at a new truth. For I recalled the tensed, grim, sparkling faces of my soldier friends while I was throttling the mongrel; I coupled that memory with what was passing now; and at last I had found the great and perplexing truth I had been seeking.

I had wondered what war was. Now I knew. It had been war when I had been at the throat of the mongrel who had so wickedly assaulted me when I had not harmed him.

At last I had the explanation. The sympathy, the present remarks of the boys rendered it. I knew the meaning of the brown suits of severe appearance; the strange weapons; the drillings; all the pomp and the panoply and the discipline; the constant progress, somewhere.

I had seen no war yet. I had given my friends their first taste of war, kindling their enthusiasm; making them look forward to something *they* meant to do somewhere; something like what *I* had just done. We had seen no war yet; we were just preparing.

Somewhere some big mongrels of men must have attacked littler dogs of nations, and we were going to fight for the little dogs! It was a wonderfully inspiring thought. I thrilled at it, even before they put me down again on the ground as some of the officers came pushing into the ranks.

During the brief time that this scene had required we had all forgotten about the Colonel. But now everybody remembered, and as the men quickly went back to their places, many glances were stolen in his direction. But everybody was immediately reassured, and broad grins traveled back and forth through the lines.

For, though he continued to sit his horse with dignity unrelaxed, Colonel Farquhar, an imposing and truly military figure, had deigned to laugh in pure enjoyment of the situation and in appreciation of the regiment's first victory. And I knew positively that it was all right, for, as I, too, stole a glance at him, he winked at me with understanding that assured me that I would be subjected to none of the regulation field punishments.

So, while I licked the blood from my jaws upon some nice grass that was still green, though autumn had commenced, I marveled at the discovery I had made. And I was so proud that my forefathers for centuries past had raised me to become a soldier, and to win the first victory for the Princess Pats even before they got to *their* part of the war!

I was glad I had been able to show my courage, and what I could do in the fighting. Of course, I do not pick quarrels, and I would not be fool enough to imagine I could whip a bear, but if I was cornered by some monster, and had to fight – well, I would die fighting, anyway! And I have heard that is the ultimate test of a dog, or of a man.

We marched perhaps three miles through a beautiful country, in which the leaves of the soft maples of Canada were already turning, and up on top of a large hill called Fort Levis. We were given many tents, hundreds of them, and roundabout there were lovely green fields in which I loved to play, and through which oftentimes sundry of my brown-clad friends would romp with me when their duties did not confine them to camp.

How I enjoyed our stay there! But many of my comrades in khaki were dissatisfied and angry because they were not getting to the front. I heard them talking about it.

They complained that the war would be over before they would be given a chance.

"We would rather have war than this sort of thing!" they said. "That would be the *real* stuff! We want to help lick Heinie! Why all this working and drilling when we might have all the *real* fighting? They're using us as if we were rookies! I had years of that kind of work; we don't want to start all over again!"

Poor boys of mine! You saw the real fighting you wanted, and the God of Battles Who is also the God of Love knows how bravely you fought. And He alone knows, I think, just how many of you are still at the front, under the mounds of grasses marked with little crosses of wood. And He knows how well you fare, after the supreme sacrifice, in the fields of peace that lie beyond the rivers of blood and the briny walls of tears!

Editor's Notes to Chapter IV;

1) Francis Farquhar (1874-1915) was the Military Secretary to the Governor General, The Duke of Connaught. He was a long serving soldier having joined the Coldstream Guards in 1896, fought in the Boer War and won a Distinguished Service Order. Later he served in Somaliland. He appointed as Military Secretary in 1913.

Chapter V

I PLEASE THE LADIES

Soon came a day, during our stay at Fort Levis, when I was taken to a house where I met many beautiful ladies. It was rather a new social experience for me, since I had always been a sort of man's dog. But I met the situation with my usual poise, and in being introduced to the ladies I maintained my ordinary kindly dignity, which they seemed to find fascinating.

One of these ladies, and of the most beautiful of them, made a very special fuss over me. I noted that she was called a "Princess." I was given a very beautiful collar with a badge on it, and on the plate were engraved the words :

BOBBIE BURNS. P.P.C.L.I.

One dark lady, of extreme attractiveness, grabbed me around the neck and seemed very fond of dogs like me. She exclaimed that "she wished I belonged to her." Altogether, the women seemed to think as much of me as the men did, and my usual reciprocity policy was immediately in effect. There is room in my heart for love of a great many people, in addition to the supreme place that is for my Pendragon alone. So I added the love for all these nice women to that for the many fine men I had known.

A kind woman they called Lady Farquhar buckled the new collar around my neck and locked it. I absorbed all the honeyed sayings and the strokings. My picture was taken in many poses, and I sat very still, which seemed to cause them much wonderment.

"Isn't he well marked?" asked the beautiful dark lady. "I didn't know till now that he had such a lovely sable color! And that white ruff about his neck; isn't it picturesque?"

"What an *aristocrat* he is!" marveled one of them. At which I recalled a remark one of my khaki Canuck friends had made to me before I started on this call. "Bobbie," he said, "you're going to meet the aristocrats today. So be on your good behavior."

I shall always remember the happy days I spent at Fort Levis — though when the time came to leave it, I did so without whining but looked forward with eagerness to the next adventure.

The route marches we took through the country had always their exciting moments. I enjoyed every yard of the way. I grew more and more fascinated with the sight of khaki. Not only would I follow it anywhere, but I would not glance at a person who was not encased in it – except the ladies.

One day, when down in the village of Levis, I met a soldier in khaki. He was unusually kind, even for such a brown-clad comrade. I thought he was one of my "Pat's Pets" friends in khaki, and would soon take me back to the camp from which I had strayed, but I shortly found he was taking me to Quebec, instead. I could not resist him then as he had me tied to a rope, and he took me all the way to Valcartier.

I feared I would never rejoin the friends at Levis, and although I was well treated, I felt lost without them around me. In fact, "lost" was the word. I fretted; was sick and irritated; I could not eat nor sleep. I wanted my Pendy and his comrades – and mine.

Then one day, as if by magic, appeared one of those comrades of the Princess Pats. Frantic with joy, I bounded in glee. I laughed and barked and jumped. Do you think dogs cannot laugh? Well, I laughed that day!

I leaped up and put my arms around my friend's neck in ecstasy. And here is a strange thing that my comrades could never understand.

How did I know the man from the Princess Pats, even before he saw me, and before I saw his face, for I knew him at a distance? And how did I know the man who was keeping me, though he was a soldier in the same kind of uniform my Pats were wearing, was not a "Pat?" So that he always seemed wholly a stranger to me, and I pined in his keeping?

I cannot tell you how I knew, I fear, for you would not understand it. But I *knew*. I knew that soldier was from another regiment, and I sickened and brooded while he held me captive. And when the Pat arrived, why, I was a dog transformed.

It didn't take my rescuer long to make plain who I was and where I belonged, and he took me away with him. The soldier who had claimed me as his own had been telling everybody that I had come with him from Sault Ste. Marie. Of course I could not make anyone understand that he was mistaken, so had to make the best of it, but I was planning to gnaw the rope and escape from Valcartier and try to rejoin my friends when my deliverer appeared.

It took only a few hours to return to Levis, and maybe I was not glad to meet Pendy and Rob and Fred and the other dear friends again.

They all asked me where I'd been and what I had been doing, and I tried to tell them as well as I could. But it has always been a matter of deep grief to me that dogs can understand men better than men can understand dogs.

Some of those who understood me least accused me of deserting the regiment. But one of the boys who knew better than that – he was dear old Fred – waxed very indignant.

"Didn't they tell you that untasted meals and water were in front of him when he was found? And look how thin he is! He's been grieving for us! You make me very much to the sick!"

On September 26th one of my friends took me on a trip to Quebec. There we met by appointment a clergyman of a Fort Levis Church, and dined most sumptuously at the Château Frontenac. So many courses were served my friend and the clergyman that I thought the dinner would never end. But I was serenely satisfied with that, because I sat by the clergyman's chair and was given a piece of meat from every course.

The dining room was filled with beautiful ladies and handsome gentlemen, dressed in varicolored uniforms, mostly khaki. I noted various grades of Generals, Colonels and staff officers with red ribbons strung about their uniforms.

I noticed one officer with spectacular red covering most of his collar and two rows of ribbons across his breast, showing, I presume, a tremendous amount of service in other wars. As my soldier friend told the clergyman, this officer had concentrated "in expounding his occult knowledge of all the intricate and enigmatic workings of military prowess, past and present." The ladies with him listened; in fact, that seemed to be all they had a chance to do. It may be that they were sublimely awed by the discourse; I hope so.

After dinner we walked the promenade and listened to the band which played there nightly. There were not many dogs about, and I was fearful of my feet being trodden upon by the mass of humanity walking hither and thither – God alone knew where or why.

It was near to midnight when we arrived back at camp. Lights were out and sentries were on every corner. "Halt! Who goes there?" was shouted many times before we arrived at our tent. Fatigued by a busy day and night, I was asleep in two winks.

The next morning brought a bustle of new excitement. The boys were packing kits, pulling down tents, loading them on wagons and having them hauled away. I was tied to a post all morning and was in great fear that I would be left behind. But when the P.P.'s marched down I marched with them and arrived at the pier full of anticipation regarding the next adventure.

Tied to the pier was a large and splendid boat, the *Royal George*. As we were lined up in front of it there was much loading of provisions and bustle of all sorts. Fred and Rob busied themselves with the "gunny sack – extra kit" trick, and – more reconciled than I had been on the first occasion – I entered the boat in the depths of the bag slung over a stalwart shoulder. In fact, I even extracted a little malicious satisfaction in it when I thought how we were fooling those "higher up." Though I heard Fred say "he guessed they knew it, but were winking at it."

I was put in one of the staterooms and tied. The boat remained at the pier till September 30th. At 11:30 in the morning we sailed for somewhere, all day and all that night. In the morning we arrived at Gaspe Bay.

This was a large bay, holding dozens of large ships that reached as far as the eye could see. It was a magnificent, inspiring, never-to-be-forgotten sight. Out to the horizon rode the warships, some of them so distant as to seem only slightly larger than specks. The vessels rode graceful and light as gulls in the dimpling waters. Yet, too, they gave the eye an impression of bulwarks of strength, strong and steady like rocks.

During the day their automatic semaphores were perpetually bobbing signals to ships miles away. During the night their signals blinked like the flashing eyes of some uncanny creatures of the deep.

My stay at Gaspe Bay was enjoyable at first. I was allowed to run over the deck, and I went up to the officers' mess and down to the sailors' mess, making many new friends and cementing the older friendships.

I met the ladies again – those to whom I had been introduced at Levis – and they were pleased to see me. Some did not seem as cheerful as before, but all were friendly.

I grew to feel very sorry for some of these ladies. They sat in chairs and were wheeled about the deck. Their eyes looked dismal and red and their cheeks were white and hollow. From their lips fell no merry laughter and no cheerful welcome, such as I had heard from them when they were on land. Upon their faces was a wistful, anxious look, as if they were longing for something they knew was out of their reach; a sort of "I wish I were dead" look. I tried by every artifice known to dogdom to cheer them, but with little success.

I have heard since that what the ladies had was *mal de mer*. I have often wondered since how anything so horrible as that sickness could have such a pretty name!

Chapter VI

EASTWARD HO !

The second day of October was beautiful – and memorable. There were many ships in sight; warships, scout ships, sailing ships – and the hardships of those who still entertained the pangs of that awful seasickness with the French name. But most of us, including myself, were by now well over these.

My boys aboard the *Royal George* formed a ring on the decks and had boxing contests, accompanied by laughter, cheering and noise. The ladies seemed to enjoy these. All the officers were at the ringside and the ship's officers watched from the bridge or top deck. Colonel Farquhar took a lively interest in the exhibitions.

The proceedings were enlivened at one point by a breezy debate between two officers regarding the winner of a certain bout. It wound up by one of them jumping into the ring and offering his services as referee for the following bouts. It had looked for a few moments before then as if one of them would meet the other for a few rounds, and the men were hugging themselves with anticipation – but no such luck!

No two officers agreed with each other regarding the decisions which other officers were making, and there was so much faultfinding that finally an official referee was appointed and he adjudicated all the remaining bouts.

But that didn't seem to make much difference, except that it didn't do any good then for you to "kick," because what the referee said settled it. I could not see that it helped so very much. Nobody was satisfied except the men who were named winners, and those who had backed them, for a few bets changed hands, among both officers and men. It looked to me as if the referee aimed principally to please himself, and I have noticed that it is always easier to do that than it is to please other people. When darkness fell, the boxing was postponed, till the next day.

There were rumors afloat at daybreak of October 3rd that all the ships were to sail at 8:30 A.M., and some of them did get under way. Shortly before starting, a small Canadian warship went the rounds of all the troop ships, and signaled to each of them:

"Good-bye. God bless you!"

So Canada formally bade farewell to the men departing to fight under the insignia of the Maple Leaf on European soil.

Each troop ship received the signal in reverential silence. Aboard the *Royal George* we waited our turn to receive this Godspeed from home and fireside, from loved ones left behind. From the stoutest heart and the most reckless soul – and there were many aboard that craft – came a long sigh as the letters: "G-O-D B-L-E-S-S Y-O-U" were signaled to the ship. It was an unforgettable moment. The *Royal George* signaled back: "Thank you; good luck to you."

It was some little time before the sudden feeling of homesickness left the hearts of most of the men, so many of whom were destined never to return. They crawled below or walked the deck in silence more eloquent than words.

As the morning wore on, however, their spirits revived. Soon there was renewed talk of sport and a proposition was made for a boat race between picked men from each company, but it did not materialize.

All the afternoon there was drill. Each company was exercised in turn, running back and forth, up and down the decks. They had to goose-step, hop-skip and mark time. This greatly delighted the recruits, but utterly disgusted the veterans.

The veterans remembered always to register muffled complaints in no uncertain language of these tactics, condemning them as "the most outlandish tomfoolery." They were careful, however, to indulge in these outbursts in the seclusion of their staterooms.

At five o'clock in the afternoon we had boxing again and this continued till about dark. Then, a little while later, when all had quieted down, the *Royal George* lifted anchor and slowly and silently sailed away.

There was nothing much to be seen of the boats in front, behind or on either side. But occasional flashes of light, twinkling from the deep, told us that we were not alone by any means, and that our course was guarded by ships from the greatest navy on earth, silent watchers from afar.

At eight in the evening we had a very successful concert in the dining room. Much new talent – just discovered on our ship – shone or tinkled, and the jubilant notes of music fell in a delightful patter.

Lights were out at nine o'clock and everybody had to "dig in" below. There was no escaping that order; the bluejackets saw to that.

I spent the night in the butcher shop. But what good did that do me? I was tied up!

In the morning, however, I was again given the freedom of the ship, and roamed about joyously, for I had felt the last qualm of seasickness.

The convoy carrying the first contingent of Canadian troops was the largest that had ever sailed the seas up to that time; or since, so far as official censorship has permitted to be known.

The convoy sailed in the following formation:

Cruiser, H.M.S. Charybdis
Cruiser, H.M.S. Diana

Troopships

	Megantic	Caribbean	Scotian	
	Ruthenia	Athenia	Arcadian	
	Bermudian	Royal Edward	Zeeland	
	Alaunia	Franconia	Corinthian	
Cruiser	Ivernia	Canada	Virginian	Cruiser
H.M.S.	Scandinavian	Monmouth	Andania	H.M.S.
Eclipse	Sicilian	Manitou	Saxonia	Glory
	Montezuma	Tyrolia	Grampian	
	Lapland	Tunisian	Lakonia	
	Cassandra	Laurentic	Montreal	
	Florizel		Royal George	

Cruiser, H.M.S. Talbot

In this order, the cruisers *Charybdis* and *Diana* protected the front of the flotilla of transports. The *Eclipse* was stationed on the starboard side and the *Glory* on the port side. The *Talbot* protected the rear.

We still had the little sparrows on board, flying from one ship to the other, continually on the hunt for forage. It seemed so strange to see these little creatures, that I had always beheld fluttering about the trees on land, skimming across the water and over our decks.

I heard that our speed was less than nine knots an hour. All day long we were within sight of land. I heard it called Newfoundland; high, barren cliffs of rock.

After the first novelty of the ship I became somewhat bored, but this may have been because I felt a little sick again. For a while I was sick of the boat, of the food; of the water, fresh and salt. But various kind folk tended me and soon I grew better.

Nearly every night there was a concert in one of the large rooms. The air was rather stuffy, but as there was great excitement I endured the stuffiness with philosophy. I love company; I was never built for a hermit dog.

On October 5th a hubbub rose on our decks as a strange ship approached us from the starboard side. It waited within a short distance until the last ship passed, then took its place in the northernmost line. Everybody wondered what ship it could be. It was settled by some Solomon among us, who stated that she was the S.S. *Florizel*, carrying the Newfoundland contingent. As nobody disputed him, the *Florizel* she remained.

So Britain, "on whose possessions the sun never sets," rallied her forces from her widespread sunlight when Germany resorted to the blackjack to gain "her place in the sun!"

Also, the excitement which was chronic with us, whose nerves were strained with the suspense of what might lie ahead, and the enemy dangers the high seas might hold, broke out again one morning soon after the *Florizel* had joined us. Our transport, the *Royal George*, suddenly put on all steam and passed all the other boats. I thought at first, amid all the conjectures on every side, that perhaps a race was in progress. But surmises were settled when the *Royal George* took her place as a scout boat to the right of the line, perhaps fifteen miles from the others.

There she remained all day, traveling now at the same slow pace as did the rest of the fleet. For a while we all thought we were going to leave the other ships and go "on our own," but then we heard we were to do scout duty from then on during the day, returning to the column at night. The view of the remainder of the fleet was much more splendid from that distance, and we thus had a pleasure not enjoyed by those on the other ships of that grand convoy.

Much argument obtained among the soldiers whether we would be able to outrun a German cruiser if one appeared. Some claimed that the slow boats were heavily armed with many high-calibred guns and much ammunition. Then, in case an enemy craft appeared, the slow boats would close in on her and fight to a finish, while the faster boats made for the nearest port.

This appeared a plausible method of attack and defense; and the sailors and bluejackets, by their looks and actions, could be depended upon to give a good account of themselves if called upon to do so.

They had the "fighting swing," the "fighting build," the "fighting face." Even their clothes seemed cut for a "rough-house" engagement at a moment's notice. They were of the proper breed, those boys. They possessed that soft, easy, mild mannered – even harmless – look of a hand grenade, just before it explodes! They contained their share of the universal spirit – the spirit of Britain, France, America – which was to amaze Germany.

So I felt perfectly safe in their company. Anybody watching a British sailor at his work would have to feel that way.

Besides, there were the professional "battlers" lurking in the offing. Sometimes they were invisible; then they would creep into sight from the rim of the horizon. Their long gray forms glided into view, giving a thrilling feeling of power that spread throughout the transports. Their huge guns pointed menacingly in all directions. I could not imagine any enemy approaching them without these guns barking their mighty barks – that deadly bark which heralds spew as deadly as the lava from a raging volcano.

Chapter VII

IN ENGLAND

In our journey overseas each day was much like its predecessor. The *Royal George* would daily take its place as scout boat fifteen miles south of the line and return to it at night.

There were nightly concerts in the salon. On October 11th we sighted a large French warship which was traveling from a southern direction and disappeared to the north of the fleet of transports. The next day a large British dreadnaught hove in sight. He was of the latest type, with bristling guns protruding from his sides and from bow and stern. The man-o'-war entered the convoy near the center line and steamed through it till he departed to the northeast.

Came the next day, the 13th, but there was nothing unlucky about it. We were told we were a hundred miles south of Ireland. It rained during the afternoon, but the sea remained calm. A large ship, sailing south, passed the fleet.

About twelve o'clock these ships received orders to break away from the convoy and proceed "on their own": *Royal Edward, Franconia, Tunisian, Canada, Laurentic, Virginian, Royal George, Megantic, Bermudian* and the *Lapland*.

Shortly after they left the fleet, two large destroyers appeared to the southeast, first as specks which grew larger till they were within a half-mile of the new convoy. Then they slowed down and sailed with it the rest of the way to Blighty.

Our ships which had proceeded "on our own," and were protected by the destroyers, were faster than the others and we reached England well in advance of them.

We sailed to the English coast and arrived off Plymouth at about 3:20 P.M. The shores were lined with people, cheering madly for the Canadian boats as they approached the mouth, or channel. The *Royal George* anchored to the same buoy as the *Alaunia*, and the respective officers exchanged calls during the afternoon, and swapped experiences of their trip across.

At 10:30 the next morning a large British training boat made the rounds of all the ships. The decks were black with young naval cadets who were stationed on various training ships in the harbor. Never was there lustier cheering than came from these young throats as the boys viewed the Canuck troops.

During the afternoon many boats of all kinds, sailing ships and even ferry boats, when passing the warships and transports, would set the nearby hills re-echoing with the screeching of whistles, while the voices upon their decks lent their plaudits. On sea and land lungs and machinery vied in bluff noises of welcome for my beloved Pats and their comrades.

There was every evidence of unusual enthusiasm in the ordinarily quiet port of Plymouth.

Later a tug came alongside the boat and landed a revenue officer and the health inspector. The inspector gave the boat a clean bill of health and left the latest issues of English papers on board.

Two days later the *Alaunia* was taken away and the troop ship *Grampian* replaced it alongside the *Royal George*. This boat had 500 men and about 700 head of horses aboard. During the afternoon a boat came alongside with an invitation for some of the troops to have tea at General Pale-Carew's estate. Needless to say, this invitation was most popular and was accepted with no regrets.

It seemed good to feel the land beneath one's feet again; and a little strange, too, at first. The streets of the village we passed through were lined with people who were profuse with offers of sandwiches and fruit. The soldiers accepted all the gifts for immediate consumption. So, by the time they arrived at the estate, they were unable to partake very heartily of the tea!

At ten o'clock in the morning of October 17th two large tugs came to the steamer and started with it up the river. They halted at a large dock. There was a great shipyard there with many large boats and battleships. In fact, in the harbor were several unfinished battleships; fighting monsters of gray steel.

At 4:30 in the afternoon, Hon. Colonel Sam Hughes and Colonel Carson came aboard the boat, and as they were leaving they were given three rousing cheers by the P.P.C.L.I's.

About dusk orders were given to pack all kits and be ready to disembark. The Pats complied amid great excitement.

They marched two miles to a railroad station and were soon aboard a train. After five hours the station of Amesbury was reached. This was eight miles from Bustard Camp, Salisbury Plains.

The road to this camp was dry and hard, and ideal for marching soldiers. Our camp was located on a small hill about a quarter-mile from Bustard Camp. Bustard Camp consisted of a farm and two small inns. Therein refreshments were served and beds made at all hours. There was also a bar, but liquor was not served to soldiers. These inns were "out of bounds" to them.

On October 19th the Canadian soldiers received their first mail from home. The next day the battalion went to the "butts," and the humdrum of camp life was resumed.

Route marches, parades, inspections, and all the "stuff" that the veteran in the game dislikes so thoroughly were fully engaged in here. October 24th there was a grand parade for inspection by Lord Roberts. With us were 5,000 other Canadian troops. It took the Lord about twenty minutes to inspect us.

A fortnight of tramping over this ground transformed it and the camp to a veritable morass of mud and water. The daily rains started in enthusiastically to help, so that soon the quagmire was up to the knees.

Many visitors came to the camp, relatives of some of the English soldiers. They seemed greatly impressed with the Canadians. Instead of seeing a mob of partly uniformed civilians playing at soldiering, they appeared surprised to find as fine and well-organized a body of men as could be seen in any British camp.

The rain continued steadily. There was scarcely a day without its showers. The downpours interrupted parades and route marches, and the soldiers' clothing was wet most of the time. In fact, it was seldom dry, there being no fire by which to dry it.

The Canadians found the much heralded "ideal" climate of "the tight little isle" the wettest, dankest sponge in the shape of weather they had ever experienced. And the Canucks were more than ever surprised to find that the English houses were about as cold as the outside weather.

During these days I had an anxious interval. I was almost quarantined, but not quite.

A "civvie" (civilian) constable of the district notified Adjutant Captain Buller that upon a coming Monday he would call to collect all dogs that had been brought over with the Canadian contingent. There were eight of us in all; though, of course, none of the other seven was Mascot of the Princess Pats. Still, they had their rights, and it seemed to me that, as usual, officials were impertinently infringing upon these.

It appears that the British Board of Agriculture had caused a law to be passed that all domestic animals brought into the British Isles must undergo six months' quarantine regulations, this being a measure to prevent disease from being carried into the country.

The Adjutant called my Pendragon into the orderly room and read the letter to him. When Pendragon came out he was thinking hard.

I don't believe those British authorities took account of the resource of my men of the Northland.

Anyway, Pendy and Rob and Fred and others of my friends held a council of war. The next thing I knew, I was taken away quietly from the camp by some of them and led to the outskirts of Salisbury and placed in the care of some kind persons. They took my collar off; the one that the nice lady had given me in Canada. I could not figure what it was all about, but Pendy said I was not to worry, so I did not. Then they went away.

It seems that before they returned to camp they bought another dog, a mongrel of low degree, and put my collar around his neck and led him back to camp in my place!

When that constable person appeared on the designated day at the headquarters of my Pats – he had heard of their Mascot, of course – and demanded me to be sent to quarantine, they handed over this mongrel with a display of great grief. My Pendragon asked the constable to be allowed to keep the treasured collar, so he graciously allowed him to take it off the mongrel's neck. Then they led him away to quarantine.

Fred almost sobbed in the constable's hearing. "There goes the last of Bobbie Burns, the most aristocratic Mascot a regiment ever had!" he quavered.

The constable looked first at the mongrel, then at Fred. There was a pitying look upon his face, as if he feared grief had robbed my friend of his reason. "Aristocratic! That mongrel? Huh!" But Fred was always a joker.

Then, after a day or two, my comrades came to the town for me, replaced my collar, and I capered merrily with them back to camp. On the way I met some of the Pat's officers. They grinned at me and winked, as if it were all a rare joke.

I have always felt that my friends prevented me from suffering some fierce fate.

On November 15th the P.P.C.L.I.'s received orders to pack all blankets in bundles of ten, and all kits, and make ready to leave for Winchester, twelve miles from Southampton. Southampton is a city of about 120,000 inhabitants and is on the southeast coast of England.

As the Pats were leaving Bustard Camp, the 1st Brigade of the Canadian Army lined the route of our march for perhaps five miles in the direction of Amesbury. As the battalion approached each of their brother battalions gave three rousing, rhythmic, army cheers. The circling hills echoed and re-echoed with this enthusiastic farewell as "Pat's Pets" marched by with their usual "swank" and cockiness. Little did they realize that they were listening to the last Canadian cheers that most of them would ever hear.

At two o'clock on the morning of December 4th, at the new camp at Winchester, a fire alarm sounded, rousing the Princess Pats and the whole brigade. Here the Pats had an opportunity of measuring the thoroughness of British army discipline and alertness.

In qualities of quick decision and almost simultaneous action, the K.R.R.'s (King's Royal Rifles) and Shrops (Shropshire Light Infantry), were distinctly on the job at that early hour of the morning.

They were at the scene of the fire even before the Pats were, though they were a half-mile further away.

They dressed and proceeded their half-mile to the fire while the Patricias were garbing and doing not more than a hundred yards to it.

The results of the fire were disastrous to the Pats, for two of their best officers were severely burned in it.

The blaze was among the tents. A tent sheltering Lieutenant Papineau and Captain Stewart was consumed, and these two officers, who were caught asleep, were severely burned about their heads and faces. They had narrow escapes from death as they were hauled from their beds amid the burning embers of the tent and floor. They had to be immediately sent to a hospital for treatment.

They were not able to accompany the battalion to France but rejoined it later.

Ultimately Papineau was killed on the Belgian front, in 1917 after a military record of great efficiency and valor. He had been promoted to Major on the field.

Captain Stewart, after similarly gallant service, was eventually made Major on the field, and was acting in that capacity when this chapter was written in the spring of 1918.

Major Stewart was with Captain Scott in Scott's dash for the South Pole. It will be recalled that Scott reached there thirty days after Amundsen, of Sweden, achieved the ambition that had baffled explorers for so many years.

From December 4th till 9th occurred a series of rains, which seemed even wetter than usual, making a morass of the camp and grounds. It was very cold and dismal rain, too, and it discouraged the men and also myself.

Confound these climates where the sun is almost always taking a vacation, say I!

Editor's Notes to Chapter VII:

1) Sir Sam Hughes (1853-1921) was the highly controversial Minister of Militia and Defence, 1914-16. He was a flamboyant and difficult character, known for his raising of the First Canadian Contingent at Valcartier and the Ross Rifle.

2) Sir John Wallace Carson (1864-1922) was Sam Hughes special envoy in England. He was in charge of the Canadian Forces in the UK until 1916.

3) Field Marshal Lord Roberts (1832-1914) or "Bobs" as he was affectionately known, had led the British Army through many successful Colonial Campaigns and was seen as the savior of the British Army (and by extension, savior of the British Empire) during the Boer War. At the beginning of the war he was brought out to wave the flag, but he contracted pneumonia and died in 1914. Buried St. Paul's Cathedral, London, England.

4) The Adjutant was Herbert Cecil Buller (1881-1916). He was a long-serving British Officer. His career started in the Rifle Brigade in 1900. He was a member of the Governor-General's staff when war broke out in 1914.

5) The officers burned were Talbot Papineau and Charlie Stewart. Papineau (1883-1917) was from a well-to-do French-Canadian family, with deep historical roots in Quebec. He was killed at Passchendaele on October 30th, 1917. His body was not found after the war and he is commemorated on the Menin Gate Memorial, Ieper, Belgium.

Charles J.T. Stewart (1874-1918) was from Halifax, Nova Scotia. He served with the Patricias from 1914 and rose to Lieutenant-Colonel in command of the Regiment in 1918. He was killed in action near Cambrai, September 28th, 1918.

Chapter VIII

BILLETS AND PIPES

I have heard that some good gray poet – I have forgotten which one, as most poets grow gray at it, though not all of them are good – once wrote these lines:

> *"Of all sad words of tongue or pen*
> *The saddest are these: 'It might have been.'"*

To this sentiment, those of my original "Pat's Pets" friends who survive, recollecting the incident which I now relate, will subscribe.

During that early December, when the weather was so soggy, the soldiers of my battalion were suddenly ordered to select billets among the houses on the outskirts of the town of Winchester.

Needless to say there was much elation over this order, and reports swiftly spread through the ranks that henceforth the men were to be billeted out, and that the discomfort of muddy grounds and cold, clammy, wet tents would be speedily and automatically ended.

Now their damp clothing could be dried at night and they could sleep in comfort on the floors of various buildings!

The effect upon the battalion, after the first trips to formally select billets, was magical. My boys all worked with a will that was surprising. Instead of the grouch that had been becoming chronic, it was a case of mirth and song, and those who couldn't sing – and God knows how many soldiers there are with no ear for melody! – tried to, anyway.

"When I get to billets," observed Fred, "you can bet your shirt that I'll trot out my jane in style!"

"Wait a minute," interposed Rob, the poet of the "Soldiers Three." "This glad occasion inspires my muse afresh. You know she's been developing ringbones and spavins lately, in all this muck. But I feel her jumping within me. Just a second now! I've got it! Listen to this!"

> *"When foxy Freddie draws a billet*
> *Sequestered from the damned old rain,*
> *He'll grab dull care and straightway kill it,*
> *A-hiking with his piking jane."*

"Just for that," observed Archie, the pessimist, "I hope to God you get bullets instead of billets!"

When I first knew Archie in Canada he was an optimist, but since he struck England and its mud he has been beefing so hard that his face was crinkled like a bulldog's. He was the best little killjoy in the regiment. He was always prophesying that things would be worse, and so far he hadn't missed a bet.

But how that boy could fight, as he proved later! He just kind of naturally took out his grouch on the Germans.

Just now, however, his cynical prophecies that there would be no billets were received with scorn and derision.

"That's all right!" growled Archie, "but I can tell you poor stews this; that you ain't going to get hoarse counting up the billets you'll draw!"

Amid friendly curses he went away, while the boys continued to exult over the comforts that would soon be theirs.

"Tomorrow or next day," they had decided, they would be in billets. Spick and span they would step from them of an evening, having obtained leave for a couple of hours, and their "janes" would meet them at the doors, and together they would wander through the sogginess and dream love's young dream, for Cupid is an extra good comrade to the fellow in khaki.

There was a dance listed which some of the boys hoped to get leave to attend. Wait till they should swank to it from their billets!

Up to now the words of the blasted pessimists had come true; too true! But there was an end of that. The coming billets were ushering in a new day!

Hopefully they awaited the orders to move into billets. They waited for a couple of days. No orders came – and as if in fiendish appreciation of this state of their suspense, the elements started elementing even more earnestly than they had been doing.

But after those two nights, still in the soaked tents, came another order to select billets, this time in another section of the town.

"Blimy!" exclaimed one English soldier, "I wonder what was the matter with those other billets? Folks must ha' kicked!"

Sergeant Wilson went to the new section with a party which included Fred and Rob.

He knocked at the door of a humble cottage, rather small. He saluted as a fat little woman opened the door.

"Madam," asked Sergeant Wilson, "how many of our men can you billet in your home?"

"Mighty!" replied the woman in dismay, using a term much in favor in the region. "H'i cawn't billet h'anyone! We has on'y these two 'ere rooms for me husban' an' me an' the two bybies."

"That doesn't matter!" replied Sergeant Wilson sternly. "It's military necessity, and we must have these billets. You should be able to accommodate six of these men on the floor of one of the rooms."

Fred and Rob and the other looked inside appreciatively. How much nicer would be that strip of new clean carpet to lie on, instead of in the mud which comprised the usual soldier's bed of late!

"Well," replied the woman, "h'if H'i must, H'i must!" and she shut the door hard.

So it went, till a number of visits had been made by various detachments, and the men returned to camp in high spirits. That night, or the next, orders would surely issue to leave the soggy tents and proceed to billets!

But two more days drifted by, while the boys remained anxious and mystified.

Then they received the shock of their lives.

There was blandly handed them the information that this had been merely *practice* billeting! That there would be no *real* billeting in England. That was reserved till they should reach the front in France.

For some days thereafter, Archie, whose dark prediction had again been proved true, merely *looked* those four ancient and hated words, when used in this order: "I told you so!"

He did not dare to speak them. If he had, his comrades would have murdered him by some ingenious new slow method.

Various happenings proceeded, but I hasten to a joyous one that was a red letter one for me. For how I had longed for this happy day to arrive, yet feared that it never would. And when it did, it seemed almost too good to be true!

Since I had joined the Princess Pats at Ottawa, there was but one and only one thing connected with the regiment that made for my annoyance.

It is the memory of those hellish bagpipes of unhallowed and unregretted associations; those wailing, undulating, yowling contrivances that irked my tufted ears for many moons; that drew my howls of protest as they skirled under golden sun, or silvery moon and the scandalized stars!

How many months had I endured those barbaric strains, worse than the shrieks torn from the souls condemned of a host of hated cats!

The morning of that 17th of December, 1914, a morning soon rendered glorious in my vision despite the gloom and the rain and the mud thereof, – I made this discovery that filled me with so much of simple joy.

I saw my friends of the bagpipe band – who were good, talented fellows, all of them – packing those instruments of sorrow.

A little careless and gentle inquiry on my part elicited the news that, within an hour, those harbingers of harikari would be rolling in a van to the station, en route for Aberdeen, Scotland, for safekeeping during the period of the war.

I found a dry spot of land and rolled blissfully upon it; I barked and tittered and mouthed my delight with all the power of the two sound lungs nature has given me. My heart was filled with love of all things living, and I was perfectly willing to let the dead past bury its dead.

I scampered about, making friends with everybody, trying to tell everybody what it was that I was so happy about – and most of them understood. My smile was never wider, my eyes never brighter, my bark never pealed more clearly than in that happy hour.

But this life is made up of reactions. I have always noticed that when you are happiest, a sorrow inevitably follows it.

It was so with me now.

There was a preliminary bustle through the ranks of my regiment that told me that it would soon be leaving for France.

And I found that I was not destined to go to the front line trenches with my beloved Pats!

No; this stay at Winchester was my last with them, as a regiment. They were a fighting unit now, and I was not to be exposed to the dangers that would constantly confront them.

They would sail across in advance of me, and I was to be left to be taken with the transport, which would carry over the quartermaster's supplies, the horses, the artillery, etc.

My friends, in arranging that I should be in the rear lines instead of the front trenches, explained to me that it was for my good. They claimed that a lively and live dog was more companionable and satisfying any day than a dead dog.

Though bitterly disappointed, as the day for their departure drew near, I had, perforce, to yield that this view was reasonable.

Pendragon told me I was to stay with those of the rear; that I was not to wander away; that I was to be a good dog. He said there would always be friends back with me, so I should not feel lonely, and that I would see all there was to be seen; and by that he did not mean wholly with physical eyes, for he knows the eyes of my spirit, and realizes that it is given power to see more than can be seen by the spirits of men.

I thoroughly understood what he told me, and I am proud to

remember that, during all the time we were at the front, I gave not the least bit of trouble. I did just what I was told to do and stayed wherever I was told to stay. The seriousness of war had by now been impressed upon me.

Nevertheless I had ample opportunity to gather the story that I give you in the ensuing pages. Through the days and nights the grim thunders of the great guns reverberated in my ears. I saw many terrible and heartrending sights; with the eyes alike of the flesh and of the spirit. My friends caught me to their breasts and told me with trembling voices stories alike of joy and of sorrow; always I was in touch with those who fought, who were about to fight – and who had fought and found peace eternal. I could see their shadowy forms across the border; could catch the messages which their spirits transmitted in the language that is subtler than that contrived by stumbling tongues.

Though my body was not in the front line trenches, my spirit was there, and I saw many a sight in visions, and heard many a word, that the speech of men later confirmed for truth.

It came, therefore, that my boys set off on the last hike ere they crossed the Channel to the French front, with their Mascot left to follow, and remain behind them. I watched them wistfully – and when they disappeared from view my spirit was with them.

Editor's Notes to Chapter VIII:

1) Sergeant George Wilson, #1751; born Glasgow, Scotland, 1883; previously served 5 years in the Inniskilling Fusiliers. During the Great War was wounded three times; April 16th, 1915, June 2nd, 1916 and August 14th, 1918. Struck off Strength, September 1st, 1918.

Chapter IX

ON FRENCH SOIL

Bright and early on the morning of December 20th began a furore of preparation. Kit-bags, transport wagons, tents; everything of any use around the place was packed and the boys lined up for a march down the road. They marched and rested and then marched again. It seemed a very long way to the place called Southampton.

People lined both sides of the streets for miles and miles to say good-bye to the Canadians. They cheered and shook hands with each soldier as he passed, and many a gallant Canuck, too, was kissed by old and young. There were men, women and children all shaking hands at once for miles and miles along that road. The streets were packed with masses of good English folk, bands were playing and all hurrahed like mad.

They marched to the Southampton docks and were put on a large and beautiful boat. There was plenty of room, though there seemed to be thousands on board. The boat left the dock about 7:15 in the evening, and for the first time each soldier was served with hard slabs of eatables that looked like dog biscuit and what the boys called tins of bully beef. There came a time when I ate some pieces of this dog biscuit and bully beef.

From either shore many searchlights were playing on the waters, and these wavering beams came also from surrounding warships. Many warships and more transports were about, and the rays played about the craft till it was well out in the Channel.

The night was inky dark, enshrouding a calm sea. The effect of the myriad searchlights, splitting the gloom, was indescribable. The surrounding gleams seemed countless, mysterious coruscations from every angle in the gloom. So the ship moved on stealthily in the calm sea through the maze of lights, it being impossible to tell where the water ended and the shore began.

The men were sent below. Some of them were nonchalantly asleep in a few minutes. Others did not care to sleep, and strolled about through the night with their heads bent, thinking. I knew why they were thinking so seriously.

Now there was an essence in the atmosphere that told me the supreme step had come; that soon they and I would fully know the hateful meaning of that black-and-red word, war.

My friends were up early, when it was still dark. It was six of the morning, though the gloom was still that of night. They could see the lights from the shores of France as they bestirred themselves and made ready for the order to leave the boat.

The lights of the warships were still flickering around the transports. There were rumors that they were to land as soon as the tide came in. Meanwhile, the ships continued to travel slowly in circles, which they did for hours.

It was 1:30 P.M. when our boat sidled carefully to the dock and we prepared to march off it. Our tall Adjutant Captain Buller was the first Canadian officer with a fighting battalion to set foot on French soil to fight for the threatened liberties of the world.

It was destined that he should not return, but would die a fighter's death at the head of his men. The thought of death, associated with him, would have seemed incongruous in that moment, as he walked blithely down the gang-plank. It was as if he were on parade, with his easy active gait and cheerful swing. So thousands have stepped since down the gang-planks – and never returned to Blighty – nor to Canada.

It chanced, after this, that my Pendragon was the first "man o' the line" of a Canadian regiment to press foot upon the soil of "la belle France."

Because of this fact, I still retain a sense of real, *bona fide*, grievous injury, the injury of a pal denied his just right!

For the shoes of a large number of soldiers, Canadian and otherwise, pressed that soil before my four pads had a chance at it! For, you see, I did not come with Pendragon down that particular gang-plank.

I wish it had been different. I wish even that I had been in that accursed gunny sack again, over Pendy's shoulder. I had been "sneaked" by various frontiers. Why couldn't I have been sneaked past the last one, the supreme one?

This France seemed to be quite a different country from England. Its friendship was probably as sincere but less noisy. How I loved the noisy friendships of Canada and England!

So my Pats started in to make some noise of their own. How proud was my spirit of them when it heard how well they were succeeding! It may have been that these French, in the months since the war had started, had become more hardened to it than the Canadians who were just coming into it; that it had become somewhat of a monotony to them. But the spirits of "Pat's Pets," landing at last for the fray, enjoyed a swift reaction through this cause, and it found vent in the noise they and I loved.

The uproar was deafening. My Pats made noises imitating Indians and Africans and all kinds of native peoples. They sounded just like them, too, for my friends, the pick of Canada and largely made up of veteran fighters, had traveled throughout the world and had made every form of noise known to the human race. The result now bordered upon the inhuman.

It appeared to me that the good French people were filled with awe at such unusual actions from men on their way to do battle in a real war. Such behavior might have been in place at a movie rehearsal – evidently reflected these French peasants – but prior to a life-and-death struggle, it was very odd to them.

They gazed at the Canadians as if they constituted a band of escaped lunatics. They were wide-eyed and wide-mouthed, absorbed in wonder and fright. From their aspect you would gather that they thought us a band of disguised Huns, who somehow eluding the British navy had come from the rear and were now doing a war dance just before attacking them.

The Canadians were acting much differently from the British "Tommy," or in fact from any other troops they had seen going into action. The Canucks seemed like a big theatrical troupe before the start of a play, or like delirious warriors, plied with some fascinating drug, going to their death with frolic and laughter. No college sophomores had ever paraded with more noise or abandon after a victorious football contest or baseball game.

When they had, perforce, to stop and rest lungs and gesturing limbs for a moment, those bewildered French people would cautiously come a little closer, rubbing their eyes. They would catch hold of a soldier's arm, or stroke his uniform or his rifle. This they did to make sure they were not dreaming; that these were indeed men from a friendly young Power overseas who had come to fight with their *poilus*.

Soon, too, they were overjoyed to find among the Canadian ranks some men of their own flesh and blood, who could talk to them in their own tongue; whose hands, even, gestured like their own while they were talking. After this, their attitude showed they quickly gained confidence, and soon were enthusiastic over the Canucks, after the excitable fashion of the Gallic race.

That the spirits of the Canadians were noisily expressed was a matter of no wonderment. They come from a land of sharp contrasts in temperature; where in the summers, even in the regions close to the Arctic Circle, the warm sun pours flame down upon the fruitful black loam of the land; where in the autumns the maple leaf which is our insignia turns to crimson and gold in a night; where in the winters our world is covered with a soft robe of fleecy snow as white as purity itself, and the crackle of a twig in the frigid stillness sounds like the snap of a pistol; where in the swift-blown springs in a trice is accomplished a miracle in green and bloom and fragrance.

Well, after some time, order was restored, and the men cheerfully complied with the brusque orders of the officers to "fall in." They were marched to very wet grounds on the top of a hill. It was quite dark before they reached camp. All were tired and sleepy as they tumbled into the tents.

There seemed to be less tents to get into than had been the case at Winchester. There were about sixteen men to each "circle" tent; they had to sleep so close together that all were quite warm. If a man wanted to leave the tent during the night he had to walk over – and upon – the others. As the night had turned bitterly cold, and there was but a single blanket for each man on a wet ground, the matter of sleeping was not the most comfortable diversion in the world upon that night.

With all the discomfort morning came much too soon with the usual "parade," "number off," "form fours," "stand at ease," etc. As usual, too, there was the wait of an hour or so for the officer, only to be again dismissed.

At 1:30 in the afternoon they were ordered to pack up again "in full marching order." Followed another wait, this time of some hours, then they marched several miles through the town of Havre to the station, a dirty old building surrounded by as much mud as we had wallowed around in at Winchester.

It was well after dark when they were issued four days' rations and piled into small dingy flat cars. These cars looked to be constructed to accommodate twenty Frenchmen each. Yet, for this emergency, into each of them was wedged forty-three men of more than ordinary dimensions – which is to say, forty-three Canadians.

But all were surprisingly good-natured. It was the combative instinct working; they were glad, at the expense of any discomfort, to be getting each moment of slow progress, nearer to the fighting line.

There was room in these cars for only half the occupants to lie down at once, while the other half stood up. They alternated fifty-fifty in the process, and in this way all "carried on" for four long days and nights.

Meanwhile, you may be sure that the men did not forget to comment sarcastically upon the arrangements which had not been made for their comfort. It's pretty tough, being so crowded that only half of you can lie down at once!

To have enough room for each man to lie down; of course, that would be showing altogether too much consideration for the men who were doing the fighting, they said. Naturally, the twenty-odd officers could have several cars for their comfort, with their servants; but too much comfort was not good for common soldiers, especially just before they were to be killed. It would give them too good an opinion of this old world, and make them want to remain here a little while longer!

That may have been the reason for the lack of comfort given the men who no longer felt like "Pat's Pets," I have decided, in thinking things over since. For undoubtedly it is a fact that the less a soldier gets to eat, and the less comfortable he is, the more reckless he becomes as the hour for battle approaches; especially if he is promised a rest when the engagement is over.

That accursed train would stop for hours like a balky horse, and apparently with no more well-defined reason than that animal would have; would wander along a mile or two farther, and then take another rest of several hours!

Many a complaint was registered, unheard by any in authority, during this weary journey of restless days and nights. Many a curse was uttered, though I doubt if the ever-listening angel recorded these justified outpourings of irritated spirits. Many a silent wish was registered for a few comfortable hours in a home train, like the trip from Ottawa to Montreal a few months before.

From the way in which my friends sized up things afterward, probably this was all part of the plan to stiffen them for rigors to come. As they looked back on it, there had been a gradual elimination of all accustomed comforts during the months of preparation for the trenches.

So it happened that the Pats had first-class coaches in Canada, second- and third-class coaches in England – and finally drew the roughest, smallest and most rattley-bang box cars in France, in turn! These were all graduating steps toward the dugouts and trenches.

It was a benevolent plan of bringing on the hells, one after the other, to the final inferno at the front that embraced all the fifty-seven varieties.

If it was their object to stiffen the men by these means for the ordeal to come, they succeeded, all right. They were certainly a stiff lot of soldiers when they detrained!

Chapter X

"MARCHONS !"

My poor boys were nearly at the end of physical and mental endurance when they heard those first wild rumors that they were to detrain at last. I mention them as wild rumors, for they started in the morning and it was night before the actual event occurred.

The P.P.C.L.I.'s must have looked a tame and dejected lot – quite in contrast to their blithe spirits on landing on French soil – when they got out of those devilish cars. You could hear their joints creak.

My comrades stiffly "numbered off" outside that dismal looking station "somewhere in France." Our brave fellows were quite a contrast to the snappy bunch that marched through the city of Ottawa that beautiful morning in August. It seemed now so long before! And it was 9:30 of the night of December 24th, Christmas Eve, that found them thus, unhappy magnets of the hearts of all loved ones at home, among the holly berries and the vacant chairs; hearts that were now yearning for them across the seas, wondering how they were faring.

How they were faring! Here was another of the manifold grim ironies of war, this Thing they had come to seek.

They were – waiting. The same old weary waiting for somebody or something; the pathetic waiting as usual; the daily and nightly wait of army life. Very wearying and exhausting was this wait, the reason for which was always so obscure and mysterious to the men in the ranks. Why? They could not ask why; no reason was ever given them; theirs was only to wait, wait, wait – and *wait*!

Only the man o' the line and his God know what a torture is stubborn, dragging, sullen silence when he is wearily *waiting*.

In one of those strange divining dreams of mine I waited, too; my heart filled with sorrow, as my cocked ears listened to the murmured exchanges between the boys who were so shortly before imitating Indians and cowboys and black cannibal kings in the exuberance of their joy at reaching French soil, to fight for human liberties; these poor bound slaves of the sternest of human discipline, *waiting*.

"Let me put my pack down. I – I can't stand this – another –"

"God! boys, catch him before he falls! There! ...Bill! are you hurt?"

"No. Let me lay here, that's all. Don't bother me! Don't – bother –"

"But, Bill, old boy! You'll get all wet there, in the mud!"

"I don't care! Let me die here; leave me! I tried to stand it, but I'm at the end o' my rope! Why don't we march? God! I could stand *that*. But this *waiting*! ...Let go of me, Barney!"

"But, Bill! You can't do this; you'll catch your death! You're game, Bill, you know that; good old Bill!"

There was an instant's silence; then again Bill's drowsy voice.

"Yes; I'm game. Help me up, boys, I'll stick it! Bring on your hounds!"

So it went along the line, for many a gallant fellow temporarily toppled from the line while they waited in the mud, after that hell's journey in those constricting cars; toppled and somehow scrambled to his feet again, to wait on, with glazed eyes and sobbing breath, while through the night seemed to peer, icy cold and cruel, the ogre orbs of the iron ghost of discipline, the brutal tyrant of war.

I am positive that, if this dreary wait had endured only a few minutes longer, hundreds of our less fit must have fallen exhausted by the roadside, unable to move; – and why?

Could anybody give a satisfactory reason why so many hundred good, courageous, honest Canadian volunteers – *volunteers* all – should have been left by that roadside for nearly five hours on a cold, wet, raw night, standing at "attention," holding up their heavy loads of equipment? What gross neglect of duty was here? Even a collie dog would know enough to meet his friend at the train when he expected him!

But it was not until about 2 A.M. of Christmas Day that Pat's bedraggled "Pets" were at last put on the march. They were told that the distance was "about a mile," but many more of the men staggered out and fell by the wayside even before the mile was negotiated – and five miles more were covered before they were ordered to halt at some farm buildings beside the road!

There they waited at attention for another dragging interval – *outside* the buildings.

Then somebody casually discovered that the battalion had come too far! So they were marched back again, about three or four miles, or nearly to the point from which they had started.

My boys thus stood about the roadside, or were kept marching back and forth, the whole night long. It was a rather strenuous constitutional, to be sure; especially after the box cars. But why use brains when so much strength and vitality are available for exercising?

And brains, after all, are of no use without muscle; therefore develop muscle first and brains may develop itself. It was worth trying, anyway.

"It's the greatest game in the world, and not one for weaklings," declared one. "War is not a pink tea, and if we can't stand the first blast, like this, we have no business in it!"

"That's right!" declared another. "We're not weaklings in mind or in body!"

So those of the stoutest courage rallied the others by putting them to a moral test. "We wanted to be over here," they argued grimly, "and we're here. So, for God's sake, let's not welch!"

"That's right!" came the answers. "It's up to us to show the stuff we're made of, no matter who's to blame!"

That intrepid spirit, the spirit of Canada, ran all through the ranks during that memorable series of marchings and returns. In a way, it was a triumph of the Christmas spirit, at least in courage.

Throughout, I trotted in dreams along with them, back and forth through the mud, trying feebly to wag my discouraged brush under their rallying calls to one another.

At last – it was in the small hours before daylight during one of our numerous "rests," we became acutely sensible of the deepening of a sullen muttering we had been hearing at intervals during the long night. Now it swelled like thunder; only in it was a sound that I found far more sinister than thunder; something that set me trembling, so instinct was it with menace, with destructive malice, with death.

The next moment I heard a group of men discussing the sounds which heralded the approach of dawn of Christmas Day. It was the thundering of the guns.

So it chanced that we heard the voice of the Thing we had come to find before we saw it.

Some of the boys were serious when they heard the big guns barking, but others referred jokingly to the sounds, and appeared not to mind at all.

I woke, whining, from my dream.

It was 7:30 in the morning when the boys were ordered into the buildings of some farms to sleep. If there was ever a welcome sleep for the worn-out Pats, this one was it. From these farms the rumbling of the cannon was increasingly perceptible, but you may wager that it did not keep them awake very long. And they enjoyed a deep sleep till after noon.

Nearly everybody awoke with spirits revived. Most of them seemed to find inspiration in the roar of the guns, which was now continuous.

It seemed to act upon them as a call to battle. The complaints issuing from the ranks were lessening. Many began to take a certain pride in the fact that they were experiencing their first hardships. These, they added philosophically, were only a taste of what was to come, or "the real thing." These rare souls, with the reaction produced by a little rest, already seemed to positively enjoy themselves; even more than when comfortable in the Exhibition Grounds at Ottawa!

At 2:30 in the afternoon the battalion was marched out about two miles to dig reserve trenches. The noise of the guns increased, and was at first quite jarring to the nerves. But it was odd to note how soon they grew used to it!

At 5:30, without having suffered any serious mishaps, they marched back to billets. So the programme now ran from day to day; marching out a few miles to work in wet trenches. The boys worked always ankle deep in mud and water, and sometimes the mire reached to their knees. Always heavy rain clouds made it their business to pour their watery burdens down upon them. Then the weary march back to billets; and thus on, for every day except Sunday.

New Year's Day opened with the never-failing damp cold so hard for Canadians, – who were used to crisp, dry cold – to endure, and with occasional flurries of sleet and snow. All thoughts flew home, overseas to dear old Canada, where the ground was then covered with a pure carpet of white and the golden sun glistened through the frosty clouds.

And here they were in a difference – a difference of mud! There was a dissertation on this difference between two of the boys, when they rose:

"The sun," remarked Arthur fervently. "Where did I ever hear that golden word?"

"This rain sure has my Angora bleating for mercy," answered Bill, the man who had nearly sunk with fatigue when we left those horrible box cars. "What did you say about a sun?"

"I said it!" reiterated Arthur. "Sun, why hast thou forsaken us, confound thee?"

"Ah!" flung back Bill in disgust, "why wouldn't it forsake us? What respectable sun would be hanging around to shine on Europe, filled as it is with godless Huns when it has God's country, Canada, to filter its rays on?"

"Fall in!" cut in the sergeant.

On this dismal New Year's Day the entire regiment was paraded to a field, perhaps three miles distant. There were other battalions waiting in this field when "Pat's Pets" arrived.

There the whole 80th Brigade was congregated. I don't know how long *they* had been waiting, but if their experiences had been like those of the Pats, they must be loving Sir John about as the sheep loves the wolf or the chicken the falcon!

At last, however, they were visited and inspected by Sir John and other gentlemen of a more or less distinguished military appearance. Of course, the usual showers of rain and snow had to interrupt the ceremony. No ceremony or work of any kind was complete without exhibitions of this peevishness of the elements.

It seemed that, even if the showers showed a disposition to be accommodatingly late, in arriving, the military powers would dawdle sufficiently so that the boys should receive the full fury of the elements when they *were* unloosed.

The Pats stood at attention for an hour or more, awaiting the arrival of the General and his staff, – and the other troops had been there before they arrived! The irony attaching to this inspection of 6,000 men was that, no matter what the verdict might be, the brigade was booked to go into the trenches in a few days anyway, and it seemed to them the chief office of the inspection was only to aggravate the tempers of my boys and make them wish they were in the front line trenches.

I think may be, if the General had heard some of the grumblings, perhaps he would have been on time for the next inspection, or perhaps asked the platoon sergeants to act for him!

After a long wait and a chill occurred the inspection, which required less than eight minutes for 6,000 men!

Then the brigade marched to their various quarters. A raw wind was blowing; there was frost in the air; it was bitter cold. My boys were glad when the exercise of walking to billets warmed them again. There hot coffee and cognac soon made them happier.

Next morning saw the resumption of route marching and trench digging by the regiment, each section trying to outdo the other in digging large and safe ones, *à la camouflage.*

Yet what the Pats had now to endure was joyous play, compared with what was to come!

At 9 A.M. on January 5th, orders were issued to pack all kits for full marching order. All blankets and equipment and quartermasters' stores were piled in the transports and limbers.

One may imagine the feverish excitement that spread at this prospect of real contact with the enemy. "Be ready for the firing line"; so read the orders of the day, and everyone was anxious to have that "whack." As rumors had it, they were to relieve the French somewhere.

So, at 8:30 A.M. Canada's foremost battalion was in the road, waiting the order to march. The first day's march covered about fifteen miles. There were but a few short stops, of about ten minutes each.

It was rather a hard trial on the feet, for the Pats had grown used to turf. The cobblestones seemed uncommonly hard. The boys could scarcely withstand the first day's forced march, and some of them wore the soles of their shoes even with the foot.

They were being paced by the greatest marching army in the world; the professional British Indian soldiers who were used to forced marches of twenty-five or thirty miles a day in search of the mobile Indian hill tribes.

But the Canucks were game, and brought up the rear of the 80th Brigade with the "swanky" swing they were famous for. They never dropped a yard in the pace set by the K.R.R.'s in front of them. They were more than equal to the stern test!

However, on the second day, the pace began to tell even on the pacemakers. The Canadians saw a number of the professionals passing to the rear, unable to stand the gaff they had themselves introduced!

"Hi! Tommy!" yelled my friend Fred, as he noticed one discouraged East Indian fighter limping to the rear, to receive attention for his swollen feet; "blessed are the pacemakers, for they shall inherit the earth!"

Tommy Atkins paused and cast a sour look at Fred, swanking along as if he liked it. Fred had hiked through too much of Northern Ontario wilderness to mind this breezy trudge in the open.

"Aw!" answered Tommy, "you'll stop by and by!"

Editor's Notes to Chapter X:

1) Field Marshal Sir John French (1852-1925), later Earl of Ypres; a long-serving British army officer; commanded the British Expeditionary Force (which included the Canadians) in France, 1914-1915. He was dismissed after the failure of the Loos Offensive in December, 1915.

2) 80th Brigade, 27th Imperial(British) Division was made up of British Regiments who had returned to England from various Garrison duties from across the Empire. It initially included the 4th Rifle Brigade, 3rd and 4th King's Royal Rifle Corps, and the 2nd Shropshire Light Infantry.

Chapter XI

THE TRENCHES

We were all bundled into the village of Voormezeele. The Colonel and Adjutant occupied a room about sixteen feet square in an inn. A partition divided this room from the bar or "pub," one of those Flemish country *estaminets*.

The natives were purchasing their refreshments as usual, and were to learn later that one of the greatest bodies of fighting men that had reached the Western Front had their headquarters in the room next the bar – and were to reflect later, too, that many of the soldiers whose playful mood amid laughter and song now diverted them, were about to march to what should prove their last resting place.

For a uniformed crowd besieged the bar, calling for their pick-me-ups as on Piccadilly or Broadway, but instead were given sour beer. The natives marveled and goggled, standing in groups with eyes, mouths and ears open, absorbing the spontaneous sounds of Canadian merriment. They apparently expected to see trials by court-martial ordered, and shootings at dawn.

But theirs were only the little offenses of the bottle, and late hours. So, the natives were disappointed as they stood about watching the Canadian soldiers. Later some of the boys were taken to the orderly room next the *estaminet* and got their C.B.'s (Confined to Barracks) for a few days.

The regiment was quite fatigued and stiffened from the exertions they had undergone, but after a night's rest they were the same "cocky" Pats, happy and singing and prancing out for another try at the cobblestones of the Flemish road.

The boys started at 9 A.M. They had been told it was a nine-mile march to the spot where they were to relieve the French. It was easy marching that day. They arrived at an open field an hour before dark. There, shorn of all kitbags and extra accoutrements, they ate a hearty meal and were issued twenty-four hours' "iron rations." The meal comprised all that could be eaten, for all British believe in fighting on a full stomach.

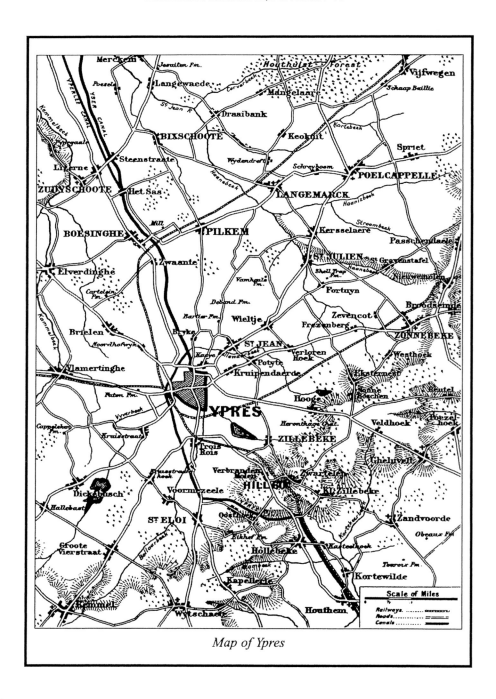

Map of Ypres

After dark each company commander was given charge of his own company, and was supplied with a guide who was to lead the men to their first experience in the trenches.

The mud in the roads and fields was up to the knees in many places, and was soft, yet sticky and unyielding when the foot was wholly caught in its grip. Then every step was taken with an effort. Occasionally a man had to be lifted out.

The P.P.C.L.I.'s, the first Canadians to fight on European soil, relieved the French on the moment appointed in the front line trenches, at nine o'clock on the night of January 6th, 1915, at a point called "Brasserie Road." This was perhaps five or six miles from Ypres.

The approach to these trenches was over an open country road. The trenches were situated about halfway to the top of a hill covered with brush in which had been dug the German trenches. It was easy to locate these German trenches through the presence of a stream of red lights in front and on either side of this wood and parallel with it. All this could be seen from a flat at the foot of the hill. To the right of the road was another small wood in which were located the headquarters of the Pats.

On the way up this hill into the trenches the Pats caught their first glimpses of the stretcher bearers carrying the wounded down the hill. Some of them joked about the wounded on the stretchers.

"I wish I had his job!" said one of our boys. "Going back to Blighty!" And several men laughed nervously.

The marching was slow, and made slower by many sudden jerky stops. "Hole to the left! " would be passed back in low tones; then, "Trench to the right!" These were words of warning, as it was very dark and the boys were picking their way. Also the word was passed back, as they neared the trenches: "No smoking!" "Oh, mind your own business!" fretfully muttered one Pat; though he promptly extinguished his "fag," nevertheless, mindful of the lynx eyes of the Heinies that were doubtless alert over the parapets of their trenches.

It may seem to the layman that those of our Pats who joked about the wounded were callous, but I would like these captious critics to put themselves in their place. Remember, their nerves were strained to the breaking point with this first grim experience of the trenches, and not a man who saw those stretchers but who instinctively thought that perhaps he would be soon decorating one. The attempts to jest were only to keep up their spirits.

This sight of the stretcher bearers was the first view of war vouchsafed the Canadians as they worked their way slowly on. They were as close to the Huns now as the barbed wire would permit. The spit and crack of bullets dropping here and there, close to them, now made the more superficial spirits take a somewhat serious view of matters. This was no movie show, but stern reality!

As the Pats moved along, there occurred some low-voiced bits of picturesque recrimination:

"Oh, shut up! This isn't a hurdy-gurdy affair."

"Well, what do you care? You'll be dead and in hell in the morning, anyway!"

So the front line trenches were reached amid swearing and joking and suppressed laughter. They marched in close formation over an open road to within one hundred and fifty yards of the Hun lines, then entered the trench. The supports were perhaps fifty yards to the rear. They consisted of two small dugouts with a sort of open trench about two feet deep. In this men sat and sat and waited till morning. In the front line trenches there was a dugout about every twenty yards. The trench was about two feet deep and had a parapet about two feet high.

As a matter of course, that night and the next day were wet. So was the second day, and a cold north wind whistled through the barbed wires. Nothing had been seen of the enemy except flashes of his Mauser rifles all along the line; and at night, along his trenches occupied by thousands of men, a long line of star lights shooting up in a continual stream.

The Pats looked on each side and saw the red fire spitting from the myriad muzzles of their comrades' guns. They knew that each flash meant a departing bullet aimed at the enemy trenches, and they wondered how many of the bullets found their marks.

Such were the thoughts that flashed through the minds of men in the trenches. The men wondered how far away the enemy was; if they had one line of men or two in front; how many men occupied each line; if their trenches were any better built than the Canadian trenches.

They would look and look over the parapet; look till their eyes were sore and weary and watery; look for some moving object, something to shoot at! At times they were anxious to give an alarm of some kind, just to let their comrades in support know that they were doing their duty, if nothing more. Some of them were anxious to cry aloud, just for the reassurance of their own voices in the darkness.

They would stand musing, with guns in hand, ready for any emergency, keyed to extreme tension. Occasionally some of them would shoot their guns at random, just to assure themselves that the weapons were in good working order.

Then in the mental whirl would leap thoughts of friends at home. What would *they* feel about it? Then the thoughts of the deaths of innocent women and children; Louvain and the ravished nuns. The story of four babes sent to bed early by father and mother, with kisses; the call of the parents at a neighboring house; their return to find police and firemen digging out the mangled corpses of their children from the ruins of their beautiful home, destroyed by a Zeppelin bomb. And my blood – the blood of a simple, honest, peaceful dog that cannot comprehend such cowardice and such iniquity – ran faster in my veins, and I longed to leap at the throat of one of those murderers!

Man; "the noblest work of God!" What blasphemy! Man, who can be guilty of crimes that beasts would scorn to commit! Prating of "being formed in the image of God"; the God man's acts shame and cause Him to question His Scheme of Creation.

I once heard one of the Pats describing how he had winged his first German. He was telling an interested circle of comrades.

"Somehow I felt that this time I was not to be disappointed," said he. "I felt a fierce longing to see one of those faces, the faces I had in mind, shaped like a pig's, with wide round chops and a low brutal forehead.

"It had been quiet. I think the Heinies must have figured we were all asleep, or felt a contempt for us. Anyway, suddenly I caught sight of one of them approaching the parapet with his sneaky, treacherous gait.

In a sudden flare, a light from our trench, I saw his fat German face close up, seeming to leer at me. In a fraction of a second my rifle was at my shoulder.

"I took a bead. Crack! He went down in a heap. He is there yet. He hasn't moved since he dropped – and he will never move again!"

A long quivering sigh broke from the lips of the men who had been listening. I sighed, too. We were all watching the face of the man who had been speaking.

It was as cold and relentless as if it had been carved from stone. In it was the spirit of Canada, that was willing to suffer in torment and go through the valley of the shadow of death to avenge the devilish wrongs the Hun had foisted upon the world.

They all agreed, did my Pats, from the outset that it was a fight to a finish, for a knockout, a survival of the fittest, and that a "no decision" affair would not go. This was the stand of the flower of the manhood of Canada, at the very outset of the stern game; and that now above their graves their spirits cry aloud against any faint-heartedness that, carried into effect, would render their supreme sacrifice in vain!

There was, however, none of the pomp and panoply of war of which they had dreamed. Since they had left Canada it had been a case of valor wallowing in mud and rain, and now this condition was intensified.

Final realization of which brought the deeps of philosophy, as deep as the mud itself.

My "Pat's Pets," so plastered with mire that I doubt if the lovely Princess would have recognized her heroes, drew one deep sigh for illusions forever dispersed, and immediately settled into trench ways like veterans.

Chapter XII

"SOME SHOOTING!"

Trench life, I gathered from reports brought back to the rear, was something calculated to stretch the nerves tight as fiddle strings.

You had to stop and stay there, look and listen for somebody or something, and you had to conserve your energy, too. You might need it in a hurry, and all of it at once. So you had to sit tight and watch your chance, like an Indian. And what men were better fitted for that little trick than my Canadians?

Were they not from the regions where the red skins roam?

Were they not the sons of men who conquered "the tall and uncut," and who, through centuries of associations, absorbed the red men's cunning; which, added to the white man's wiles, makes so formidable a blend? So, as in the poker game which the white man taught the red man, my Canucks now calculatingly thought things over and "sat tight" to win.

But it was a wearing-down process for both sides. The piercing north wind drove the rain against the faces of the men in the trenches; they were soaked to the skin; the mud was nearly to their knees in the bottom of the trench; their muscles and joints cracked when they moved.

My Pats counted the hours till the relief would arrive. Only twenty-three hours! My civilian reader, you will never know how long an hour can be. You have to inhabit a muddy trench to know that!

Twenty-three hours! Then my boys would shiver, as much with discouragement as with cold. If only there might be a touch of Canadian frost to freeze this mud! If only one might get out and run up and down the road to get warm!

But that might not be. The trench was but three feet high. One half of it was mud and the other half water. There was no chance of making the trench deeper; had the boys attempted that, they would have been drowned in more mud.

The water was always pouring into it from all sides and there was nothing to bail it out with. If the trench had been built up equally on both sides, it would have been a case of drown or be shot. There was no system of drainage, but fortunately the trench was lower in some spots, which enabled the water to run out at those points.

Asleep in my warm quarters, far back of the firing line, I shivered and yelped during that night of pouring rain. For my spirit was with my friends in that muddy trench, where my body would have been had it been allowed the privilege.

In spirit with them I quaffed the brimming cup of misery. My life in these dark hours took on a new expression. My point of view had always been that of joy in living. I had been convinced that all earthly things were for the comfort and sustenance of God's creatures; all of us. But now, what?

It seemed to me that all the world was turning into an uncompromising morass. My spirit world became a furious, fuming, fermenting tempest; a thing discordant, irreconcilable with what I had believed. I suffered the supreme hurt, so terrible to animals with two legs or with four; the cynical hurt of utter disillusion.

For now I realized the depths of misery in the world – and realized that the misery was man-made!

Then, too, I was learning of the pitiful limitations of man, man whom I had deemed supreme. I had looked upon him as omnipotent and everlasting. But now, in the dramas and the tragedies of the trenches, already beginning, I had discovered that he was only an animal like us others.

Man, after all, lived and died, felt cold and hunger; shook and faltered under the thongs of the stern test like all animal creation.

The long night – that first night of vigil in the trenches – wore on, while my spirit fared in the rain and slime with my comrades. It heard the perpetual crackle of rifle bullets, the crunching bellows of the heavy guns; it marked the nervous strain that seemed agonizing enough to unbalance the strongest mind or weaken the stoutest heart.

After I had wakened and risen, too, my spirit fared with my boys in the gray daybreak. It heard my comrades, Rob and Fred, who had fared shoulder to shoulder through the long night, talking together.

"We've just found how long a night can be," Rob was saying. "Now we have a chance to figure on the day. Will this day ever be over?"

"I don't know," replied Fred, with a sorry grin. "But I know this. It has my goat that hard that you can hear the poor critter blattin' clean back home to Canada!"

"Ah!" cut in Jake, another of the comrades, "what are you two beefing about? Didn't expect to hit any palace over here, and lap your chow off any gold plate, did you? You'll have to put that off till we get to Berlin. Then – believe me! – we'll have a bobtail Tux and a waiter's apron on Bill, and set him to hustling steins!"

"Hi! fellows!" called another, low enough so that his message should not carry across No Man's Land. "Look over there, at the Heinie's shoulder! He's using a shovel on the trench!"

In an instant my little group of boys were looking eagerly through the peephole, watching a smudge of gray, first appearing then dipping under, at a parapet of one of the Fritz trenches at the foot of the wood. It was the shoulder of a Kaiserite, who was stolidly shoveling and unconsciously exposing himself to view.

He was too far away for my comrades to tell you what he looked like, but I can tell you, for my spirit can see far. He wore a round gray hat on his bullet-shaped head. He was one of the uncounted masses of the humbler classes raised in Germany, especially for cannon fodder, to goose-step to death at the command of the man with a foppishly curled moustache and a withered arm; the man who *also* claims to be cast in the image of the Almighty with Whom he affects palship!

The dull face of the shoveler belonged to a low order of intelligence; in him was no atom of initiative. The top of his head was not more than an inch or two above his large crumpled ears. Like so many of the Kaiser's Junker-ridden subjects, he had two ideas. One was the Fatherland. The other was that the Fatherland would pension him when he grew old. In a word is here shown how cunningly the rulers of Germany have obtained their hold upon a stupid people.

The gray shoulder was never wholly out of sight now, and it presented a fair though moving target for an expert shot.

Immediately a low but earnest discussion began among my friends regarding who should have the honor of a crack at the Fritzie.

"Whoever fires must never pick out his head," waggishly observed Fred. "He's got a bean like a peanut. But his shoulder is ample."

"Cut out the merry twaddle," urged George, "and give me a wallop at him!"

George was a good shot, but Joe came into the conversation with a gentle reminder.

"You know, George, I beat you in practice. I'm not saying anything – but I beat you."

"That's right," acknowledged George, reluctantly but like a true sportsman.

So Joe took his rifle and drew a good steady bead on the swinging shoulder, aiming to just skim the parapet and get him low, where there would be a chance at the vitals.

His friends watched at the peephole, with sparkling eyes and silent with suppressed excitement.

With the report, from the Pats' trench rose a concerted yell of savage triumph.

The Heinie had sprung into the air, to fall limp in the bottom of his trench. The next instant the amazed Patricias sprang away from the peephole, at which commenced the insistent tapping of death.

The law of the trenches is the ancient law of "an eye for an eye; a tooth for a tooth." But the Pats had not expected so instant, so overwhelming, so deadly a demand for reprisal.

Immediately, against the steel plate that was slit for the peephole, rattled a regular fusillade of rifle bullets – and soon some of them came through the slit though no Pat was at the moment in range of them.

The bullets which whizzed through the peephole buried themselves in the opposite parados one after another, in rhythmic succession, launched from the muzzles of rifles in the hands of Germans hundreds of yards away. My little group of Pat's Pets, careful now to avoid the caresses of these vicious little messengers, felt such wonder as never before had held them.

"Some shooting!" at last said George to Joe, whose successful winging of the Heinie had drawn this hail of vengeful wrath. His tone was trembling with the wonderment he felt.

"Well, rawther!" chimed in my Fred, imitating the English accent. His voice, too, despite the attempt at levity, reflected the general tension that was spreading through that trench.

But Joe said nothing. Then the others, too, fell silent, as though dazed, while several more bullets skyhooted clean through the peephole to kick up the dirt in the rear of the trench. The parados wall was fast becoming reinforced with metal through the loving attentions of the Kaiser's marksmen.

Now all eyes became riveted upon Joe, long accredited one of the best marksmen in Canada.

The boys ceased speaking; an unusual thing; just watching Joe, to whom that day was being given, as well as to the rest of them, an unusual experience.

Joe was sitting there in silent awe, like some unbeliever who was being forced to accept the evidence of something incredible; before which all his past ideas of the limits of efficiency were crumbling.

His black eyes narrowed and sparkled as he continued to watch the steel plate and the slit through which the bullets continued to come with paralyzing frequency. It was as if something deadly infallible were pumping missiles at that little mark.

For hours my boys – some standing and some sitting – continued to watch that fusillade, which the Huns continued without interruption. They watched in fascination, saying little, combating a feeling of dismay; reluctantly admitting a conviction that the powers of this foe they had come to fight were better than the best that had been previously known.

There were other lookout points, commanding a wide range of vision, that the Huns did not and could not discover. Through these each Pat looked by turns as the impulse moved him, seeking to penetrate the secret of this marvelous shooting, which had been prevented thus far from claiming human sacrifice only by God's mercy.

But the sharpest eye could not yet detect the explanation. Nothing appeared visible on the German front. Nothing moved or stirred. There was nothing to be seen but an implacable line of sandbags and earth. Yet the bullets came in showers and with deadly exactitude.

No puff of smoke, no whiff of any sort, revealed from whence they came. What manner of fighting was this? A hidden enemy contriving to spew death without revealing himself? Bringing a sense of unreality to men who had so often won victory in practice shooting against the champions of the world; and who had been ready at any time to stake their lives upon their skill against any champion?

Here, however, all traditions were set at naught. There was something stealthy and horrible about it. There was nothing to be seen to shoot at in reprisal – yet the enemy's bullets now came through that single bull's-eye – slender as it was – in showers, seemingly in cynical boastfulness, to show the world what Germany had thrust up its brutal sleeve for the world's undoing! And the clever Canadians, crack shots as they were, were held helpless!

There were practical men among the Pats. They were doing some deep thinking.

There had been some hours of this and the men were sitting about moodily. There was no talking. Finally Joe rose and walked silently to one of the observation points the Huns had not yet discovered. Joe was half-Indian and half-engineer. He took nothing for granted; nothing but facts appealed to him.

He applied his eye to the slit and stood there silent for a long time. His piercing gaze constantly sought No Man's Land and the German parapet, six hundred yards across it, from which the constant hum of death was proceeding. They were making a day of it.

"Do you see anything, Joe?" finally asked the big Boer and crack shot himself.

"Yes," he replied brusquely. "There are a number of suspicious looking holes and black spots. That's where the shots are coming from.

"But I tell you, boys, there's no use of trying to get even, *this* way. Our chance must come in the open, I think. We can't compete with this devil's work. We haven't the rifles.

"You'll find that, for shooting from cover, they've got something we haven't got. Somehow, they've beat the world.

"But, by God, I'll bet you we find their bayonets are no better – nor as good! And after all, when it comes to the showdown, the infantry will fight it out in the open, with steel, man to man, and not like sneaking rats!"

How many times, in the ensuing months of war, was Joe's prophecy of those earliest days to be proved true!

Then the boys began speculating upon what manner of devilish device it was that enabled those Prussians to shoot from six hundred yards as if the distance had been six!

They knew that no human being could do such shooting without the aid of some uncanny helping artifice. Not one man, but a line of them were showing staggering skill. And from that distance bullets were coming clean through a slit one-and-a-half inches deep, while the rattle of the bullets on the plate sounded like hail!

It was agreed that Joe had undoubtedly called the turn. The answer must lie in one of Germany's secrets of war preparation. It was now uncovered, though the means were not yet discovered.

Certainly such "efficiency" had not been prematurely displayed by Germans shooting in the various meets in days of peace. Trust the wily military powers of the Fatherland for that!

Later, in shock of battle and its red aftermath, the Pats were to learn the explanation of the riddle which at first bewildered them.

When Teutonic prisoners were captured later, and their rifles were taken from them, the mystery was cleared. Never had rifles been constructed with such marvelous telescopic sights; such construction, in every way, ahead of the times!

It was all apart of the destructive science which Germany had been craftily pursuing for forty years. Add to this mechanical perfection the human element; men docile and rather stupid, cogs in a social system, devised by autocracy, which provided that the son of a butcher should also be a butcher, yet trained for a prescribed period in the arts of war that made of him a dead shot; and you have the frightful peril that civilization faced in the dark days which ushered in the world's war in the summer of 1914.

Editor's Notes to Chapter XII:

1) The Nationalities of the original members of the PPCLI were; 690 from England, 157 Scottish, 96 Irish, 7 Welsh, 105 Canadians (including three French-Canadians) and 43 from other countries. Private John Coetzee, #759, was a South African Boer from Capetown, who had fought with the British in the Boer War. He was killed May 9th, 1915 and is buried in Ypres Reservoir Cemetery, Belgium.

Chapter XIII

THE RELIEF

Still endured that forced inaction which seemed, somehow, to be the plan of "procedure," and which had irked my comrades since they had enlisted. First had been the delay in leaving Canada; then that in England, and now, in France, it appeared to the boys that they were only marking time!

Crouching in the front line trench, in the rain and mud, they began to use the soldier's privilege and growl about this, as soon as they felt a little used to their new surroundings.

"I can't understand why we're *here*, of all spots!" ran the comment. "Why aren't we advancing along this wood, so as to gain the high ridge? Yes, or why not retire to this little ridge behind us? It surely looks to me as if the Fritzies have all the best lookout places, and there's no need of it! I'll bet, too, that their trenches are dryer than ours; their beans may be thick, but they use 'em!"

So the talk ran, but be sure it was echoed by many another regiment than my Pats, in both sets of trenches. For it is a characteristic of all soldiers to do a lot of "beefing," and when the action begins to forget it and fight like hell itself.

It was in that first dark, dismal, stormy night of which I have spoken, with bullets zipping, whiz-bangs and "winnies" popping and whining, creating death on every side, that my friend Captain Newton received his mortal wound. He was the first Canadian officer to be killed while fighting for justice on European soil.

My fancy could readily picture the last look of grim determination on his fighting face. And the spirit which spread like a consuming fire among the men when he had fallen; the spirit embracing the Mosaic law of reprisal!

Now that blood had been shed as a sacrifice, it would be henceforth fiend against fiend. The world has learned, since the film of the latter day Attila's challenge to the Anglo-Saxon and his Allies has been unrolled, how uncompromising can be the just wrath of the Canuck!

Upon hearing of his fate, I recalled my first meeting with the

Captain, back in Canada. It was in the village of Fort Levis. We were on one of the route marches I loved so well, and were resting on the summit of a hill.

The Captain called me to his side and stroked my back, while we talked together like brothers. He had one of those rare low voices that I love and he spoke words that were pleasant to my ear.

Flushed with health, the picture of splendid young strength, he drew me to him in the sunlight and looked deep into my eyes. He put his cheek to mine.

"Poor Bob!" he said, "you like this sort of thing, I know." I wagged my tail to tell him how much I liked it.

Some cattle were grazing in a nearby field. He pointed to them.

"Wouldn't you like to be there with them?" he asked.

I ran over toward the cattle, whirled, and returned to his side.

Just then a sergeant took me by the collar and began to tell me what a wonderful dog I was. He addressed the Captain and a lieutenant by his side.

"I wonder how Bob is going to like the music of the big guns? I'll bet they frighten him; that is, if he hears them. I think the war will be over before we get there. The Germans will retreat directly to their own Country."

The Captain and lieutenant said nothing, but they smiled at each other, slightly and significantly. I understood that smile. They thought the sergeant was too optimistic.

And now my sunny Captain was the first epauletted victim of the Huns, who had no thought of retreating!

When the news of his death reached me I felt more miserable than I can express. I felt that I wanted to be with my boys while they were facing dangers; I wanted to share their dangers.

What pitiful wrecks of humanity now daily began to come back from the front! M y friends who had but a few days before been so filled with vitality and the ardor of life! I met them, and I knew deep sorrow at witnessing the ravages this war had made in them, in only a few short hours.

It was not only the wounded; such sights as I saw in wounds of the body were horrible enough. But there were sights that were worse; and they were the wounds of the mind.

"Shell shock," the doctors called it. I understand it was the effect of the men being too close to the thunderous noises, the booming that we were always hearing at the rear. I could not understand it exactly; but I came to know the fearsome effects.

I ran joyfully up to some of my friends who had come back from the front – and they did not know me. Worse than that, they would stare past me as if I were not there at all – and when I rubbed my body against their legs, seeking a caress, they seemingly did not feel it. They stared with glazed eyes – at nothing; their faces were blank and drawn and white; when they tried to talk they only mumbled meaningless things.

They were like men walking in their sleep, in the grip of some dark dream which they could not shake off. They were not trusted alone; they were in the care of others, who led them about gently, as if they had been blind men. Yet they were not blind; they could see; *yet they did not see!*

What a terrible fate! It is one unknown in my world of dogs, save sometimes in those weird days of heat in August, which always depress me so.

I tried so hard to make these friends, who were now strangers, understand and know me. Then I would creep away reluctantly, shivering, and lie down and watch them in dumb wonder. It seemed to me that theirs was a sadder fate than if they had been killed in the trenches. For if a bullet struck home or a shell exploded, it was only the body that was killed. And with these poor boys – God help them! – *it was the mind!*

My inner knowledge told me that the mind of man or beast was the immortal part. But if that mind were destroyed; could there be resurrection beyond?

I can only discern these truths. I cannot read the answer beyond them. I can only have faith – and wait. And that I do!

These days were certainly filled with bitter education for me. I had seen men hunting and killing moose and deer in my Northland. But I had not imagined that they hunted and killed each other, to say nothing of horses. For they ate the moose and deer. So it seemed a wicked and useless waste of life to me! To kill for sustenance is to my traditions – which, of course, date back to my father, the wolf – the first law of nature. To kill for the lust of killing is degeneracy. And it is in this abyss of blood that autocracy plans to keep the shuddering world!

Wet feet, water from above and mud and water below, thus attended my Pats' initiation into trench life. But they all managed to keep their spirits well buoyed up till the second night, when they expected to be relieved. Their casualties for these first hours had been very light. A few were reported missing; that terrible word in army reports which usually comprises the unidentified dead. Fighting a good fight, they fell to the glory of their race.

It was a "snipers'" battle. The keenest eye that ever narrowed behind a rifle sight could not "plug" a silver dollar with every shot at five hundred or six hundred yards. Yet this is practically what my boys were required to do to compete with the improved Teutonic telescopic sights of which I have spoken.

Misguided and misinformed mentally about what they were up against; at first believing that conditions were equal, the Pats gallantly coped with a vastly superior equipment, and successfully, but sooner or later too many of them were caught.

Many of them would go on swimmingly for days, and each day would see several new "nicks" cut in the stocks of their guns. Such was the record of Sergeant Brown. He was the best shot in the battalion. He cared little how much he saw of his mark, so long as he saw *some* part of it. He would often fire in one bullet after another to see how many he could fire without missing the hole – but finally, he, too, got careless. All were agreed that, if he had possessed the German telescopic sights, not a Hun he faced could have matched him.

On this night of the expected relief, No.4 Company waited for what seemed ages for the relief that never came. Every minute seemed an hour and every hour a month through that long wet night; demonstrating anew that time is measured most exactly in suffering.

They watched and waited alike for friend and foes. The Brasserie Road was lined with dead French and German soldiers which had fought the issue to the red finish in No Man's Land. The French had driven the Germans from trenches, the Pat's held, but at awful cost. The foes lay as they had fallen – in many cases in death grips, many men falling as they had driven the bayonets home. Some lay quietly, relaxed, and it was plain to see that death had come mercifully in an instant. Others had twisted and writhed in their pain before they succumbed to red wounds.

Such were the sights that greeted the eyes gazing through the twisted strands of barbed wire.

The icy winds of the North Sea, always sharp as cold steel, were doubly so on this bleak night of extra waiting. All wearing apparel seemed like porous cheesecloth in the shrieking wind and driving rain. It was cruel!

Not one Enfield rifle in hundreds was now fit to be used, because of the mire, and not one soldier in fifty was able to stand up straight, to say nothing of using his rifle! My boys were so utterly exhausted!

If only the enemy had known their condition it seems inevitable that they could have rushed the trenches and captured them, but perhaps they were no better off. The north wind was playing no favorites; its congealing breath was against every man. With the mud it made war on all. The reason he did not attack then is because he recoils from taking a chance.

It was purely psychological – and it explains why Fritz did not win in his first desperate dash – and why he will be eventually beaten and his bombastic pretensions crushed to powder.

It is why his years of cunning mechanical preparation went for nothing. He was against a fighting essence that sets at naught all his preparation. For in the great gamble of war *the ideal gamester is the one who wins.*

Since returning to my Northland and thinking things over, remembering what I saw, I know this. That with Russia and Roumania gone; that with the East in the grip of Germany; that even if Italy, exhausted, were to make peace, the hordes of the Hun would in the end be beaten.

Why? Because, in a battle to the death, they have aligned against them three great nations that *will* – and *do* – take chances. I mention them in the order in which they entered the conflict.

France, that Hun propagandists despised and flouted as a foolish weakling among nations; France whose irresistible dash is only equaled by her steadfastness.

Britain's army of millions of "contemptibles"; British fighters of whom, early in the war, a German general complained that "we have them beaten, but the fools don't know it!"

America's army of Yankee nerve and speed and fighting spirit; traditionally impatient of any method of warfare that hesitates to take a chance, and of tenacity that matches that of the parent British stock.

Against this trio of Powers – even with the aid of Japan to Britain in controlling the seas not counted nor the moral force of the great bulk of civilized lands rallied against Germany – what chance has the Hun in the ultimate trenches?

I have seen; I have heard; I have digested. Therefore I prophesy. Defeat for Attila is as certain as that tomorrow's sun will rise!

Reverting to our unrelieved position in the trenches, Lieutenant Pearse sent word back that his men were nearly perished from cold and hunger, and that either food or relief must be sent. Answer was received that "perhaps" relief would come before 6 A.M.

My poor boys waited, with hope revived. At last 6 A.M. arrived, 6:15, 6:20, 6:30; at last broad daylight – and no relief.

Not one man in a hundred felt equal to another half-hour without a rest. But a phrase recurred to them:

"Canada expects that this day every man will do his duty."

They were sons of that race to which Lord Nelson signaled so many years before, in one of the greatest hours in the history of the English people. So – they hung on! Canadians would be the last to show the white feather!

Another weary day of rending hunger and agonizing cold passed with abominable slowness. But an expression of will to "stick it" appeared on every man's face. And they did "stick it," in a fashion that brought honor to the sons of the young nation across the sea. Through drizzling, dragging, desolate misery crawled the hours of that last dreadful day – and no hope came till *another* dawn.

Through the night my boys held to faith in the cause and to hope in their friends; and only these powerful forces seemed to keep them alive till the hour of relief. It was a stubborn mental fight over matter; and obstinate matter, too. Many men, when relief did come, had to be assisted out of the trench as they were too weak to extricate their feet from the sticky Flanders mud. Two men died that night from cold and exposure, without the contributing cause of a single wound.

The German sentries must have surely been asleep, or they would not have overlooked that relief finally coming up after daybreak!

Each minute the approaching men were exposed to fire seemed an hour to my boys, who feared that the fire of the enemy would begin and stop the advance.

On they came, however, over the open fields and, roads, in plain sight of the enemy, for we had then no communication trenches.

Joe, one of my friends, poked his head high above the parapet; for all the world as if deliberately to draw the enemy's fire. But he was not thinking of the enemy; he was thinking of the relief.

Unconsciously his cunning Indian instinct was asserting itself. His black eyes were sparkling; and so widely opened were they that the whites circled all around the twinkling pupils. Evidently Fritz was decidedly off duty, for not a shot was taken at the fifty or more heads that, in uncontrollable excitement, followed Joe's above the parapet.

The men of the relief kept coming; slowly, slowly, over the wet, sticky, muddy ground, for at every step their boots sank deep in the mire. Sometimes it seemed to the watchers – keyed for the possible fusillade from the German trenches – that it took a full minute for some of them to extricate their plodding feet from the quagmire.

Were they really moving? Yes ; they were coming – closer, closer.

"Praise God!" almost sobbed one Canuck.

"Shut up!" fiercely admonished a comrade. "The Fritzies may hear us. They must be waking up now."

The exhausted Company was relieved by another at 6:30 in the morning, without an enemy shot being fired! It was one of the miracles of the war, and my Pats who survive are sure it had not happened before, nor has it happened since!

The Lieutenant entered with his men as coolly as if on parade. Came a few hasty words of whispered instructions, and the relieved men, half-frozen, started back over the road on which the relief had come. They had been in that trench for seventy-two hours!

How such a sizeable body of men had escaped the notice of the enemy, less than two hundred yards away, baffled us. They must have had lookouts but God is good to His own. Perhaps the lookouts took the relief for an attacking force, and figured they would let them get nearer so as to rake them with machine guns. Or perhaps the lookouts were asleep. That is my opinion. Else why, in retiring, were not the relieved men fired upon?

Editor's Notes to Chapter XIII:

1) Captain Denzil Onslow Cochrane Newton; born in England, 1880; served as Staff Officer to the Governor-General; first PPCLI Officer to be killed in the War. Died of wounds January 9th, 1915; buried Dickebusch Old Military Cemetery, Belgium.

2) Sergeant Frank S. Brown, #1246; "The Poet of the Pats"; born Waterford, Ontario, 1893; son of Rev. S.G. Brown of Almonte, Ontario; promoted Sergeant in September 1914; joined PPCLI in the Field in January, 1915. He was sniped on his first trip to the trenches; Brown has no known grave and is commemorated on the Menin Gate Memorial, Belgium. A small book of his poems entitled, "Contingent Ditties And Other Soldier Songs of the Great War", was published posthumously in 1915. Some of his poems had already been published in The Ottawa Citizen.

Chapter XIV

" FOREVER... AMEN ! "

My relieved Patricias arrived at a small wood south of the road. There they remained all day in supports; and it was quite a comfortable change from the front line trenches, for this half of the battalion. For they had such comforts as straw to lie upon and dugouts for coverings.

But here was no security, if one were careless. Each man who ventured into the open to try to improve his position was fired at by German snipers posted in a wood on a hill overlooking the dugouts two thousand yards away from them.

Think of the marvelous efficiency of those improved German telescopic sights! Men firing at others from concealed positions over a mile away – and too often winging them!

The men who had to go into the support trenches that evening had a hard night of it. A bleak wind drove the rain through their clothing as if it were a pure cotton fabric instead of all-wool serge. But serge or canvas looked alike to these Belgian rains. They could penetrate almost anything!

"Is that why the Belgians put straw on top of the tile roofs of their houses?" asked one of the boys sarcastically.

"Oh," rejoined another, "I guess it isn't quite sharp enough to drive through tile!"

"I don't know," retorted the first man. "I believe it could drive through cold steel itself!"

It was the same with the Canuck army boots, or even the famous Canadian water boot, the *Penetanguishene*, so called by the Indians to describe its water and wear qualities.

It seemed that nothing could resist the penetrating drizzle of that rain, though it must be recorded that the *Penetanguishene* withstood it better than did anything else. It possessed the element of toughness that must enter into all Canuck articles of wear, intended for a land where the weather, the seasons round, runs to extremes.

Yes, and this element of toughness and fibre enters into Canada's living creatures, too, from men to moose!

Where is there another animal to compare in speed, strength and vitality with our moose, who is so ungainly that he is almost beautiful in my forest-trained eyes? Watch him as he successfully battles with an Arctic winter, contending with his enemies to the death! He emerges from the cover in the spring round and fat – and he has fattened on adversity!

Before the war the world did not know my Canadians – but it knows them now! They are fierce upholders of a primal law that is the essence of their blood, the law of the survival of the fittest. And they fight now in order that liberty, the fittest of all human ideals, may survive.

The intermittent battle went on for two more days and nights. Parties "carried home" to the Hun in his stronghold, giving no quarter and asking for none. The Canucks knew and accepted the fact that the Hun was ruthless. The grim record since those days is ample evidence that, in the man's test, the Hun learned to respect and fear the Canuck.

After two nights in the support trenches the battalion was marched to billets at Westoutre. The billets were two large barns only a few hundred feet from the village. The machine gun crews, headquarters staff and quartermaster occupied houses in the village.

It was here that a concert was given Lieutenant Pearse. At this affair was sung for the first time the famous "Louse Song." Also a trench song that has since become famous, "I Want to Go Home."

Our barns, like all Flemish stables, were very dirty. The water was thick with dirt and could be smelled many yards away. However, all had the chance to clean and dry their clothing, and this was something to be thankful for.

What a state that clothing was in! Trousers, tunics, overcoats, were thickly caked with mud. In some cases it had even penetrated to the underclothing. It was sticky; in consistency it resembled some putrid, ill-smelling glue, only that it was slippery and nearly as hard when dry.

On January 14th the battalion moved again, this time about a mile nearer the firing line. This farm was prosperous, as Flemish farms go. In the barns were many head of cattle. It proved quite a comfortable place in which to lodge.

Eagerly the boys looked about them and found that conveniently nearby they could buy coffee and brandy, besides eggs and bread and other comforts. They planned for an enjoyable time there, but the next day they were ordered back to the trenches.

My Pats were in support trenches this time, at a place called Shelley Farm. For forty-eight hours they did fatigue work. Then the battalion was ordered back to Westoutre, a march of five miles. They arrived tired and dirty, much pleased with rumors that they were to be sent to an adjacent village for much-needed baths. For days they had not been able to pay themselves any accustomed attention, and the filth, dirt and vermin were abominable.

But did this dream of baths materialize? Not just yet!

That is, in no official form. But many of the boys contrived, somehow, to get into a little more presentable condition. They were learning, though, that conditions were more primitive than had obtained in any preceding war of modern times.

After a rest of four days orders were issued that my boys pack up and proceed to the trenches again; this time to St. Eloi. The trenches were within fifty yards of the German lines, and the P.P.C.L.I.'s had to go over open ground for several hundred yards to enter them.

In doing so they passed the noted great St. Eloi Mound. This Mound of black earth, which gave the impression that it had been built at some time for a memorial, was remindful of the relics of the Mound Builders in America, save that the latter mounds are round instead of square.

While the Pats were marching toward the trenches they were exposed to German fire, and it was then that Lieutenant Price and several men were wounded, some fatally. Lieutenant Price, one of the finest of fellows, died in a couple of hours.

The trenches were shallow, with mud and water knee-deep. To the left they were not even yet consolidated, so it was necessary during the night for my Pats to assist the engineers in doing this work. This was not the pleasantest of nocturnal occupations, for the Germans, at that point less than fifty yards away, were sniping the whole night through.

While engaged in this particular shift, on the next day, January 26th, my gallant friend, Lieutenant Fitzgerald, was shot through the head. He died within the hour.

It was a sad day for our Company, which missed him deeply. I knew him well, and when I think of him there come to me memories of the famous knights and chevaliers whose names are imperishable in song and story. His was a personality which commanded alike the love and respect of those who knew him. For he possessed the qualities which endear man to man.

A gentleman he was, of one of the noblest and most courageous of Irish families. His was the charm of the best of the sons of the Emerald Isle, which has sent so many such sons overseas to grace with laughter and fascinate with good-fellowship the various realms of the world.

Considered in an earthly sense, mine is a terrible story — if we stop at the destruction of the bodies of such splendid men as Fitzgerald. But – by virtue of my faith and my vision – I look beyond and am comforted – for I see their spirits waiting yonder in the fields of green that lie beyond the fields of blood.

The Germans shelled our trenches severely, but they seemed unable to place their shells where they wanted. I think the Pats were too close to their own lines for them to be able to shell them accurately.

Time wore on and it drew near the hour for the relief. Just before the desolate dawn, when the field was still wrapped in darkness relieved fitfully by the flashes of the star shells, and the big guns on both sides were sullenly thundering, Major Gault of the Pats called to his side my Pendragon and three other men.

The little group stood together in the trench.

"Jack," said the Major soberly, "these two poor fellows must be taken care of."

He pointed to two huddled, miry, bloody bodies lying in the bottom of the trench. They had entered it to fight with their comrades. It had been their last battle. Following the gesture of Major Gault, the four men he had summoned viewed the mangled dead figures of Lance Corporal Murphy and Private Crook.

Major Gault gave the remainder of his order. "Men, you see that ruined house, five hundred yards back there? Take along a spade and bury them in the back yard. Then proceed to billets."

Crook had been killed by a bullet through the neck, and a shot through the leg had finished Murphy, who had bled to death. The four men of the burial squad lifted the sagging weights out of the trench and started with them for the appointed place of sepulchre in open view of the enemy.

They had to proceed across an open space already swept – early as it was – with rifle fire from the German trenches, between two and three hundred yards away.

Could the Germans see them?

It seemed hardly possible not to see them, for dim gleams from the east portended the swift approach of dawn.

Yet, all the way to the improvised burial plot, the bullets spattered about them in the mud.

There must be no time lost, else there might be more than the two bodies to bury by the time the spot was reached.

Because of the need for haste, a pair from the squad of four each took a body. Grasping it by the arms they pulled it toward the back yard. The inert forms, even the heads of the dead men, were dragged along through the mire. This did not matter. The essence of them that still lived and breathed the breath of immortality was now far beyond the possibility of hurt or the touch of degradation.

When the detail reached the back yard dawn was breaking. Like ghosts in the lessening darkness, that was now subtly changing to the gray mists of the morning – mists chill as death itself – now appeared the moving forms of the detail to the foe in the Hun trenches, a foe which the scenes of this war were to prove had degenerated to the barbarities of the Dark Ages. For it had respect neither for the living nor for the dead.

"Jack," said one of the men, "we must hurry, or we'll never get out of here alive. They've seen us, all right; their fire is thickening."

So it was arranged that the grave – one to accommodate both bodies – be dug by the men working in relays. One man was to work as fast as possible, another to relieve him at the end of a minute, and thus on till the work was finished. For each moment that the task should endure, death stood at the elbow of the digger.

As the moments crawled by, the light grew stronger and the figure of the grave digger clearer among the writhing mists. The other three men would crouch behind a protecting brick pile in the vicinity, awaiting their turns.

There was no doubt that the German riflemen were training their weapons on the successive ghostly figures toiling with the spade. Bullets spattered thickly about them. How it happened that none of the missiles found a living target was always a matter of wonderment to the members of that detail.

It was as if the Lord of Hosts, mindful of the nature of their errand, protected them.

At last a wide grave was dug, some three feet deep, just enough so that the two bodies should be decently covered. Swift progress had been made, digging in the mud.

Into the grave the two bodies were hurriedly rolled and the earth thrown upon them till a sizable mound was made. Meanwhile, the rain of bullets had grown thicker. They kicked up the mud at the feet of the men; they rattled against the brick pile; they whistled in the damp air, through the rising mists, close to the ears of the detail. While in the east, slowly, sullenly, as if in protest, kindled the bleak dawn.

All was done now but the last office; one attended with risk that was now almost prohibitive. But to leave them there, like that; the men of the detail could not do it!

"Jack," suddenly said Private Harry Bristow, now Major, serving on the Western Front, "let's stand there, and you say the Lord's Prayer before we go."

He had voiced the thought that had been in the minds of four men.

They circled around the shallow grave. It was growing lighter. Immediately the rain of bullets, falling about them, was intensified.

It had grown light enough so the Huns could see what their errand had been.

This made no difference – to the Hun.

Came the words of the immortal prayer, spoken not too hurriedly, despite the risk; passages interspersed by the fall of bullets of hate, in men's defiance of the Omnipotent message of love:

"Our Father Who art in Heaven. Hallowed be Thy name..." Crack! A bullet, striking a wet bank, threw mud into the face of one of the four men who were standing with bared heads.

"Thy Kingdom come; Thy will be done on earth as it is in Heaven. Give us this day our daily bread, and forgive us our trespasses as we forgive those who trespass against us."

Ping! Splush! A bullet penetrated a tin utensil at the feet of one of the men. Another stirred the mud a foot away from another of the detail.

"Lead us not into temptation, but deliver us from evil, for Thine is the Kingdom and the Power and the Glory..."

Crack! ...crack! ...crack!

"Forever... Amen."

Dawn was accomplished.

Was beginning another day of hate, of horror, of hell.

The sun was rising over the fields of death.

Amid a fresh fusillade, the four men of the burial detail, miraculously unharmed, hurried from the new-made grave and hastened to billets.

Editor's Notes to Chapter XIV:

1) Lieutenant Charles H. Price; born Manchester, England 1884; served in the Boer War; killed at St. Eloi, January 24th, 1915.

Lieutenant F. Fitzgerald (real name R.G.R. Mansfield); killed in action at St. Eloi, January 26th, 1915. Both are buried in Voormezeele Enclosure No. 3, Belgium.

2) Andrew Hamilton Gault (1882-1958); was the founder and financier of the Regiment; wounded February 28th, 1915, May 8th, 1915 and lost his leg from wounds received June 2nd, 1916. Commanded the Regiment from November 1918 to March 1919.

3) Lance Corporal John Henry Murphy, #1740; killed in action January 25th, 1915. Private Charles Crook, #1552; born England 1875; served Boer War. Killed in action at St. Eloi January 26th/27th, 1915. Both are buried in Voormezeele Enclosure No.3, Belgium.

4) Private Arthur H. Bristow, #1504; born England, 1880; wounded May 8th, 1915; subsequently commissioned into the British Army.

Chapter XV

TRENCH LIFE

It was that night when the Patricias were relieved and went into billets at Dickebusch. Their sleep was certainly that of the just – "about tired enough," for they had not closed their eyes for three nights.

On the 27th of January they left again for support trenches at St. Eloi, and remained there till the 29th.

On the last day of January the first draft from England arrived. Some of the men left there when we came over arrived as reinforcements, and brought with them other Canadians from the 11th and 12th Battalions. Our casualties, counting cases of illness, numbered 300 or more up to that time, so the help from the "tight little isle" was welcome.

My Pats spent that day in Dickebusch billets, and toward evening they began to prepare to leave for the trenches again. One company was luckless that night. It was slated to hold trenches on Shelley Farm, but for some unaccountable reason the detail was unable to find those particular trenches. In the effort to find them the men were marched back and forth for several hours parallel with the German lines.

It was miraculous that no casualties occurred during that erratic hike. The night was bright, and the Huns could hardly have escaped seeing these big fellows slipping and tugging along, in full marching order, across the open country.

Their steps were accompanied by a staccato of rifle fire. The bullets clicked or zipped, the sound depending on whether they struck in soft or on hard ground. They were falling uncomfortably close. Sometimes there would sound a sharp crack, as if a rifle had been shot close to their ears. This always meant that a bullet had landed well within range, and invariably brought such signs of agitation as sudden starts, or curses, or perhaps uneasy laughter.

That there might be no monotony, sometimes there would sound a prolonged *s-s-s – zim-m-m-m*, a sound impossible to adequately describe, but as full of malice as an evil-tempered rattlesnake. The hissing disturbance would last for several seconds, and invariably

PPCLI Cemetery, Voormezeele, Belgium.

meant that a bullet was ricocheting in the general direction of the detail.

Altogether, that march back and forth, to find where they belonged, was a severe test of the boys' nerve, but they underwent it in fine style and finally found their trenches and entered them with a swing as if on parade.

With their rifles glistening in the moonlight, and the star shells of friend and foe shooting skyward in all directions, there were but two slight casualties, hardly more than flesh wounds.

On arriving at their trench, by the way, they ran into a fire about as hot as what they had been undergoing – but this latter fusillade was purely vocal!

The poor boys they were relieving had been due to leave the trenches at ten o'clock at night – and the relieving detail did not wander in till two o'clock in the morning!

They were received with a volley of sarcastic grumbles.

"Hello, what-t'-hell! Been having a little supper after the show? What's her name? Are your spats on straight?"

"Hi! fellows, look what's blew in! My word! if here ain't the Rookies Brigade, an' they've brought their knitting along. I say, Girls, tell us the latest scandals!"

"Hey! Bill! Pipe the Bunch what has come to play with us! Open a chocolate box for 'em, an' get out the rocking horses!"

"Aw, the hell with you!" growled a tall Canadian, the first of the relieving detail to recover from the unexpected warmth of this welcome to-our-trenches. "You poor prunes must roll your fags with leaves from Joe Miller's Joke Book! If you'd been out where we've been the last four hours, you'd been leggin' it back, curse you, and you wouldn't ha' stopped till you'd swum to Blighty, neither!"

So, snarling at one another, they separated; the men who had waited to be relieved, and the men who had waited – while marching hither and yon – to relieve them.

Summing it up, it was certainly hard on both sides. It could be laid to the unintentional blunder of the guides, who chanced to be new at the game.

This new detail was to remain in the trenches only twenty-four hours, but for a reason unknown at first, they had to remain an extra twenty-four. But as this was not an especially hard part of the line, there was no complaint at first, and the boys enjoyed a distinctly novel experience. They roamed about the trench and No Man's Land in the moonlight, did some needed work on it, and enjoyed a social interval with no interference whatever from the enemy.

It transpired that this was only because the enemy was interfering, with all his powers, at other parts of the line!

There were distinctly two playing that game, and unfortunately the enemy was equipped to be the aggressor. He had all the machinery known to modern science. He was using it to the full extent of his brutal capacity, in defiance of all just rules as preconceived by Canadians and other white men of the world. He was bombing women and children; he was firing at litter-bearers, *tending the wounded*, and at details who were burying the dead. He was maturing his Satanic plan of releasing poisonous gases; a device yet to be loosed.

Just at present, however, his efforts along that line were momentarily legitimate, even for a Hun.

He was attacking at different points of the trenches, while that portion of the front line trench held by this new detail, which had marched several hours to find its station, was left unhindered.

This was all very well for the first twenty-four hours, for the boys had rations to cover that period of time. But, for the next twenty-four, while they waited to be relieved, it was a different story.

It was impossible to relieve them. The men who would have done so, in the natural order of events, had been obliged to enter other trenches to help hold them against attack. It is through such exigencies as these that men detailed for twenty-four hours in the trenches often have to remain forty-eight, seventy-two, even longer, till the strength of an attack somewhere is spent and it becomes possible again to strike a balance of forces. In war it is always the unexpected that must be coped with. For this reason, as time went on, the Pats began to get a clearer idea of the perplexities of the officers, and their patience and philosophy deepened with the weary days.

Under the circumstances, the detail was lucky to be relieved in forty-eight hours.

It was at ten o'clock at night that the relief detail came. The majority were so weak they could not walk to billets, and the officers had to send for transport wagons.

"Ye gods of war!" exclaimed one of my friends, "is it come to pass that the private soldier is getting recognition from the British transport?"

It was so; but so serious was the state of many of those men that they could have never got back to billets without this jolting but welcome aid.

Those who entered the wagons, many having to be helped into them

The burial of the Princess Pats.

by the officers, were asleep in a few minutes under circumstances that seemed incompatible with slumber. Fancy being sunk in the deepest sleep while lying in the bottom of a wagon without springs, rumbling and bumping over the roughest of cobblestone roads! It was a depth of slumber that reveals the depths of exhaustion.

It was difficult to rouse the sleepers when the wagons arrived at billets. The men's feet were so sore that yells of agony were heard when they removed their shoes. In the morning their feet were so swollen that they could not don the stiff roughened leather again. However, they adopted the expedient of hobbling about barefoot for a while, and were then able, though with much pain, to wear their boots, though without socks.

This first rest was in improvised billets in a wood, slightly southwest of Dickebusch. They were then marched about six miles to some barns near Westoutre. It seemed a long and tiresome tramp to men whose vitality had been lowered by their constant exertions, which were constantly sapping their strength – these men of the strongest of strong battalions. And they were accepting their trials grimly; now mostly in silence. The *esprit de corps* of the army was spreading.

Among all their trials, the men's feet were now giving them the most trouble. To undergo such heavy marching, after a man's feet were frostbitten, required at least as much nerve as most men can muster! However, there were no quitters. But there were complaints that the transport should be requisitioned more frequently, for while men were hobbling with frozen feet to and from details, the horses were resting!

It was realized, however, that war was war, and that orders must be obeyed. "Do or die" is the motto of the army. Indeed, some men did drop out, more dead than alive, and were carried to their quarters, game to the last, their wills unbeaten though their bodies had been forced to succumb for the time being.

In such a case, the steps came draggingly, heavier and heavier, while the legs above the suffering feet shook and shook like leaves in a raw wind. Then would come a thud as the poor fellow fell in a dead faint on the cobblestones of the road, to be picked up by his comrades as if he were a child. They would carry him to the side of the road and others would relieve him of the weight of his equipment and distribute it among themselves, as extra weight. Then they would march on, and he would lie and rest for a while, finally staggering up to follow them with hobbling steps.

The inhumanity in war brings out a corresponding humanity in the hearts of men toward their comrades! It is wonderful, the flashing sidelights which bring out the weird contrasts in the Jekyll and Hyde scheme which seems to rule the world!

My boys, in moments of battle, presented the awful semblance of wild beasts unloosed in the arena – and in the lulls which brought a fleeting breath of peace, their hearts were like the hearts of little children!

But tired were the boys, it was always with a martial stride, with at least a suggestion of the swanky dash which had endeared them to the hearts of Canadians, that they invariably swung to their destination, whether it be the billets or the trenches.

So it was with this night of which I have told. They were aroused early the next morning, February 8th for rifle inspection. It was the first time this had been ordered since they had gone into the trenches, and it was no easy matter under the circumstances to get themselves spotless.

However, they rose nobly to the occasion and stood on the roadway for an hour or more for their usual waiting till the inspecting officers should arrive.

It was inevitable, of course. It was necessary to get the rifles cleaned and keep them clean. Besides, the Pats' officers were put to as much trouble as the men. They, too, had to make themselves spotless before inspection, and everybody knew that all such orders came from H.Q.

Always the officers of the Pats shared the men's rigors as they did their triumphs. They endured the same hardships; were just as sensitive to the vagaries of the thermometer; did the same amount of marching; had perhaps as little to eat; the same scanty allowance of rum.

In fact, I have known times when they have had less of rum; when they gave their portion to some suffering man o' the line and went without any themselves.

Reflections like these passed through the minds of the privates as they stood in line that morning, waiting to be inspected. "We're all in it!" So ran their thoughts. So they cheerfully stood in the road and obeyed the commands of the N.C.O.'s over and over again, "just to pass the time away," and counteract the piercing blast of the wind. Such elementary commands as "'Shun! (Attention) Form fours! Stand at ease!" etc., were thus repeated many times during the hour of waiting.

But with all the philosophy which the men had been forced to cultivate towards headquarters, it was hard to acquit them of some measure of blame for keeping the men waiting in a freezing wind which lowered their vitality, already sapped by their experiences to a degree that rendered them more fit for a convalescent hospital than for this test of endurance. However, it was all in "a soldier's day."

At last the officers arrived for the inspection. *At last!*

On February 9th the Pats were paraded in order to make wire entanglements for the front line trenches. All worked at this with that sportive spirit and jolly good will that the volunteer soldier injects into all his work. Also, many of them were set to making willow baskets to hold earth to reinforce the parapet. This was more like play than work for them, and the very novelty of it was refreshing and broke the monotony of trench life, more especially being out of range of the deadly guns.

The Pats were proud of being among the pioneers of the Allied armies in France, and no Canadian nor English regiment was more anxious to be the first to try everything that was going. "Try everything once;" that was the feeling.

Thus far the boys had certainly succeeded in their desire and wish, and were to the forefront. They had been first in fighting, first in hardships, and last to shirk. In fact, they had no mind to shirk at all. They might kick and fume and fuss over trifles; that was the privilege of a British subject! It was their right to exercise it upon any needed occasion, and they did. Had not their forefathers fought and died to insure to posterity the full and free discussion of all affairs?

That was the difference between the men of such nations as the British Empire and America, and those of Germany. The latter were docile, fawning fellows, with the spirit of individuality crushed in their breasts; led about by their noses by officers they had been taught to revere as supermen, or even gods.

No Canadian, nor Englishman, nor American sees his officers through any such rose-colored glasses. Not one of them could summon the blind idolatry that is lavished upon the fat and overrated Von Hindenburg, even though each of the three nations possesses minds in military command that are keener than his.

So the Canadians, in these early days of the war like the British, and as the men from the United States were to do later – viewed things as they were. They respected the sterling qualities of their officers, and gave credit for them; and they saw as clearly their mistakes, and exercised their God-given privilege of criticism. They might so fume – and "let off steam" – but when the big tests faced them, they battered into the most sullen obstacles without thought of quailing, without word of complaint, with the white feather and the "streak of yellow" unknown.

Chapter XVI

" MERCI, KAMERAD ! "

Hardships were now beginning to tell heavily upon the battalion. The grim vicissitudes of war were taking their toll. Many men were falling ill, through various causes. The platoon to which my soldiers three belonged, which a few days before had a strength of sixty-four men, had only twenty-three upon an early day in February, 1915, able to answer roll call. This was the case with the whole battalion. At that time the largest platoon had thirty-two men, where it should have had forty-eight or more.

My Patricias were among the most "durable" men on the Western Front – as they are yet. Consider, then, what must have been the state of affairs throughout the whole Allied army in that bleak winter!

Friday, the 12th inst., the boys again left for Dickebusch and took their places in the trenches. It was at six o'clock in the evening when they fell in for that march. They proceeded at a fast pace for about two miles, and were then loaded down with bags and shovels.

These were the best trenches they had yet occupied, and were further away from the German lines. They ran through a hollow, and the boys could get into and out of them quite easily. However, there was always something to keep the otherwise joy out of life, as one of the boys observed with forlorn humor. For the day and night were bitter cold, and they shivered and were wholly unable to keep themselves warm.

Came Saturday, the 13th. This time it brought ill luck, though a phase of it to which the boys were well accustomed. For it rained nearly all day.

Again the boys were doing fatigue duty and digging trenches. This work helped to keep them warm, and they were glad of the change, and got fresh water and tea. Ensued a dreary night of waiting and watching for the enemy – but morning found them all still well and cheerful.

At ten o'clock that night they were relieved. Trouble, which it appeared had been quiescent too long, attended the process. They were shelled while leaving the trenches, and lost two men.

Somehow the Huns must have learned the men were being relieved, and have known the road they were taking out of the trench, for the fire was deadly accurate. Finally, after much stopping and resting, they arrived at Dickebusch and remained there all night, leaving at 9:30 next morning for their old billets in the same barn. It had grown to feel almost like home for them, and was a welcome place to rest their weary bones, to wash up and to scrape off the uniforms once more.

But those uniforms had grown to be sad-looking objects to swank in!

After another night's rest and a brush-up, they fell in at 1:45 P.M. to proceed to another official bath. It was as welcome as had been the previous laving-bees. They obtained a complete change of clothing and marched back to billets feeling cleaned and freshened.

So the days passed, monotonously enough. But there was an excellent little wad of excitement on the way, the boys were to find.

It was on Sunday, February 28th, that my Pats were ordered to pack up and "stand to." The boys were restless; there was an intangible essence in the air which promised action. I felt it too, in my place far back of the front line trenches, and through it was warned to visualize what was to come.

My "Pat's Pets," grimy and bedraggled "Pets," now, marched for about six miles to a place about a mile from Dickebusch, amid laughter, song and gaiety, the same as they had acted upon their arrival in Havre, France, as this night promised the long anticipated crack at the enemy. There they camped for the night.

There were rumors of a bayonet charge. My boys were much excited at the prospect. Fred summed up the general feeling.

"Ah, for the chance to tickle their cursed ribs with the cold steel!" he exclaimed vengefully. "I hear they don't like that, a little bit! They'd rather snipe from under cover, and shoot up a burial party, and pull off a few little hero stunts like that! Let's see how much good Fritz is, standing up against a corn-fed Canuck in a little sticker duel!"

At five in the afternoon they were ordered to fall in and march to St. Eloi. They were reinforced by about 500 men from the 11th and 12th Battalions of the Canadian Contingent. As they were put in a separate company, they firmly believed that the rumors of a bayonet charge were correct, and hopes ran high.

At about midnight they were lined up at Shelley Farm ready for the attack. But before this, all had been doing fatigue duty and standing to most of the night.

Most of the boys were by then exhausted, and as angry as they were tired. For hours they had struggled through mud knee-deep, carrying heavy bags and doing other pleasant little duties that had taken most of their muscle and wind.

It was because of this that they were angry. The ambition of fighting men had been stirred – and all the energy had been consumed in the strenuous muscular efforts of the laborer! They had been ready to make the supreme effort of their lives against the Germans, in the first bayonet attack upon their lines, and now they felt more like crumpling down in the mud for a sorely needed rest.

They were marched to the road, then were ordered to halt. Part of them were separated from the others, and then only the best and strongest of the boys were selected to attack.

It fell upon No.4 Company and the snipers to furnish these attackers. The 13th and 14th platoons were the attacking platoons. Part of the 15th and 16th platoons were designated to comprise a shovel party, which meant that they were to level the German parapet and destroy the trench as much as possible.

They were marched along Shelley Farm and given the final words of instruction. Just before daybreak they quietly started for the German trenches.

Those who participated in that little episode, who have survived the rigors of the world's war, will never forget that memorable moment. The silvery moonlight made the night like day. In its wan sheen glittered some hundred bayonets, though, because the position of the moon was behind the column, this sinister glitter could have been scarcely detected by the Germans in front.

The men marched slowly to the spot where it had been arranged that the attack should start. Occurred a moment's pause, while nerves were cruelly strained as men waited, with tensing muscles, for the magic word, "Over!" that would usher in a new chapter of war's experience, thrilling, fascinating, full of dash; the first trench raid.

The order came.

The distance across No Man's Land at this spot was only about fifty yards.

With a concerted lithe bound forward, the first Canadian bayonet charge of the world's war was on.

It was accompanied by a yell, in unison, that satisfactorily carried to the Kaiser's minions in that trench the spirit of the Canadians who had come to take it.

In my dreams – the true dreams that unrolled for me as from a scroll the happenings of the front – I heard that yell that night, even as I saw the forms of my friends, head down and bayonets fixed, charging like mad moose across No Man's Land in the moonlight. It was a sound to set the spines of the enemy tingling, as it did in that first moment of surprise.

Like the roar of an angry lion challenging for a duel to the death; like the throaty yelps of a pack of wolves bounding toward their quarry, were the outcries of my Pats as they surged forward.

Gleamed and flashed the bayonets in the moonlight as the men who had been selected first to baptize Canada's steel with blood ran across No Man's Land. A man fell here; another there; as the defending fire leaped almost instantaneously from the German trench; for the men within it were far from being taken by helpless surprise.

The Pats saw their pals fall, but there was no stop. They only dashed the faster across the intervening space to the opposing parapet.

To the cries of challenge was now added a deeper note; growls of revenge for the comrades toppling in the ranks during that wild run.

They were close to the trench now. The defending machine guns were tittering; showers of bullets were falling among them, claiming their toll. Not a shot was fired in return. The Canadians were depending upon the cold steel; the steel that Joe, who was half-Indian and half-engineer, had said that Fritz would dread, and come out distinctly second best against his Canuck foe.

The next few minutes were to prove that Joe's foresight was true!

Amid a shower of German bullets, from machine guns and rifles, the Canadians gained their parapet and leaped down into their trench, which was not guarded by barbed wire, being the head of a sap – and the bayonets all fixed for business!

There was an exchange of shots from small arms at short range, but as the enemy actually closed, it was the bayonet that Jack Canuck depended on as against any other weapon.

And with the flash of the moonlight streaming into the trench and illumining the deadly blue-white, clashing, thrusting steel, came the craven whine, the Hun squeal of fear that Allied raiding parties have come to know so well; the hypocritical yelp of baby-bombers, murderers of women, Red Cross destroyers, when faced with the steel-points of justice:

"Kamerad! Merci, Kamerad!"

Was mercy shown the merciless?

Well, some prisoners were taken back to my boys' lines.

Which brings me to an exciting incident of that trench raid; one in which my Pendragon was concerned, and which I will now relate to you.

Remember, I was far back of the front lines that night; far behind the crack of rifle fire and the clash of steel. From where I was you could hear only the big guns booming in muffled thunder through the hours of the dark.

But in my divining dreams, I saw the scene in which my Pendragon figured; saw it as clearly as if I had been there with him.

I suppose it was because the incident harked back to primal days that, at the first of my dream, it seemed to me that I *was* with him.

It seemed to me that we were in a setting unnumbered ages before that of the present; away back in the era of the primordial. We were in a bleak plain, facing a towering forest of strange and monstrous twisted shapes, which looked as if it might be an abode of horrors.

Forth from this forest was coming a strange beast, with fearsome growls. I cannot describe the appearance of this monster; it was too terrible.

Dashing toward this weird brute was my Pendragon, with a snarling shout of challenge. He was my Pendragon, though strangely different. He was bearded; his hair waved in the wind; he was only partly dressed in the skins of wild animals he had killed. Above his head he was waving a great bludgeon; he was to do battle with the monster that was approaching.

It seemed to me that I was bounding beside him; Pendragon who was my idol then as he is now. But then, even as he was different I was different; for I was not then a collie dog. I was a wolf; Pendragon's first brute slave that he had tamed and taught to do his bidding.

With snarling cry I was bounding with Pendragon toward this beast that we were to attack together.

Just as we were about to close with it, this aboriginal dream faded into another; the second dealing with present truth as I have no doubt did also the first with past truth.

After my Pats had captured the trench and the last of its defenders who were still able to run had apparently retired, my eyes seemed to follow Pendragon. He was the only man of the Princess Patricias who habitually carried an ax. It was an Indian-like lifelong habit formed from years of battling with the Canadian wilds.

The ax was an ordinary engineer's tool and he always had it along in place of an entrenching tool. And it was to be demonstrated at once that it was rather a handy thing to have in a pinch.

With the dispersing of the Hun defenders Pendy had laid his rifle to one side at the head of the sap. The trench was reinforced with large

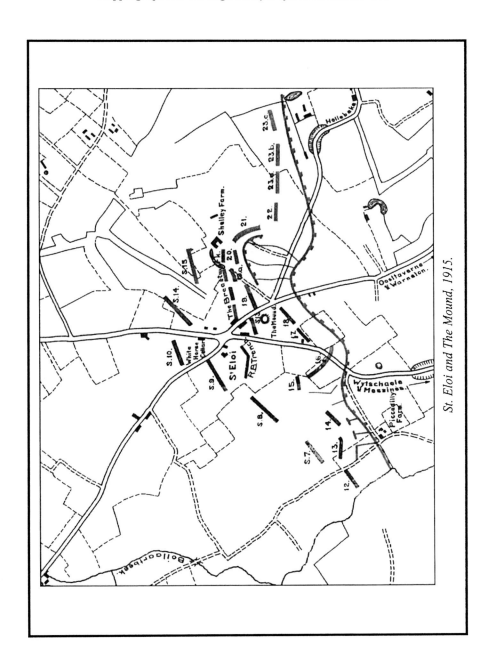

St. Eloi and The Mound, 1915.

heavy timbers and supported by "lagging," which is a miner's term for lining. It was certain that the trench had been built by experienced miners. But what miners had built miners could destroy. There were good miners with the Pats.

The Pats were busily engaged changing the interior arrangements of the trench, cutting down the woodwork. I could see their forms clearly outlined in the sheen of wan moonlight which crept into the ditch.

Suddenly my heart seemed to stand still with fright. All the Germans had not been evicted from that trench!

At least, there was one left. I saw the crouching, gray-clad figure creeping stealthily from a side sap; I saw his face, convulsed with hate; I saw his eyes, gleaming cruelly in the moonlight. I longed to spring at his throat, and sobbed in my sleep that I could not, for I was miles away!

Now, secure as he thought in the shadows, the Hun was raising his rifle. But the eyes of my comrade, Jackson, were alert. He was working across from Pendy, though further up the trench. He chanced to turn and see the crouching figure, just aiming with the rifle.

It was too far for Jackson to reach. But my Pendy was almost within arm's length of the Prussian, though with his back to him. He was still smashing away at the timbers.

"Jack!" yelled Jackson. *"Behind you!"*

Like a flash Pendragon whirled, instinctively swinging the ax back over his shoulder. I saw the whites of his eyes in the moonlight as he glimpsed that crouching figure. The Hun was just about to pull the trigger. But he never pulled it.

Pendy swung the ax home. He was just within reaching distance. The sharp corner of the blade caught the Hun in the neck. He fell like a chopped tree.

Jackson walked up and looked down at him. "I guess he's finished," he said grimly. "Say, Jack, let's swing him on top of the parapet."

He was still wriggling as they grabbed him and heaved him up there. He made a fair target. He didn't wriggle long. The parapet was raked with machine gun fire from German emplacements farther back, in revenge for our successful raid. So the Prussian, who had thought to slay and sneak away, was finally finished by the fire from his own comrades.

That incident required about a minute, all told. The whole attack was over in thirty.

A shot here; a shout there; but mostly quiet work with the steel and the sight of figures in field gray scrambling madly to avoid it. They clambered out of the trench, yelling with fright, scurrying like rabbits. Their vaunted "stonewall" defense had been knocked to pieces at sight. The ripping contact with bayonets had taken care of that. It is a man's weapon which they abhor as the civilized world abhors their sneaking, treacherous, cowardly fashion of digging in trenches, into clouds, underseas, to fight, and their battering and sinking of inoffensive neutrals to gain their own ends.

What were left of the Germans rushed back to their second line. The trench was in the possession of my Pats.

However, the victorious "Pats " were inside it only long enough to discover how much deeper, better drained and altogether more comfortable it was than those first trenches of the Allies. Doubtless, with their passion for system, the Germans had been secretly practicing at digging trenches for many years before they elected to start the world's war.

Of course, the Pats knew they wouldn't be in the trench long. Orders are orders; and unfortunately, too, as the casualties the next morning were perhaps more than if the trench had been consolidated and held. But the British army was learning, and if the price of tuition ran high, perhaps it was worth it.

Not more than thirty minutes were spent by my Pats in the trench they had taken, but they made those minutes busy ones. I have spoken before of the will with which Canucks attack their tasks; whether of construction or destruction.

When the word arrived to leave it, that trench was a sight for gods and men. Dugouts and breastworks were destroyed and the trench was shoveled half full of its original dirt. The timbers lay in twisted heaps. It would be easier for the Huns to dig a new trench than to bother with the old one!

The Pats left well satisfied. Their casualties were very light considering what they had accomplished.

They arrived at dugouts a half-mile further back at daybreak. There they remained all day.

They heard the Germans were so angry at the raid and the resultant losses, that during the day they opened a terrific enfilade of fire on No. 3 Company. They used all kinds of shells, band grenades and trench mortars, trying to revenge their own losses.

As they had no artillery with which to reply, the men of gallant No.3 had to lie flat and take everything that was coming. There was no immediate retaliation possible, and their casualties were correspondingly heavy.

Nothing of importance occurred during the next few days. My Pats did fatigue duty, and after it returned to a barn behind the line. A rest of two days there, and a return to the trenches at Shelley Farm, completed their turn in the trenches for that trip.

That was the longest turn they had in the trenches for some time, and it was the most disastrous. Their casualties were very heavy.

They started for the rest camp March 11th.

Editor's Notes to Chapter XVI:

1) German attacks on the St. Eloi front continued throughout February 1915, on several occasions they broke into the British lines. Counter-attacks involving British units of the 27th Division drove them out but with heavy casualties. The Patricias were often in support of these attacks. On the night of February 27th/28th, 1915 a "reconnaissance in Force" was mounted by the Canadians. The attack was successful in breaking into the trenches on The Mound. They held their position until daybreak and then withdrew. Later in the war The Mound was destroyed by shelling and explosions from underground mining operations. During the Raid of February 27th/28th the Patricias suffered 17 casualties.

Chapter XVII

NORTHERN LIGHTS

Came a dark night, not long after the first trench raid, of which I have told. In my sheltered place back of the battle lines I shivered and moaned in slumber. For in my dreams came phantoms to whisper and to warn me, and presently there stole through my brain the blackest shadow it had ever known.

How free from sorrow had been my life in the years before we had come to seek this Thing, and found it in blood and tears!

I knew the mockery of dreams first, on this dismal and memorable night, with a glad vision of the past. Rex, the collie that had been left behind in the Northland when we crossed the seas, seemed again to be bounding with me along the shore of Nighthawk Lake on a rare summer day. Pendy was building the fire while Fred, whose clothes were piled on the bank, swam in the lake.

Then, following the unaccountable depression that suddenly crept over me, came the drumming of footsteps, running to us from the forest. Rob, my comrade, the dreamer, the poet, who had so often stood with me upon the hilltops while we watched the outspread grandeur of God, burst from the path into the clearing, shouting wildly as he came:

"War! War!"

Next I saw three men clasping hands on the shore. I heard three voices sounding in one, the voice of Canada:

"We're on!"

My "Soldiers Three"!

Then my vision flashed to the present; a scene of this sodden night in Flanders on the Western Front.

Two shadowy figures stole like ghosts from the shelter of the Patricias' trench out into No Man's Land, at the other side of which stretched the Germans' barbed wire with the trench beyond it. Despite the darkness, all was plain to the eye of my spirit as I muttered in my sleep.

It was one of those errands – foolhardy if you will, but necessitated by the grim game of war that now led this pair onward to the listening post.

I recognized them as they crept forward stealthily. Rob was slightly in advance. Immediately behind him was Jim.

Rob was whispering back over his shoulder, soft as a breeze, as they went cautiously on through the inky blackness.

"I wish I was back in good old Canada now!"

"There's a lot of snow up there these days," answered Jim, as softly.

"Oh, I love the snow! Any place, any spot; from the Hudson Bay to the Great Lakes; from Prince Rupert to the Straits of Canso, would do me tonight. I'm sick of mud!"

A star shell from the German trench lighted the dark sky above them. They huddled in a shell hole to escape observation. Bullets from friend and foe, constantly exchanged through the night, fell close to them and sent mud spitting in their faces.

Presently there came a lull. The listening post was only a few yards from the enemy wires.

"It looks like some of those Canadian devils were in front of us again," was heard from the German trench in low grumbling tones.

Immediately there was afforded the daring Canadians an opportunity they never missed. The flare of a star shell, from a point that made it impossible for the Germans to see them, crouched in the shell crater, revealed to them a dim form upreared above the Teuton trench, striving with sharp eyes to pierce the gloom and ascertain if there were really intruders present close to the barbed wire.

"Can you see him, Rob?" excitedly whispered Jim, very low.

"Yes. I can just get 'six o'clock' on his knob on the sky line," replied Rob, meaning that he had drawn a deadly bead on the Hun's head. "Duck when I pull!"

In that very instant he fired.

They dropped into the deep sheltering crater, and hugged the earth.

"You got him!" whispered Jim. "I saw him tumble in. Good old boy! And it's not the first one for you, either!"

"I know I got him!" whispered Rob grimly in reply. They lay quietly for some moments, for star shells were falling thickly. The Huns' suspicions were aroused, and with these blue-white flares, like the livid lights which the poet Dante conjured in the hell of which he wrote, they were searching No Man's Land.

Then:

Bang!

There came a terrific explosion. One of the Germans – through mere chance – had thrown a bomb directly into the crater wherein the two men were hiding.

In Jim's horrified sight, poor Rob rolled to the bottom of the crater.

"Rob!" whispered Jim shrilly, "are you hurt?" There was no answer.

Swiftly Jim was at his side; he bent over him. Blood was trickling from his head and a red stream gushed from his neck with every throb of the pulses.

Setting his teeth, in defiance of the swarming death which menaced the action, Jim leaped upright and rushed out of the crater into the open, setting his face toward the Canadian line, for which he forged in a desperate dash. He had but one thought; he could not carry Rob alone; he must get help; there might be a chance if action were taken quickly.

Star shells were now shooting up by the hundreds around him. The entire German trench was in commotion, evidently fearing that a raid impended.

Shots rattled around Jim, for he was plainly visible to the Teutons. On he went in his headlong rush, and not a bullet struck him. Leaping a ditch here; jumping a crater there, he pressed on till a magical word stopped him, a word of one of his own vigilant comrades:

"Halt! Who goes there?"

"Friend!" gasped Jim. "It's Jim!"

"What's the matter?" asked the sentry, recognizing him now and lowering his rifle.

"Tell the sergeant Rob is hurt bad, in the crater to the left of the listening post. We must get him in!"

Immediately it was done. "Pass the word back for five men to get in a wounded man from crater to left of listening post!" ordered the sergeant. "Here, Jack!" he cried; "you go, and you, Fred!" And with Jim, who turned back with them to guide them, he called two other men. He told them to get Rob in as quickly as possible, but they needed no urging.

The party started, stumbling into shell holes and tripping over uneven ground till they came to the spot. The German line was now in a furore, and they had to stop and hide many times to avoid the Huns' alert sentries. But, partially due to their own caution but more due to a Higher Power, they arrived at the crater without accident, and without the enemy apparently being aware that they were there.

There was now no sign of life in the limp form of their comrade as they picked him up tenderly. They dragged rather than carried him to their own trenches, for the star shells were still searching No Man's Land, and the need for haste was imperative.

Within the Patricias' trench they laid him down. His clothing was soaked with blood and water. His face was gory, and his neck; and where the skin was not red it was blue-white and cold.

"Pass the word back for the rum!" ordered the sergeant. His voice was shaking. All the regiment had loved Rob.

The rum came quickly. They poured it in the mouth of the dying man. But he was unable to swallow it.

They feared that he was dead. They searched for signs of life. Yes; he was still breathing faintly.

Came a ghostly groan. The fiery liquid in his mouth had revived him somewhat. He opened filming eyes; to stare blankly out over the wide waters that were darker and deeper than those of Nighthawk Lake.

Then, broken and faint, came the mumblings of words, breathed in a thrall of delirium that mercifully softened the agony of his passing. The words of a poet and a patriot; the words of a brooding spirit that had loved its land, and for that land had yielded up the supreme sacrifice:

"Canada... Canada... Canada! my heart... my love... *Canada!*"

Those who stood about him, with bared heads, were deathly still. From the detonating steel of friend and foe, there in the black night, came the orchestration of the soldier's requiem; the rattle of rifle fire; the bursting of bombs; the diapason of the great guns bellowing in the rear.

Came his voice again; strangely strengthened; ringing with an exultant note:

"Oh, God... Great Spirit of Truth... my soul... give it back to Canada... let it rest there... in peace, in purity... under the snow!"

His soul... under the snow! An emanation of the Divine, of the courageous, of the unconquerable; an essence to forever inspire the generations yet unborn; the generations of the lion heart, of victors, of men; the essence of deathless will that comes to quickened dust from its parent soil – under the snow!

The little group stood and watched; among them my Pendragon and Fred, those two who had struck hands with him that day in the forest, this stricken poet of the "Soldiers Three"!

Again came his voice; dulled, drowsy, a little bewildered:

"Where's my hat, Eva? ...What's that coming down the road?"

After a moment, once more he spoke, now in a whisper, so faint that they had to bend their heads to catch the words:

"The lights! ...The lights! ...Green, yellow and red ...dancing across the sky. ... Oh! *the – the – Northern Lights!*"

His voice ceased; his head fell back; he twitched once, then lay still. His comrades stood motionless, saying no word.

His spirit had fled in quest of the Northern Lights; to the silence and peace and purity of the snows.

Editor's Notes to Chapter XVII:

1) It is very difficult to put a name to Rob. He may have been a fictitious character, although throughout the book Munroe's detail usually allow for positive identification. The only miner and original No.4 Company man killed in the period specified by Munroe, was Private Roland C. Fruen, #1513, who died February 27th, 1915. He is buried in Voormezeele Enclosure No.3, Plot III, Row G, Grave 2.

Chapter XVIII

SHELL SONGS AND LAUNDRY

For a few moments, as if it were to fill in a lull between battles with a talk "around the circle" in billets, I am going to pass on to my friends of the laity, who have not experienced the actual shocks of war, various information of the field that I gathered while abroad. These bits cover a variety of matters, from shell songs to a spy's laundry code.

One often hears the friends at home speculating upon such questions as the noises made by different projectiles, and whether you can actually see them as they are hurtling through the air. It is a subject which intrigues the popular imagination.

You can hear them sing in many keys, and you can see them, too, from various angles. The latter experience is the more horrifying, and soldiers have actually been known to have been killed through fright at seeing these monsters swoop toward them, with the resultant deafening explosion. That is "shell shock" in its most acute form. Men have been killed, too, merely by the crash when they have not seen the object.

Remember that "shell shock," from which so many soldiers have suffered since the war began – some of them never to recover – is purely a mental disorder. The nervous shock transmits itself to the brain, and the terrible results follow. The effect ranges from a mental dislocation to a complete snuffing out of intelligence, or even of life.

I will give an instance of the most disastrous effect of shell shock.

During a sharp exchange of courtesies between the rival trenches, the boches landed all "whiz-bang" and a "coal-box" simultaneously upon the parapet of the front line trench, held by the Pats. My Fred was right back of them and in between, and on either side of him was a comrade. The two projectiles landed a few feet apart and terrific explosions occurred with but a few seconds between the two.

The noise almost ruptured Fred's eardrums, and always after that the hearing of one ear was impaired. He was, however, unhurt. Recoiling at the detonations, he glanced down. His two comrades were stretched out in the trench, under his feet.

Thinking the shattered metal had felled them, he called for aid. Men came running and found the pair dead. There was no visible wound. They were stripped. To the amazement of all beholders there was not a wound, not a single abrasion, on either of them!

The finding was unmistakable that their hearts had fairly stopped with shock as the explosions crashed above them.

By the way, my Pats christened a number of those early munitions of war, and those of them which are still in use in the ever-changing crucible of affairs are still known by the picturesque nicknames given them by the Canadians.

The whiz-bang and the coal-box were thus so named by the Patricias. The coal-box was so diagnosed and monikered by the Pats at St. Eloi. Also, the whiz-bang was thus identified for future reference at Polygon Wood, during which argument, instead of an occasional "stray" as before, the Teutons began "to send 'em over mighty rough, and in unrighteous profusion," as one Pat put it.

The coal-box was a large 8 or 10 inch shell containing a black powder which, when it exploded, looked like the soot of a ton of coal oozing out of the ground which has been so thoroughly cratered in this war, and in so many ways. Hence, the graphic nickname was a real inspiration.

One cannot see this shell coming, but he can hear it, all right. It has a grumbling, purring, droning song like that of a high-powered motor car eating up the road, and this sound grows louder just before it explodes, for all the world as if a motor car were driving straight at you. The boys used to say that you could get out of its road if you knew where it was going to light, but unfortunately you never knew!

Its contents are not H.P. (the boys' term for high explosive), but it is a shell that has done damage enough. The explosion releases a whoof and a crack, simultaneously.

The sound of the explosion which resulted in the christening of the whiz-bang is self-explanatory. It is just that; a prolonged whiz-zzz; then the rim is knocked clean off the cipher with the bang.

It is a three-inch shell about fourteen inches long; either contact or time-explosive. Off on the ground or off in the air it goes, and either fashion is fully as unpopular. The coal-box, on the contrary, is purely a contact affair. In the case of the whiz-bang, the riot commences when the cap blows off.

A 15-inch naval gun shell you can neither see nor hear coming, if it chances to fall near you, but if you are at a distance of anywhere from two hundred yards to a mile away from it you can hear it, all right. It, also, possesses the motor-drone song. This shell contains a ton of high-explosive material, all told, and when it lands a lot of land or other impedimenta under it immediately changes position. The boys used to argue whether this was a 15- or a 17-inch shell, and the point was never decided.

I am dealing, of course, with the troublemakers that my boys of the First Contingent found. Of course, in the liberal education of the world's war, details of offense and defense change every day.

A highly interesting bit of acrobatic munition deviltry, too, was the *Minnenwerfer*, which the boys cut down to the gentle feminine sobriquet of "winnies." These playful little offerings were also dubbed "sausages."

There was no trouble in seeing them all the time they were coming. They were fired straight from the trench by some hellish mechanical device, and they could be seen coming leisurely from the time they left it till they paused to caress whatever objects, human or otherwise, they encountered.

They twisted and turned on the way, and before they began to make up their German minds to explode, they wiggled in the air like an animated sausage. Their motions were very deceptive sometimes. You would make up your mind they were going to pass, and instead of this they would do their best to fall short and drop directly on top of you. Sometimes, the boys declared, they even came back to hunt for you!

These sausages were two or three feet long, three or four inches thick and exploded a black powder. They made far more noise than destruction. In approaching they made no sound. They were so slow that they were alike easy to see and impossible to hear till their ultimate bark.

My reference to their being more noisy than destructive must be taken with qualifications. They were by no means harmless enough to encourage anyone to approach and pet them in the instant they landed!

There were lesser objects, too, which made the "swish" that a baseball makes in whistling through the air. Of such description were the hand grenades the Germans were making and using that first spring on the Ypres Salient. These would often explode, and as often not. They caused equal consternation in either case, for they were deadly little missiles when they fulfilled the kindly hopes of their Hun makers.

Some of the big projectiles I have mentioned would sometimes explode close to a man, and he would be preserved from injury seemingly through miraculous intervention. Such a case was that of a big fellow of the Pats who, comrades averred, was blown actually twenty feet by the bursting of one of these big shells immediately next to him. Severely shaken, of course, and thinking he might get a few days' leave on the strength of such an experience and go away to relieve the monotony of trench life, he applied for such leave at headquarters.

But he hadn't received a wound or even a scratch in his mad flight, so he was turned down!

"But," he persisted sadly, "I was blown twenty feet! A lot of the boys saw me go!"

He was an extra big fellow, hard as nails. The officer looked him over thoughtfully. The soldier's hope revived.

At last the officer spoke. "Crandall, report for duty to commanding officer in Trench 21 at once!"

So that was the only satisfaction Crandall got. Trench 21 was one of the roughest in the Ypres Salient!

One of the boys who went with the First Contingent, and returned late in 1917 because of wounds, told some Canadian friends that when he left the trenches the Germans had a brand new trench mortar bomb working that got his goat.

"They have it trained like a hunting dog," he declared. "It's fat and lazy, but persistent. It comes bumping and rolling along the ground in the craziest way you ever saw, bouncing this way and that. Then it hops up on the parapet and looks down at you and grins in a fiendish manner. You all scatter, of course. It takes its time, picks out the biggest bunch, chases it, and flops down among them. Then, and then only, it explodes.

"I tell you the thing absolutely refuses to go off all by its lonesome. It insists on finding a crowd before it will explode; sort of human photographer detonator affair."

Severely cross-questioned, he admitted that he might be exaggerating a little; but anyhow, "it seemed that way."

Nothing was more "jumpy" in this shell warfare than to watch the course of one of these big 15-inch shells of which I have spoken. You could not see them if you stood at the side, but if they passed directly over you, you could glimpse them, coming at incredible speed though thrown from guns eight miles back of the lines. Their song was a peculiar blend of swish and moan. These shells were as tall as a man, and they invariably fell point first in an arc. After the explosion there would be a crater that you could put a house in.

During those early days the Canadians and English were much hampered by the work of spies, as they are yet. But I scarcely think – though the arts of war "improve" so rapidly in a world's struggle like the present – that anything in the spy line of today can surpass in ingenuity the two instances I will content myself with mentioning.

In both instances – God save the mark! – the culprits were Belgians. However, these citizens of the country whose outraging by Germany, when she tore up the "scrap of paper" of international treaty, roused the civilized world, were among the least worthy of King Albert's subjects. They were stupid peasants. German gold, appealing to their cupidity, won their help for the Kaiser's cause. German slyness devised the means by which they gave the daily information the Almighty's understudy – or is the Omnipotent supposed to be understudy to Bill? – sought for Hun purposes.

One of these spies was an old Belgian laundress; the other an aged Belgian farmer.

One day the Canadians, within whose lines was the laundry, summarily took the old woman off duty. The evidence was completed, and it had hung daily from the clotheslines.

Shirts, socks, underwear, what-not; these formed the basis for a very clever code of information.

The clotheslines were in full view of the German lines. So many pairs of socks; so many shirts; so many pairs of drawers; they all meant something. Constantly the Hun had been advised in advance, for many days, of various Canadian deployments and employments.

After the laundry stopped, so did the leak.

Now for the other instance.

For a long time a British battery was kept busy moving. No sooner did they find a fine spot, however masked and camouflaged, than the Hun batteries would be dropping shells close to them.

This went on for some time. But it stopped very suddenly, with the arrest of the old Belgian farmer referred to.

The old rascal's fields showed some very eccentric plowing. He plowed a fresh field almost daily, in triangles. And the apex of each new triangle pointed directly to the fresh location of the British battery!

The day the farmer was arrested was one of freedom for annoyance for the battery, which had been moved once more. And it was never molested again from that particular source.

No more did the old woman toil in her laundry, nor the old man in his field.

What became of this aged and unpatriotic pair? Military justice posts no bills. But they do say that such spies as these, caught red-handed, are – without regard to sex – stood against a wall for the attentions of the firing squad.

Chapter XIX

THE WOUNDS ENDURING

Of all the cruel truths the war taught me, this was the chiefest. That the saddest fate is not that of the man who dies gallantly in battle. The supreme agony is that of Love that is left to live in loneliness, with the wounds enduring.

Think you that the man of the line, who has died, bore the heavier burden? It is not so. That was laid by Fate on the frail shoulders of the mother, the sister, the sweetheart, the wife.

From the first theirs was a suspense keener than any felt in the trenches, for a danger seen and faced is half conquered. Death for a soldier means release from pain and sorrow, and, as I know so well, life and progress in the realms beyond this one. And the remainder of this life for the woman he loved, and who loved him, means loneliness, tears, a bitterness of continued waiting – how long?

So, again at peace in my Northland and recalling those scenes of the red past, I remember Tom Hattrick. And while I feel regret at his passing, my deeper grief is for the girl he left behind. For, I repeat, Love is the most grievous sufferer in this war.

It was during the Patricias' first bayonet charge of the war, of which I have told you, that death came to Tom Hattrick.

He was a tall, stalwart, handsome Canadian, a Calgary man who had enlisted with the regiment as a private. He must have surely earned a commission had he lived, I have always believed, for he was a young man of splendid attainments and fearless gallantry and resource.

He fell, torn with machine gun bullets, while racing, with fixed bayonet, beside his comrades over No Man's Land toward the German trench. It will be recalled that the trench was held but a little while. As soon as the men retired from it under orders they carried Tom back with them, toward Shelley Farm and the dugouts.

He was then unconscious. An examination swiftly disclosed that there was no hope. His life was swiftly ebbing away. So his comrades gathered about him till he should breathe his last.

Finally his eyes opened, but in them was no recognition of his trench mates. Rather, after the fashion of eyes that are about to close for the last time, they looked beyond his friends in their muddy uniforms, fresh from their triumph over the Huns, to a thrilling scene and into a dear face of the past.

His dry lips opened. They faintly breathed a name: "Etta!"

Those who stood around him did not know Etta. But I knew her. And – stirring in my sleep in my shelter far back of the lines while I beheld him dying, whispering that name – I moaned with the memory of it, with the thought that in a few moments Etta would be left alone.

For I had been with them on the night they parted in England; as it proved, forever.

It was at Winchester. I was accompanying them, as I was a favorite with both.

Arm in arm they walked down Morn Hill. Her brown eyes were wet; her cheeks flushed; her breath came haltingly, broken with sighs, through her inner turmoil. For her boy, – as so many others, Canadian and Americans alike, were to do – had come overseas to find his mate. And the next day he was to cross to France with his comrade Patricias!

Slowly and in silence they walked to the famous Winchester Cathedral, built hundreds of years before. Instinctively the lovers turned up the lane and mounted the few stone steps. They entered the first end door that stood ajar.

Unnoted by either, now, they being completely engrossed in each other, I followed them. There chanced to be no other person in the cathedral at this hour. I lay down in the shadows just within the entrance and watched them wistfully, with my muzzle between my forepaws.

They walked on till they came to the old sepulchre of one of England's earlier heroes. There they stood together, seemingly intent upon the carving on the tomb. In fact, they did not see the carving; they stood there as had stood innumerable pairs of lovers before them, absorbed in each other; in love; in life. So passioned life had stood so many times in that spot; the aura of chill death and drifted dust contributing only a subtle melancholy to touch with added tenderness the flower of dreaming love and life!

So the dead hero in the tomb before which they stood had once loved and dreamed, and sorrowed, for love leads its myriad votaries on alike through sunlight and through shadows.

The bond between these two, on this modern night in the Winchester Cathedral, was the same as that which had bound together so many human hearts within the storied walls for centuries gone; the hearts which I know continue to love beneath the skies of the beyond.

Here men and women had knelt and worshiped on the eve of knights' departure to do battle in a foreign land; just as they do now. Here, through the ages, in sanctuary of these walls, had so often been required and granted love's sacrifice and love's renunciation!

Etta spoke at last. Her low, soft, vibrant voice was trembling.

"Tom, how long do you think it will be before they give you furlough for England?"

He answered a little huskily. "I am told that ten per cent will be returning in the spring. If so, you can depend that I will be with them. I shall have a record good enough for that, my girl. God knows I have the incentive; to see you!"

They moved away from the tomb and took seats together on an old wooden bench, a relic of the earliest days in the oldest church in England. Tom's arm stole round her waist.

"Etta," he urged, "why can't we be married tonight? Let us go, right now. Why delay?"

Both his arms were about her now, hungrily he looked into her lovely face. Her eyes were downcast. She came closer to him, now hiding her face upon his breast.

His voice had grown hoarse. "I can't leave you behind!" he declared. "How can I ever leave you?"

His love overwhelmed his spirit like a storm. Impetuously he clasped her closely, showering kisses upon her hair, her cheeks, her lips. She made no move to resist; she lay passive, in his arms.

How could they part like this? he protested. If she loved him, she would marry him at once, this night. Why wouldn't she?

Then she found voice to remind him of the rules governing marriage in her church; of the publishing of the banns; of the respect she owed her family, who were rigid in their notions of propriety under such circumstances.

"Don't you see, Tom?" she pleaded, her voice scarcely louder than a whisper. "There isn't time now; and you must leave tomorrow. But I wish Oh, I wish I had said yes when you asked me before! How I wish it!"

"Then say yes now!" he pleaded eagerly, his soul spurred by the coming inevitable parting on the morrow. "You love me, don't you? Then prove it! Forget the church rules! We can go elsewhere and be married more quickly! Come with me, now!"

"Tom!" she half sobbed, "I – I couldn't! There are my people; we must think of them. Don't you see? I – I *can't!* Wait till you come back, on your furlough."

But apparently he was not listening. He cut in, a little bitterly, because of his disappointment.

"*Conventions!* Dear, don't you see that it is *people* that make conventions; it isn't God! Even if we didn't abide by them at all, it would be all right, in His sight! Etta!"

He was again clasping her, almost roughly; fairly smothering her with his caresses. She was shaken as if in a storm; there was a low moan deep in her throat; the tears were streaming down her cheeks. At last agitated speech was wrung from her; words uttered so low that he could hardly hear them.

"Tom! dear Tom; be kind to me; *help me!*"

The effect was magical. His native chivalry had been stirred to its depths.

"Kind to you? Yes, little girl; I'll always be kind. Be brave! And I'll be brave, too. I do want to be good to you!"

The pressure of his embrace had relaxed; now she rested, breathing unevenly, in the hollow of his arm.

Suddenly she burst into a hysterical fit of weeping. He held her closely, smoothing her hair, comforting her, calm now for her sustaining, mindful that the tempest of his own emotions had loosed hers.

"There, there, Etta! Poor little girl! Don't cry so; or cry all you like; it will ease you."

For a time she cried the more freely, finding in the feminine measure of relief a certain relaxation. Finally she lay spent, with an occasional low sob and with broken sighs, in his embrace.

Now he stood up, assisting her to her feet while he contrived a bleak smile.

"Well, Etta, I must take you home now. How dark it has grown! I hadn't noticed that.

"So it's all right, little girl," he was telling her with forced cheerfulness. "We must both be brave. And I'll be back on furlough in the spring and we will be married then, won't we?"

"Y-yes," she quavered, clinging the more tightly to his arm. She bit her lips to keep from crying afresh. For black thoughts were flitting through her brain; thoughts as black as ravens. Stubbornly she fought to drive them away, but they persisted.

Why had she denied him? Why not, for the sake of her love, have defied all convention? What if – what if he – *never came back?*

She almost screamed aloud in terror as that thought came. But his voice, still with its note of forced cheerfulness, was sounding again.

"Well, Etta, here we are at the door. Bobbie Burns, where are you? Oh, here he is. I thought probably the old boy had followed us in. Stick close, Bobbie, and we'll seek the outer air together."

So we groped our way cautiously through the narrow passage at the rear end of the cathedral. Not a light could be seen anywhere; the dismal darkness of war overhung the city. Several times Etta collided with the stone fencing before we reached the sharp turn leading into High Street.

At last we reached that thoroughfare, and here we had to exercise great caution in getting across unseen.

The street contained many pickets who were gathering in the soldiers on the eve of departure. The military police and "red caps" were especially numerous on this night. They were combing the city from all angles. They were not in the mood to receive explanations, and to be caught after hours meant trouble at headquarters.

Etta knew this, and in her concern for Tom, and the accompanying excitement of their crossing the street unseen, the pain of their coming parting was in some degree alleviated.

The justice of the situation, from the standpoint of military discipline, could not be questioned. On the morrow was not the great 27th Division, England's finest Indian army, to which was attached the P.P.C.L.I., leaving for the front? Embraced within this division, the picked manhood of the Anglo-Saxon race from every part of the Empire – and with many men, too, from the United States and most of the other nations – would be marching to Southampton to board the boat for France.

The orders were sudden. So many a heart throbbed heavily that night in and around the town of Winchester; many a happy plan was upset; and, could they have looked into the future, the morrow's parting would for many a soldier be the last, and for many a loved one would

"Life be never the same again."

So, when they had safely crossed the street, and I stood waiting for Tom, one of the finest of the Canadian frontiersmen destined to cross the Channel, he and Etta stood in the shadow of a cross street down which she would presently hurry to reach home. And pride shone in her eyes, too, pride through tears, as she looked up at him.

"My boy!" she whispered, "you will come home to me on furlough in the spring?"

"Yes, dear, and we will be married then."

"I wish – Oh, I wish – "

"I know, darling. But the time will pass swiftly. You'll be surprised to see how quick the spring will come. I won't say goodbye. Just – till we meet again. And remember, I love you!"

Swiftly, after a lingering embrace, he hurried away, warily eluding the pickets, with me after him. The camp was situated in the outskirts of the town. We crept in through the back way, and avoided the sentry.

Meanwhile, Etta hurried home. In her heart was the sunlight of hope – and the shadow of dread.

Months had passed since then. Spring was approaching; the spring that was to have witnessed the bond that should follow their tryst, Tom's and Etta's.

Tom had received his furlough. But he was going to a strange country – to wait for the girl he loved.

He lay on the ground, bleeding, in the pallid light of dawn. His comrades were gathered about him. His face was grayer than the dawn.

His stiffening lips moved once more, to frame a single word, breathed ghostly faint:

"Etta!"

They he lay very still.

He had laid his burden down. The woman was left to carry hers alone – how long?

Editor's Notes to Chapter IX:

1) *Tom Hattrick is probably Private Thomas B. Haddock, #1663; born St. Mary's, Ontario, 1876; served in United States Infantry; lived in Beadle, Saskatchewan. Killed in action at St. Eloi, February 28th, 1915. He is buried in Voormezeele Enclosure No.3, Belgium.*

Chapter XX

ST. ELOI'S MOUND

My Pats started for their rest camp at Westoutre on March 11th. The barn which served as their rest camp was as uninviting as all Belgian barns. It helped to enclose a square of which the other boundaries were the dwelling house, the horse and cow stables and the outbuildings.

Within this square was a sort of deep vat-shaped excavation where drained the refuse of surrounding buildings. This excavation seemed a Belgian habit, and, on all the farms, was filled with vile-odored refuse. So the surrounding atmosphere was stifling and unsanitary, making the barn a wholly unhygienic billet.

On March 13th came the order that the Pats should sleep in their boots, clothing and equipment. This meant that there would be little rest for them after they rose. The expected strenuousness was more than realized, and sooner than looked for.

It was at 6 P.M. that they got orders to be on the road in five minutes in full marching order. The whole battalion was returned to Dickebusch, where the boys assisted in recapturing trenches that had been lost by their own divisional troops. The assistance rendered proved not so much in a sanguinary sense, but it was given with a royal will and a hearty wish to accomplish whatever was desired. After remaining up all night and wallowing in mud, the Pats were not in the best of shape for attacking a well-organized enemy, equipped with every death-dealing artifice that the brutal Hun imagination could devise.

But the Pats were perfectly willing to give it a try. Indeed, they were anxious to come to grips with Fritz. They wished to exhibit their fighting mettle. Their spirit was that of the man who has trained constantly and earnestly for many months for an ordeal of strength and skill and gameness. Always, with tingling pulses, he is looking forward to the day of the great test. So were the Pats this night, eager for the fray. They would show Heinie what real Canucks could do with the steel!

They had, of course, no chance to sleep at all, for they moved quicker than had been expected when the order was given to sleep in boots and equipment. The circumstance that called for this night assignment was this:

The Germans were hell-bent on taking the high ground at St. Eloi, including the famous mound, of which I have made mention before. This ground had a wide range of visibility for many miles in all directions, as the rest of the surrounding country was low and flat.

The Huns took the 82nd (British) Brigade by surprise during the night of March 12th, and succeeded in penetrating the front line trenches and overwhelming the Leinsters (Royal Canadians), a British battalion. But although the Huns used mass formations and drove over the gallant Irishmen in the front line trenches, they did not succeed in reaching the supports, though they fought to secure them through that night and the following day, the 13th.

It was then reported that they were massing other troops in the rear and were preparing to make a supreme sacrifice to obtain the only high ground held by the British on this front.

In this ambition, however, the Huns were destined to encounter even more trouble than they caused for two years to come, and finally to lose out altogether. No more staggering blow to German military arrogance was to be dealt than those which, for many months to come, proved more effective than those of the "mailed fist," and finally proved the gray-clad vandals, instead of supermen, foemen who were not so good at delivering the wallops as those they faced.

Although the Germans, during the next two years, captured this high ground several times, it was always recaptured. Finally the Huns lost it entirely, and at the time of this writing they are miles to the rear of it.

The 80th Brigade, which attained fame as the "Stonewall Brigade," and to which the Pats were attached, was taken from its regular rest period and ordered to recapture the ground taken by the Germans the night of the 12th.

Thus it was that the Pats, ordered during the 13th to "sleep in equipment," had no opportunity for sleep. But with a fight in prospect, this worried them not at all! The six-mile march to the scene of battle was accompanied by the latest songs and ditties and much laughter.

Two battalions of the King's Royal Rifles were billed to make the attack, supported by the Pats. The Pats occupied the left of the ground, and were to retake the trench known as "The Barrier."

The right half battalion (Nos. 1 and 2 Companies) was stationed in front of The Barrier. Nos. 3 and 4 Companies were stationed perhaps a hundred yards to the rear. If Companies 1 and 2 could not capture The Barrier, Nos. 3 and 4 were to dash over the ground and try their hand at riding roughshod over the Kaiserites.

Companies 1 and 2, however, in a concerted dash, succeeded in retaking the trench rather easily, finding it more thinly defended than had been expected. There were a number of German casualties – few being sustained by the Pats – and what were left of the Teutons stampeded in disorder to the protection of their rear lines.

The fight continued for several days. The Pats continued to hold The Barrier and staved off repeated and savage counter-attacks. During this time the members of the regiment accounted for many Germans, but sustained quite a number of casualties themselves.

The K.R.R.'s, the gallant British detail that was set to take the mound, had a far more difficult position to storm, however, and many a brave man fell in the execution of his duty. They succeeded in recapturing the surrounding trenches, but the mound itself, bristling with machine guns, was a different proposition. It was too much to expect that a thousand men, or less, could have taken it, however determined their effort.

Because of the slenderness of British resources in that early part of the war, the Canadians and English had no artillery preparations and the fighting was wholly sustained by infantry against German infantry *and* artillery. There were no trench mortars nor hand grenades in the position of the K.R.R.'s. Just rifles they had, and the "long knife," as the bayonet was known. But they did plenty of red work with these. How Fritzie did hate that "long knife," to be sure! As the spring would disclose, he vastly preferred the poison gas, when released by himself, and during which attack he might remain safe in the rear of it and chortle at the thought of foemen stifling and dying. Except, indeed, when the wind changed, and brought to him the reprisal of the "biter bitten!"

The losses on both sides – but particularly the British – in the fighting about The Mound were very heavy, when it is considered that this was purely a local operation. If a tank had been there – it was before the introduction of that device in the theatre of the Western Front, of course – a single one of the monsters, it is safe to say, would have climbed the mound and dominated and captured it in a jiffy.

During the many months of fighting for its possession that ensued, The Mound was captured, recaptured, blown up, rebuilt, and mauled like a bone in the teeth of two maddened and contending dogs several times. The issue was decided in the "Big Push" of 1916, when the British finally pushed the Huns back and retained the battle-scarred eminence permanently for themselves.

The base of this mound was about 150 to 200 feet wide. It was about 200 feet long. The slope ascended at an angle of about 70 degrees. The summit was from 20 to 30 feet high.

Not much of a hill to have caused so much trouble and blood. But it dominated a peculiarly flat country, and each side figured that it needed it in its business.

The Mound of St. Eloi wakens some of the grimmest recollections among surviving veterans of the British and Canadians who fought there or in its neighborhood on the Western Front for two years.

Chapter XXI

" WITH – THE BOYS! "

After sustaining their share of the ordeal in The Barrier trench, my Pats retired to a farm about a half-mile from the village of Dickebusch, and after partaking of an issue of well-earned rum they had a fairly comfortable night.

On March 19th they returned to the front and took their position in the same old trenches. They arrived in the midst of a rush of acknowledged perplexity and confusion. Nobody seemed to know what deployment to make, or anything tangible about arrangements.

Colonel Farquhar had to be here, there and everywhere, seemingly almost simultaneously. He would rush up to the front line trenches and then rush back, as he insisted upon seeing to all the detail himself.

The Adjutant warned him that he should be more cautious, but he knew no fear. He seemed to believe that no bullets of the Hun brand would do him harm. Besides, he insisted, he must see that all went well in front – and he must be as far in front as the wires would allow.

Added to the apparent anxiety and uncertainty of those in control of the situation, the weather was very bad and the nights very cold. The fighting was savage. The Huns were bent on breaking through at St. Eloi; they attacked it first from one side, then from the other. They showered a cruelly continual bombardment on either side, with no reciprocal returns from the British. It seemed to many of the Pats that it was a case of good men and willing muscle being pitted against machinery geared with devilish brains.

However, at present the war machinery was not to be had by the British, and their war brain was temporarily flustered, doubtless from that very lack.

In such a case, with the nervousness from "higher up" filtering through to the men, splendid leadership was the most golden of assets, and this the Patricias enjoyed to a superlative degree. Colonel Farquhar remained cool, efficient, indefatigable. His vigilance was tireless, and his good example reacted upon his men and renewed their confidence.

The strain was increasing. By now even those Pats in supports were compelled to work day and night digging new trenches, deepening old ones, putting up wires, building death-trap dugouts and preparing for a new line of defense if necessary.

Such was the hurly-burly rush upon a dark, wild, memorable night. Everybody was rushing hither and thither after no well-defined plan, so far as could be seen. It was known that there was a night and day shift of the Germans, who had been re doubling their offensive efforts. There was always about an hour between the changing of these shifts that was fairly quiet. These intervals occurred at dusk and again at dawn. But after that, Fritz invariably resumed his raising of hell.

Fritz seemed equally facile and deadly, whether he chanced to be working in the day or in the night.

It so happened on the night of March 20th, 1915; an hour that those Patricias who have survived the rigors of war will never forget.

Colonel Farquhar was inspecting the front line trenches, his busy mind teeming with the problems which every passing day now rendered more acute. He was explaining to Colonel Dwyer, of the K.R.R.'s, the conclusions he had formed, and Colonel Dwyer was agreeing with him.

"That hill over there," Colonel Farquhar was saying, "I would let go." He illustrated with sweeping gestures. "I would retake this other hill, as it dominates the other by twenty feet. Their position would be then rendered untenable – "

Crack!

His speech broke off abruptly. He crumpled and sank to the ground.

There in the sombre darkness – for the night was especially black, a winged menace in the shape of a stray Mauser bullet from the enemy trenches had passed through his body, entering at the breast.

Men sprang to his side and picked him up. They carried him back, under fire, to the dressing station.

The M.O. gave his wound a searching examination and shook his head. Then swiftly he bandaged the wound and made him as comfortable as possible.

The Adjutant sat beside his cot. The doctor's hand rested over the heart. He looked at his watch and counted the seconds. The stretcher bearers stood with bared heads and talked in whispers.

Now the Adjutant knelt at his head and pressed a hand against the cold brow. The minutes crawled by, leaden slow.

"If only he would open his eyes!" murmured Captain Buller.

"I fear he never will again," answered Major Keenan as quietly. "But I wish he would speak!" Inquiringly he glanced at the surgeon.

"I'm afraid not; with a wound like that," the surgeon told them. He had see many soldiers die.

"Yet the look in his face – it seems rational enough," said Captain Buller.

All were speaking in that strange hushed tone. As if it mattered now, when in the ears of the dying soldier even the thunders of the great guns, belching death in the black night, sounded faint, like the receding echoes of menace in a dream!

Then, quite unexpectedly, the Colonel opened his eyes. The doctor, bending over him, caught his desire.

"Hush!" he said quickly. "He wants to speak."

The Colonel tried to raise his head, but could not. He feebly moved one arm, and with a tremendous effort gasped the words

"Bury me – with – the boys!"

He had half lifted his arm. Now it fell. He relaxed after this supreme effort.

"Yes, yes!" answered Captain Buller. "What else?" There was no response.

Outside the dressing station the shells were bursting thickly. Bullets whizzed by the door. Unmindful of bullets or shells, men came and went.

The Colonel stirred again. A quiver of agony crossed his face. Major Keenan put something in his mouth.

Other stretcher bearers arrived with a wounded man of the line. The poor fellow was twisting horribly and his face was contorted with agony. He tried to murmur something. His voice was faint. Apparently he was slipping with the Colonel across the border.

The surgeon hurriedly applied temporary relief and turned again to the Colonel, the idol of the Regiment, commander of fighting men, the pick of nearly all the nations of the globe. He had led them in life; dying he dominated them; dominated them through love rather than with the brutish fear inbred in lashed and servile Huns.

The surgeon again placed his hand over the Colonel's heart. He shook his head again, but said no word.

More stretcher bearers entered with other wounded men. "They are K.R.R.'s, sir," said the orderly. Medical sergeants, orderlies and stretcher bearers stood about the commander with sombre faces, wishing desperately that he might be recalled from the shadow of death.

They watched sadly the man who had been accredited one of the best soldiers, in courage and in brain and in intelligent mastery, on the

Lieutenant-Colonel F. D. Farquhar, D.S.O. Died of wounds received in action at St. Eloi, March 20th, 1915.

Western Front. He was a man for whom the pinnacles of military authority had been predicted. But the gods of war had willed for him an early bivouac.

Again the Colonel's face twisted in agony. His eyes partially opened with a painful twitch. His fair face was ashen; his cheeks drawn and hollow; his chin had dropped; his breath came spasmodically from laboring lungs.

The interior of the building was damp; the night was bitter cold. Yet the Adjutant's face dripped perspiration as he knelt on the stone floor by the Colonel's side. His warm hand pressed his idolized commander's chilling forehead; then it shifted to search for his dwindling pulse.

There was a look of strained awe, almost of terror, in the Adjutant's eyes. His actions were automatic. Once or twice it seemed as if he would speak, but he did not. Helplessly he hoped for a few more words from the dry lips; he watched for a look of recognition, a sign of consciousness from his lifelong friend.

The M.O., who had been busy ministering to the other wounded men, came again to the cot. Again he felt the heart.

"A moment more," he said gravely, and reluctantly turned away.

No priest or preacher was there for the last rites. But once it was said:

"As ye live, so shall ye die."

The Colonel had lived a soldier's life; a soldier's death he died.

He would not have willed it otherwise. Surrounded by his comrades; with the funeral dirge of shot and shell around him; with his face to the foe till the last. He had answered his country's call; he had fought for the flag he loved; he was dying for the cause in which he believed.

"As ye live, so shall ye die."

No truer words were ever spoken.

He was gasping brokenly now; the pauses between the sobbing intakes were appallingly long. His mouth was opened wide in the effort for air; nature struggling to the last for life. In the face the ashen hue of death was deepening. The circle of silent watchers about the cot grew closer.

Came a final long shuddering gasp. The ears of the watchers were strained for the next. There was none.

Now, however, in the tortured face grew a change. O'erspread it the look of peace that comes in that last moment that is beyond finite understanding.

The pale lips opened stiffly. Toward them the Adjutant inclined his

ear.
He caught the words, breathed faintly, as if a breeze were dying:
"The – boys!"
Then – silence.

Editor's Notes to Chapter XXI:

1) Lieutenant-Colonel Farquhar is buried in Voormezeele Enclosure No. 3, Belgium. The old PPCLI Regimental Cememetery was left untouched after the war, only landscaped and headstones replaced the old wooden crosses. The old PPCLI Regimental Cemetery is now Plot III and contains 58 PPCLI graves.

2) Another book that chronicles the history of the Princess Patricias in the Great War is "Letters of Agar Adamson." Adamson was also an 'original', starting out as a Captain and later he took command of the Patricias in 1917. Adamson's letters are the best collection of Great War correspondence by any Nationality during the war. He corroborates Munroe's version of events in 1914-15. Published by CEF BOOKS, 1997.

Chapter XXII

BROTHERS MEET

Major Keenan walked to the cot where lay the body of Colonel Farquhar. He laid his hand on the breast. Then he folded the relaxed arms across the chest.

Captain Buller, the Adjutant, had continued to hold the head of the man he had loved so well. Now he laid it back gently on the stretcher. The clock showed 9:35 P.M.

Silence still held in the room though the din of battle raged outside.

A soldier's spirit, a ruling spirit, had passed on. A life story was ended; a book of promise and of inspiration was closed. Britain had lost a splendid soldier. The P.P.C.L.I.'s had bidden farewell to a leader and a friend. From Canada had been exacted another bitter sacrifice.

The following afternoon the Princess Patricias marched, carrying the body of their dead commander, to a lonely burial ground in Voormezeele. There he was laid in a soldier's grave. In the burial ground were mounds that sheltered the bodies of other members of the Patricia Regiment. So the Colonel's last words were heeded:

"Bury me with the boys."

He was laid away with all the military honors of the brigade and battalion. The cemetery was situated behind the last house to the left of the road on entering the village, which was now a demolished pile of brick and stone. Even the cemetery itself was not immune from the vicious bombardment. There lies Colonel Farquhar among the comrades he loved and who loved him.

The battalion moved to Poperinghe, and near that city they rested very comfortably for a few days that were positively happy. For a Canadian soldier, in an interval of rest, is able to emerge from the strain and behave as if he had not a care in the world, even amid the din of battle. The only shadow now, to mar concerted spirits, was the death of Colonel Farquhar, but the men were resigned to the grim inevitability of this.

The weather was lovely for the first time since the Pats had come to Europe. The sun was quite warm; there was a thrilling breath in the air of the spring that was about to be born. Small wonder that the spirits of the Pats revived; that they looked upon a fleeting vestige of peace and found it good; that the *estaminets* beckoned to them not in vain.

The proprietors of those Belgian estaminets had discovered early how freely would Canadian soldiers spend their money when they had the opportunity to do so. Doubtless, this discovery revealed to the proprietors one of the few bright spots in the war.

Whenever the Jack Canucks were off duty they would flock into the *estaminets* on all corners of the roads. There they would drink to the success of the cause; to the dear old home across the sea; to the loved one left there and to the wish to see her again. So they would sit and sip their glasses of lightest French beer, and chat, and dream, and hope wistfully, bewhiles, for the return of peace to bind up the wounds of the world, and hope that it would be granted them to return to the arts of peace fit to again take up a man's work.

How many of these dreams in the *estaminets*, when glasses were clinking cheerily and the blue smoke curled upward from the tips of their fags, were destined perhaps to be dissolved by death, to be drowned in tears!

Nothing of importance transpired till the Pats , arrived at Ypres on April 5th.

They marched through Ypres and took billets in a public school building in one of the main streets of the city. Captain Buller, former Adjutant, was now Colonel of the Pats, succeeding the commander he had loved so well and mourned so sincerely.

Ypres contained 30,000 people, it was said. Its most interesting sight was then the beautiful Cloth Hall, so called, a large building made entirely of cloth where hundreds of women were employed, making many kinds of lacework.

At about the center of the city, too, was a very curious tank, which was built of stone and stood high in the air.

The boys enjoyed themselves thoroughly during those two days in Ypres.

On April 7th the battalion again took its place in the trenches in front of Hill 60, but these trenches were only supports for the firing line, and holding them was like play compared with the ordeal of holding the previous trenches they had occupied.

This was their first introduction to the village of Hooge. It was then a beautiful place, though immediately destined to be devastated by war.

Behind it was located a gentleman's estate occupying many acres of cultivated, well-kept grounds. There was an artificial lake of about five acres, with boathouses and many boats. The woodland and castle in front of it, the gardens behind it, all helped to form a most beautiful picture.

In this woodland were located the dugouts. But as the front line was quite a distance away, the boys roamed about and enjoyed the scenery. They visited neighboring farms to secure good things; also the *estaminets* for their *cafe au lait* and other refreshments.

A few days spent in such surroundings was a pleasure rather than a task; especially when compared with previous duties in a front line trench around St. Eloi, Shelley Farm, Brasserie Road and the other salient positions!

Such surroundings, of course, were far too ideal for the vocation of soldiering in deadly earnest. Soon the Pats were removed to the famous Polygon Wood, which a little later came to be known as "Dead Man's Wood." Here they occupied the front line trenches for many days. There many a poor Canadian lies buried. Still, these were the only trenches the Pats had yet occupied from whence a wounded man could be removed during the daytime.

This was possible because of a low hollow leading straight back to the dressing station, this hollow sheltering the wounded and stretcher bearers from the enemy fire.

After a few days of this they returned to Voormezeele, which village then had 3,000 people. In common with most of the other communities of that sector it was soon to be annihilated.

There the Pats were quartered in huts, and after a rest they again returned to Ypres.

In entering the city, another battalion, wearing kilts, was marching into the same street at right angles. The Pats took them for British troops.

Immediately, however, some of the "kilties" saw the insignia "P.P.C.L.I." on the shoulders of the men of the Canuck regiment which had already won fame in this war to a degree that would have amazed its gallant members, had they known of it.

The effect through the ranks of the kilties was electrical. Everybody seemed to become cognizant at once of the identity of the Pats. A dozen of the kilties stopped short in their tracks and yelled at once greetings like these:

"Hello, Pats!" ... "Don't you know us, old kids?" ... "My God! They don't speak to the common folks, hey?" ... "Say, Pats, give us a pleasant look!"

The Pats recognized a familiar accent. They glanced swiftly across at the collection of kilties. The grinning faces, the jaunty, carefree manner, the bluff cordiality were unmistakable.

It was a battalion of *Canadian* kilties that greeted them!

At once every man in each of those two battalions, as recognition became mutually complete, halted and rushed out of the line for a general fraternity meeting.

Heedless of the thundered orders of officers and N.C.O.'s alike to remain in line, rifles were discarded, packs let down, and a scrambling, yelling, laughing mob of Canucks, half of them in khaki and the other half in kilts, danced, shook hands and slapped one another's backs there in the Ypres streets. Some even embraced, after the French fashion.

The kilties were members of the First Canadian Division and were just arriving in Flanders from England, ready to try their luck against the Hun. Their joy on meeting the Pats may be imagined. And that of the Pats, as well, because as they were attached to a British division, these were the first Canadians they had seen since leaving Salisbury Plains.

So madly reciprocal was the welcome that you would have thought both battalions had just arrived home in Canada.

Both sides volleyed countless questions at each other before they reluctantly obeyed the repeated official orders to fall in and resume their marching, but finally the hike to their respective quarters was resumed.

This time the Pats occupied soldiers' barracks in Ypres. It was a big building, accommodating 1,200 soldiers. The boards were hard to lie on, without straw, but at least this was an improvement on the trenches.

Two nights were all that was spent here. They were again moved to a place on the railroad for a few hours just before returning to the trenches.

When darkness fell they marched back to the Polygon Wood, to seek and find more trouble.

Editor's Notes to Chapter XXII:

1) The 1st Canadian Division, 20,000 strong, left Salisbury Plain for France in February 1915. After a period of training in the trenches south of Armentieres they were moved into the north-eastern part of the Ypres Salient. It was mid-April 1915. They had three kilted battalions; the 13th (Black Watch) from Montreal, the 15th (48th Highlanders of Toronto) and the 16th Western Canadian Scottish.

Chapter XXIII

TROUBLE   THICKENS

The Second Battle of Ypres was now under way. It was a test of iron. Under it, the Hun, magnificently equipped for carrying out his expressed intention of breaking through to Calais, was to fail. This would be due to his meeting stouter hearts and a leonine courage superior to his own.

It was on April 18th that the Pats took their position in the trenches of Polygon Wood, with the rest of the 80th Brigade, of the 27th Division.

The 27th Division consisted of the 80th, 81st and 82nd Brigades. The 80th Brigade, to which was attached the P.P.C.L.I.'s, also contained two battalions of the K.R.R.'s, the Third and Fourth; two battalions of Regiments known as the Rifle Brigade, and one battalion of the Shropshire Light Infantry, known as the "Shrops."

The 81st Brigade was composed of Gloucesters, the Royal Scots, the Argyll and Sutherland Highlanders, and Cameronians. The Royal Scots and Gloucesters had two battalions each. There were six battalions, by the way, in each brigade. All these Scottish regiments wore kilts except the Argyll and Sutherland Highlanders, who were garbed in khaki.

The 82nd Brigade was composed of the Duke of Cornwall's Light Infantry; the Leinsters (Royal Canadians), so called from being organized and stationed so long at Halifax. It had been years before when the battalion had been thus organized, the only British battalion with a Canadian name, of which the members were very proud. To this brigade also belonged two battalions of the Irish Fusiliers, the Royal Irish Rifles and the Duke of Cambridge's Territorials.

The Wessex Engineers were attached to the division. These units, with several batteries of artillery, comprised the gallant 27th. This organization was christened "The Stone Wall Division" by Sir John French after the argument at St. Eloi and the Second Battle of Ypres.

The 80th and 81st Brigades held the ground directly in front of

Ypres. This included Hill 60 and Polygon Wood.

To their left was deployed the First Canadian division to do duty in Flanders. To the left of this division were the French Turcos.

It was known that the Germans were massing troops in the rear for an attack. The fighting was severe all along the Salient, with threatened concerted attacks at various points.

It was now that the Germans interspersed their attacks of shot and shell with choice specimens of their insidious propaganda; which, then as now, intelligent peoples who were approached with it had no difficulty in reading its falsity and correctly analyzing its hypocritical source.

The Germans in front of the 80th Brigade, to which were attached my Pats, frequently crawled up to the barbed wire, and taking shelter in craters, exhorted their British foemen in curious fashion. They must have been picked men for this job as the defenders of Ypres noticed that they spoke English with singular precision and fluency.

The effect was weird as these dialogues were carried on in the daytime or perhaps sometimes in the evenings, mild with the approaching spring. Would arise the plaintive Teuton voice from some position of cunning concealment outside the barbed wire; would reply from their trench the sharper, more strident voices of Englishmen or Canadians, flung from the depths of the trench, for they were by no means exposing themselves to treachery. The "give-and-take" would be exchanged without the debaters seeing one another.

"Englander!" would hail the hypocritical voice of the unseen agent of propaganda; or perhaps it would be, "Men of Canada!" Almost in this voice would drip crocodile tears; the rare sentiment of a race which can at once drop bombs on mothers and their babies, and weep over the necessity of war which rendered this action necessary. For, if the infants were boy babies, they might grow up to take a whack at Germany sometime. And, if the mothers had only girl babies; well, they *might* have boy babies later, and it would never do to take the chance of letting them live!

"Hello, Fritzie, what do you want now?" would float across No Man's Land from the greeted trench in response to Heinie's hail.

"Englanders, your losses must have heavy been," would whine the voice of the Kaiserhound in reply. "Why should we fight? After all, are we not brothers?"

"No!" in horror yelled one big Canuck who, with a group of Pat defenders, was asked this question. "Say, if you ever dare to claim relationship to me, I'll cut loose on you."

The usual Teutonic appreciation of the little ironies spoken by the men of the American continent is dull. Serenely Fritz kept on. In his voice was a complaining note, similar to the song of a jigsaw: "Why fight? Enough of blood is already shed. Let us all stop. We Germans are anxious to get back to our homes and do our spring planting."

"Don't go home, Fritz;" pleaded another Canuck. "Stick around; stay right here. *We'll* do your spring planting for you. We'll plant you deep!"

Which was all the satisfaction secured by *that* particular emissary of the right-hand pal of the monstrosity known to idolatry specialists as the "German God!"

And it was all the satisfaction any of the oily tongued blond devils got, whether they addressed "Englanders " or Canadians. All along the line, from their positions in the sheltered spots to which they crawled, they whined their arguments for an armistice, in some cases gravely assuring their foes that the Kaiser would extend clemency to them. They seemed nonplussed at the indifference which our soldiers seemed to feel toward their Kaiser, and were actually shocked at the irreverent manner – many instances of which I could quote, but they would never get by the censor – in which English and Canadians were wont to speak of the "war lord" of whom his creatures had apparently made a tin god.

Especially were they grieved at the Canadians' habit of referring to Wilhelm Hohenzollern by the plain, unvarnished, democratic diminutive of "Bill!" They simply could not understand such *lese majeste!*

In these forays of eloquence the Huns were wont to solemnly point out to the British their "folly" in crossing to European soil to fight, for which crime against Sister Germania they would certainly be strafed by "Gott"! "When you were not being attacked at home you had no right to do this," they argued. "It was a quarrel between lands of Europe that did not concern you."

"Yes!" yelled back a big Pat on one occasion. "Lick 'em one at a time; that was your card, but we spoiled it. Only trouble with you is, you're thick. Did you think you could do that without us all getting wise?"

To the German appeals to "stop fighting and go home," answers were returned like this:

"Why don't *you* go home? You're closer to your home than we are. You're not defending German soil!"

Had the British known as much of the German nature as they know now, they would have unerringly recognized these "kamerad" wails from the shell holes as a Teutonic trick intended to hoodwink, terrorize and discourage their opponents. While pretending to wave an olive branch they were preparing their dirtiest trick thus far of the war, for in a matter of hours now their deadly gas would be ready for release! However, their linguistic attempt did not succeed, for nobody was discouraged.

"Go home, is it?" shouted one of the Pats to the unseen exhorter. "Why, Heinie, we haven't started to fight yet!"

With Vimy Ridge and Lens and the other grapples to follow, if that particular German still lives, he must have decided long since that the "Canadian devil" was right!

From reports received during the day before the gas attack, this tirade to try to make their opponents quit proceeded, after an organized plan, all along the line, and it succeeded nowhere.

The very next morning, bright and early, the Huns launched their first gas attack of the war, selecting the French troops as the first victims.

The swift result was that havoc was created among the poor Morocco Colonials. Many were overcome, and the others, half suffocated, rushed to the rear, leaving the Canadian flank exposed. It will be recalled that this brutal attack by gas, further violating the rules of civilized warfare, was a stunning surprise. The wonder was the resultant speed and resource of the Allies in minimizing these attacks by the use of masks, and showing the Germans, that two could play at the game by prompt reprisals.

Right here was one of the most critical points of the war. The Huns had every advantage in preparation over the defenders of liberty – save one. That was the element of fighting manhood.

History has recorded the gallant stand made by the Canadians under these most adverse of circumstances. They lost some ground, to be sure, but they recaptured some of it, and continued to interpose their stone wall of defense between the Germans and Calais.

The 27th Division deployed so as to support the Canadians. Polygon Wood was on a hill, and its defenders constantly heard the terrific fighting which developed to the left of the woodland. It was at that point that the Germans gassed the French and broke through and overpowered the few remaining survivors in the trenches. The Canadians who joined the French to the right found themselves in a precarious position on one of their first trips to the trenches.

It was in that terrible fighting to the left that Canadian troops covered the Maple Leaf with a glory as warm-hued as is that insignia of Canada and of Nature in the days of autumn. The Pats in Polygon Wood heard little of the details at the time, though they knew from the intensity of the bombardment that an awful struggle was in progress. It was in that engagement, fighting like devils against the most powerful odds; being overwhelmed, and then in fierce counter-attacks re-winning much of the lost ground; that the Canucks, despite staggering losses, closed up the ranks and confounded the Huns with such fighting as they had never seen. It was after that battle that the entire world knew Canada for what it was; a nation of Spartans that had proved itself in a day.

In this fighting at the left of the line, the rattle and din of the Canadian machine guns was incessant. They had only this weapon, in addition to the rifles and trusty bayonets, while the Germans had plenty of big guns.

Against their equipment the Canadians had, in the earlier stages of the battle, but two batteries of four guns each, occupying a position behind their forces. Through massed attacks the Germans, supported by a furious artillery bombardment overran the trenches and the Canucks, fighting like tigers, were swept back to these two batteries of field guns.

There, for some time, the gunners, swearing, sweating, fighting like fiends of the pit, held back the gray-clad hosts who swept forward to capture the guns.

Wave after wave was mowed down under the terrific fire. Under the frenzied, lashing orders of their officers the waves rolled on, closer and closer, for artillery cannot cope against such dense infantry attacks unless it is itself supported by infantry. And under the fierce hammering of the Teutons, who vastly outnumbered them, the Canadian infantry had been temporarily swept back of the guns. Many of them, too, lay dead or wounded in the trenches, and many had been taken prisoners.

Finally the Germans were almost upon the guns. The majority of the crews were dead, or lay wounded and writhing near their field pieces.

Those who were left prepared for the parting volley, manning what number of guns they could, with their decimated ranks. In firing that last round, they made history.

In manipulating the guns, they contrived that the shrapnel should explode at zero, which meant that the rain of death exploded as it left the muzzles of the guns, killing the gunners and spitting destruction in the faces of the oncoming hordes who had yelled in triumph as they came on, finally to capture the batteries.

Then the last of the gunners disappeared in a vortex of swarming Huns, frantic for vengeance.

It was the first time in the war that artillerymen, unsupported by infantry, ever performed that feat.

The last explosion, at zero, will live in the annals of the world's war, preserving the record of a deed which meant certain sacrifice for those performing it.

In the counter-attacks which followed the occupation of this ground and the capture of the batteries by the Germans, British and Canadians recaptured a good part of the ground and one of the batteries.

Surely, the Germans were discovering that there were still obstacles on the road to Calais!

Meanwhile, my Pats had seen some lively fighting in Polygon Wood, though their brothers to the left – which deployment, by the way, contained some of the Canadian "kilties" who had welcomed the Patricias while marching into Ypres – had thus far had a harder time than the Pats.

Their casualties had been severe, too, and it was during those few days that I lost two warm friends.

There was the Provost Sergeant, who had been shot through the body, but it seemed at first that he would recover. He was cheerful when taken away, and promised the boys that he would be with them again shortly. But two days later came the word that he had died. He left the memory of a gallant soldier – and a wife and three children to mourn him.

Then there was Corporal Walden, who was also shot through the body. From the first it was evident that the poor boy was fatally wounded. His young face, which had been happy and carefree, with the zest of a great adventure shining thereon, became immediately gray and pinched and drawn. The frank smile had faded forever.

With strange suddenness hollows appeared in his cheeks. He twisted and turned upon the stretcher in the dressing station, trying in vain to ease the pain, but each new position seemed more unbearable.

He would try to thank the attendants as they turned him. "Oh, yes," he would mumble, "that's better." But in a moment they would have to turn him again.

Walden had been liked by them all. Medical attendants and stretcher bearers did their best to ease his pain, but without success. There was the touch of but one hand that would do that, and the time-old ghostly figure was not yet ready to apply it.

However, Death has his moments of pity. He drew nearer. The spasms of pain dulled, grew a little fainter.

Walden's frank smile had not been banished forever, as they had thought. It came again, illuminating the face on which the death damps were gathering.

His voice came faintly. "Goodbye, boys. I'll soon be – home."

With a shock they soon discovered that he meant his *earthly* home. Their lips remained sealed before this pitiful hallucination. Not for worlds would they have told him that he was about to cross the dark river. And had they done so, it is doubtful if he would have comprehended it.

He mumbled of good times in the past; of good times to come. He would soon be again with *her*, he said; about a month in the hospital would fix him.

With such a sunny soul as his, the last moments are not of gloom. Somehow, in a state which seemed to be of mild delirium, he appeared to look forward to an unbroken life of happiness, of faith, of love, of usefulness, with *her*.

Sometimes, too, he whispered of Canada, of the love of his flag which had sent him overseas. This, too, had lain close to his heart, it was plain to see. Then his wandering thought veered again to *her*, whom he had loved deeply enough to leave and cross the ocean to battle against a cynical foe that respected not liberty nor love nor the women and children of the world. Yes; after all, it had been for *her* he had fought; for her and for Canada; and it was for them he was dying.

"Let's go into the orchard, dear," he murmured. "We can see the sunset over here; it's beautiful! Where are Jimmie and Ida? I thought they were home – "

He was silent a moment, while a bewildered expression crept over his white face. Then it lighted with a wan ghost of the smile as he looked up.

He could see none of his comrades now. He could not see even the stony-eyed angel of death, standing by his stretcher, its cold hand extended to touch his brow.

"That last parcel!" he breathed. "It was – *fine!* But the socks – were a mile too small for me – ha, ha! – dear, I guess you forgot how big my feet are! I – guess ...

"Aren't those strawberries lovely? ... Mother! what are those bells?

...Where – is ...wh – "
He was silent now.
The M.O. for the K.R.R.'s walked over to his stretcher and looked at him.
The M.O. was pale and tired and grave. For days he had been busy and the strain was killing.
He gently laid a tunic over the white face.
"Put him outside, boys," he said.
"We need that stretcher."
Such is war.

Editor's Notes to Chapter XXIII:

1) The Second Battle of Ypres commenced at 4 P.M., April 22nd, 1915, with the release of Chlorine gas on the French positions in the northeast sector of the Ypres Salient. There was an immediate and massive breakthrough, which was gradually sealed by the 1st Canadian Division. The fighting in the northern part of the Salient lasted from the 22nd until the 28th, when the Germans shifted their focus to the southern Salient. The Canadians lost 6,000 men; killed, wounded and prisoners in five days.

2) Lance Corporal Joseph Walden, #214, died of wounds April 25th, 1915. Age 23. He has no known grave and in commemorated on the Menin Gate Memorial.

Chapter XXIV

WAITING

While this terrific fighting was in progress to the left, as I have described, my Patricias in Polygon Wood had at first expected relief in three or four days. When it did not come they were not surprised, for rumors reached them of the desperate state of things to the left. By contrast with this, they were almost comfortable in their trenches in Polygon Wood!

Nature was in ironic mood throughout the days of this hell of sight and sound, of the warring phantasmagoria of the pit loosed in the shrinking world. For returning spring, placid and weirdly unconscious of the realm of blood and iron through which she showered her glories, touched with her magic fingers wood and field.

Tender leaves budded above the hastily filled-in mounds beneath which lay many a stricken soldier. In the night, during a lull in the sullen cannonade, was audible a soft-voiced breeze, stirring among the leaves. With the acrid smell of powder in the air mingled the odor of ferns and young grasses.

During the days, and even after the enemy began to bombard the wood, birds, athrill with the spirit of love at nesting time, continued to sing among the rent branches of the trees, placidly living their simple lives of peace as if in a world apart from this that man was transforming into an inferno. Even while raged the thunders of the guns, persisted their thin, plaintive, bubbling songs. But it was when the roar of the guns temporarily subsided that they sang the more loudly and cheerily.

The fierce German attack to the left temporarily won them trenches a mile deep and over a terrain from three to four miles wide. This Hun advantage left the 8oth Brigade, in Polygon Wood, exposed in a sharp salient, with Germans on three sides. Defending the 8oth Brigade was but one French battery, of four or five guns, near a farmhouse behind the Pats.

It was suddenly discovered that the Huns were firing on the brigade from three sides, and that the position in the wood was no longer tenable. So, about the 26th of April, the battery at the farmhouse had to move further back.

The Germans now centered their fire on Polygon Wood, raking both flanks of the defending force and causing many casualties. The Huns were continuing to mass troops on their front, and were bringing up more light and heavy batteries.

However, the 80th Brigade Engineers had not been idle. They were preparing a second line of defense further back to straighten out the line that the Huns had for the time succeeded in denting.

The trenches in Polygon Wood had not been overlooked by the enemy. The daily casualties from shell fire had been heavy. The Fritzies shelled the trenches every day, taking a daily toll in killed and wounded.

It was during these closing days of April, when the Canadians were fighting with all their powers, that the world was electrified with the valor of this new fighting nation from the North American continent. The fighting men of the United States – who were later to be christened "Sammies" by the French when they crossed the seas – had been known to the world before. They had written their names imperishably with their blood, over a period of one hundred and fifty years. But this other nation, of broad boundaries but fewer men, had been unknown – and now the world marveled.

And none, of all the nations, marveled more than did the barbarous Hun! A mere handful of untrained men, but with giant strength and the hearts of lions, interposed between the German bully and the road to Calais. They tripped up the blond Colossus; they bewildered and confounded him; they dealt him such a blow in the solar plexus that he ultimately went reeling away back eastward to the Russian front, to think it over!

On May 2nd the Brigade defending Polygon Wood received orders to prepare to depart. Similar orders were issued all along the line, and that night the entire division moved back to the second line of defense.

This proved to be located directly in front of Hooge, the beautiful town that was now at once destined to fall in shattered ruins, another sacrifice to the Moloch of war.

The Pats' battalion was retired to the new trenches, ten per cent at a time, in the hours preceding dawn of May 2nd, for the order to prepare had come in the night. All equipment, ammunition and food were moved back. Major Keenan, our good M.O., with the stretcher bearers carrying the wounded men, was the last to leave the trenches in the wood. The new positions were a mile farther back.

Colonel Buller, of the Pats, with remarkable foresight and military acumen, had selected an ideal ground for purposes of defense, with the front line trenches immediately in front of a long hedge fence. This hedge fence was on the crest of a raise in the land, and was used for the supports. Its position was such that the bullets fired from the front would go over the heads of the men behind the supports.

The new trenches were not so comfortable as had been those in the wood, nor were there any dugouts. Also, the men had to crouch in these trenches, as they were too shallow to stand erect in. But, what time they had, the Patricias worked on them, and they were soon in better shape than when the battalion entered them.

It was a long prelude, counting the time passed in Polygon Wood, before the test of May 8th, during which the Princess Patricias should establish in a bloody epic of courage and suffering and death their claim to a position in history approximating the "noble six hundred" of which Lord Tennyson wrote in his "Charge of the Light Brigade." A long prelude; and now the enemy's bombardment was slowly and steadily, frightfully, increasing in intensity.

The motif was deepening, throbbing, achieving a note of utter barbaric savagery toward the climax of the Second Battle of Ypres. Not one of the defenders in front of the ruined city but who felt that the most titanic struggle of the war was coming; not one of them but who felt thrills and tremors with the certainty that – at an hour and a moment that the enemy would decide, he would mass all his forces in a tremendous effort to break through, to take Ypres and from thence forge onward to Calais.

So in the days, while the shells screamed and whined, and the puffs of shrapnel writhed in the spring air, and the diabolical munitions of war made a wilderness of a garden, the men waited, feeling the black tide of menace rising. In the nights, with star shells illuminating the blackness and the sullen booming of the guns unstilled, the men waited, and felt the black tide, as raven-hued as the shadows of the night itself, drawing nearer; nearer; nearer. Still they waited, till the moment when it should reach them, and break in billows of chaos over them.

It might seem to the layman that men waiting as my Pats were waiting; with every nerve strained with the expectation of worse to come; knowing that the apex of the storm had not been reached; would be passing their time differently than they had been in the habit of passing it. Perhaps they would be absorbed in .profitable meditation, making their peace with heaven. Maybe they would be engaged in prayer. Possibly they would be drafting rude wills.

But, if he engages in such surmises, the layman forgets the basic elements of human nature.

Are the cities of lands, like Canada, saddened by the forays of the war god supine under the cloud he has brought, even with the spectacle of returned wrecks of citizens, spent with wounds; and with the reading of bulletined deaths of gallant sons?

On the contrary, the lights of the cities of Canada were never brighter; business was never more profitable; vigor never more combative.

It is this stiffness of the public backbone; a spine that will bend but not break; that proves human nature the glorious thing it is. But for this ability to defy the blackest of troubles, the world would be today going mad.

So it was with my Pats, awaiting the deadliest eruption of the Hun volcano before Ypres. Things went on precisely as before. The Pats knew that all Canada was behind them; that there was as much courage at home as in the field.

My boys were not unduly depressed nor cast down, even though the German artillery was now increasing in savagery and taking more deadly toll than had been the case in Polygon Wood. The Pats saw to it that they kept their spirits up.

On a sunny day two of them were partaking of their rations in the trench. I need hardly remind you that the soldier eating army rations is emphatically leading the simple life.

The Huns were maintaining a disastrous artillery fire. Already in that trench a number of casualties had been tallied during the day.

Said Tim, with a pleasantly ironic glance at the rude and restricted fare just now afforded by war's rather limited cuisine:

"James," to a mythical and respectful waiter, "just bring me a cup of coffee and some whipped cream. Ah, yes, James, and I'll have two muffins, with plenty of butter. And hurry, James! I've an appointment with me tailor, you know."

"Yes, James," chimed in Jake, "you can hurry right back to the kitchen with those muffins, you know, and bring me some that are better done. These are not quite brunette enough to suit me. How many times have I told you, James, that blond muffins are *persona non grattaw* with me?"

The vicious bursting of a Hun shell, close at hand, interrupted their colloquy for a moment. So loud was it as almost to deafen them. After a moment Tim took up the conversation with James, the willing wraith, quite as if nothing had occurred.

"James, when you have replaced those peroxide muffins with burnt-cork ones, you will immediately phone down to the Messiah Club and have them reserve me a man's-size table for seven lady guests for dinner tonight. I want venison and squab. Oh, say, about four courses ought to hold us; it's war times, you know, James."

"Yes," chimed in Jake, his imagination warming to the task, "and James, you ossified mummy of unrest, don't forget to put six bottles of Clicquot on ice. After that, call Younge 4-X-Y and ask – or should I say, 'awsk' – for Evelyn. Call me when you get her. Slide, James, slide, or I'll – "

Just then he stopped, looking up. Amid the noises of the bombardment there became audible a deepening thrum, as if a high-powered automobile were driving straight toward them across from the enemy trenches, and would in an instant thunder over the parapet and tumble upon them.

For a moment endured the sound, reaching its maximum seemingly directly over their heads. Then the drone, which for this fleeting interval had dominated the barbaric orchestra of chaos, passed from their hearing.

"A 'Jack Johnson'" briefly commented Jake. This was the Canadians' nickname for the big 15- or 17-inch shells which I have earlier described.

"Go it, you kinked comedian!" quoth Tim to the passed shell. "What the hell have you got to do with James, anyway?"

"Hello!" sirened Jake, in a dulcet voice, taking up the matter of his 'phone call where he had left it, "that you Evelyn? I'd know your voice in Paradise; um-mmm, peaches and cream! I got your 'phone call, sis'. Say, was your mother sore last night, when you got home? Well, tell her to remember she was young once. My God! Ev', how they do forget that; hey, kid?"

"Say Evelyn!" cut in Tim, "this is Timmy. Forget Jakie, will you? He ain't true to you; he's got more girls than he has money. I'll blow you to a good time, Ev'. What do you say to dine with me at the Allah Club this evening? Swell mob'll be there. Myself for one; Mr. Wells, the novelist; Woodrow Wilson, the pulchritudinous president; and Tom Sharkey –

"What's that, Evelyn? 'Who's Tom Sharkey?' Don't you know? Why, I thought everyone knew Tom. He's a Spanish peanut farmer, but he speaks many languages. He learned 'em in the Fiji Islands. Ya-a-s! He's awfully interesting and a bully good fellow.

"Bring Winnie along with you. I'll send James up with the car to bring you both. Ah, what you hanging up for? Mad? Well, say, go to –"

Tim stopped suddenly. With Jake he reached toward a young fellow who had been standing next to them, laughing at their nonsense.

The young fellow, without a sound, had crumpled in the bottom of the trench. A spreading blot of red showed upon his shirt over his left breast.

In an instant the pair of comedians were bending anxiously over him.

"Harry!" cried Tim, "are you hurt bad?"

Harry did not answer. He did not know that he had been hurt.

A rifle bullet had gone through his heart.

Chapter XXV

SOLDIERS – TWO

On May 5th the Patricias were removed back a mile to reserve trenches. There they remained in the trenches and dugouts that night and all day the 6th. Though they were now back of the front line there were many casualties, due to the enemy's constant fire.

On the evening of the 7th, a thickening mist in the atmosphere brought a premonition of mighty events, a climax of the affairs that had been shaping since the fatal gas attack upon the Turcos on April 21.

Right here a word should be said of how, in that emergency, were refuted the frequent criticisms of the alleged slowness and red tape at British headquarters. Such criticism, for instance, as once found expression in the words of Lloyd George himself: "Always behind."

At this juncture it was proved that, when an essential need existed for action to insure the success of British arms, John Bull was decidedly "Johnny on-the-spot."

The French, Turcos and Canadians were gassed on April 22nd. Immediately the gas was analyzed and the masks devised for the protection of the men. On April 27th, five days after this foul attack, gas masks, by the thousands, made in England, arrived on the Western Front!

Which workmanlike haste certainly indicated to the sneering Hun that the old lion's claws were still uncut!

So, when in the Second Battle of Ypres, on May 8th, the Hindenburg harbingers of hell again released their waves of gas, adding their "tear shells" as a tidbit, the British were ready for them. Of course, this was before Von Hindenburg was in charge of the Western Front for the Huns, but the spirit employed was the same.

My Pats, to say nothing of the thousands of other troops waiting in the trenches over the entire front for the smashing climax to the German attack that everybody knew would come, were puzzled on May 7th. The fire from the German batteries, hitherto brisk, arrived in desultory fashion. Shells were dropping here, there, all over, in a lazy way, seemingly without objective. One would burst near them, and the next, after an interval, would fall perhaps a mile away.

It developed that the range finders were busy. Many new batteries had been moved up for the attack, and were merely preparing – practicing, as it were – for the deadly work that the next day was to witness.

"One of the greatest battles that history ever recorded," to quote Sir John French's words after it had been waged, was about to burst forth in fury worse than primordial, because the primal savagery of it was abetted by all the devilish science of destruction upon which the Huns, intent upon "a place in the sun," had been working in the sneaking secrecy of immoral darkness for years.

New orders came. The Pats marched to the front line trenches on the night of the 7th, at 8:30 o'clock, with songs and laughter. Impatient for the test, there were seen among them none of the long faces and evidences of serious thoughts of the hereafter that men who know nothing about it are fond of ascribing to soldiers in such a moment.

Instead of such a depressing mien, the air was rent with the strains of such classics as the famous "Louse Song." This deathless epic of the war, by the way, was composed – so far as its impassioned words went – by Corporal Cooper, of the Princess Patricias. It was first sung at a soldiers' concert given to Lieutenant Price January 19th in a barn loft 200 yards from Westoutre. Here is one of its spasms:

"Lousy, lousy; awfully, frightfully lousy!–
I want to go over the sea
Where Allemand can't get me!–
The Johnsons and whiz-bangs, they whistle and roar;
I don't want to go to the trench anymore;
Oh, my! I don't want to die!–
I want to go home!"

It was sung to a tune that one would have to hear to appreciate. It was worse even than the first line!

"Allemand" was a nickname for the horrific and hell-roaring Hun.

Then, too, the boys sang the "Daddy Song" while they marched gaily to the trenches – and in so many cases, had they known it, to their graves. To the thundering obligato of the guns, splitting the silence of the night, they sang it; sang on a spring night that nature had touched with calm and that man was filling with horrors.

The "Daddy Song" contained in its finale a slamming innuendo at "daddy" that was about as subtle as the thrust from a falling load of bricks. It was sung, unblushingly and with ferocious joy, as follows:

"Where does daddy go when he goes out?
He goes out; he goes out?
Does he call at the music hall?
Or go to see a picture show?
Where does daddy go when he goes out?
Nobody knows or cares!
Mother, beware; mother, take care;
It must be nice where daddy goes!
Many brave hearts are asleep in bed,
So beware, beware!"

As for the tune – but who ever discovered what the tune was? Keeping on the key is the last thing a fighting boy in khaki does. When an average quartet, singing the chorus of a ditty dealing with the green fields of somewhere-or-other strikes one of those barber shop chords, and the tenor yells to "Hold it!" everybody within hearing distance runs!

So, roaring and bawling and shouting their songs that either a classical music lover or a highbrow, not to mention a cardboard moralist, had doubtless not approved at all, the Patricias, the Canadian regiment that held the pick of the world's fighting men, marched on through the shot-rent night to their test by fire.

The enemy's fire subsided even while the Pats advanced. By the time they reached the front line trenches the night had grown unusually quiet.

It was a quiet that was ominous. Every man jack in the battalion knew that the old adage was again to be verified: "A calm before a storm."

About five or six o'clock of the morning of the memorable 8th of May came the change. In an instant the brooding hush was broken by a thunderous avalanche of sound, tumbling through the dewy air of the morning, roaring upward to the heavens.

At a concerted instant had been loosed the heaviest bombardment thus far of the war.

The Patricias, crouching in their trenches, together with the thousands of their comrades, defending Ypres, were at first shocked, stunned, shaken to the core by the bellowing fury of the guns.

Bewildered, they crouched there, wondering at this might of artillery unloosed; such bolts of Jove, mad with the lust to destroy, as the world had never seen.

On all sides of them were falling their comrades, sacrifices to hate before ever a Hun had left his trenches to dash, massed with his fellows, across No Man's Land to the British trenches.

Bewildered, numbed, while their senses feebly questioned their vision, crouched those who continued to live beneath this hail. They watched such a shower of molten death as had remained for civilization, which had convened so shortly before in world-peace parley at The Hague, to witness.

Over an area of about a mile wide came roaring and whistling thousands of shells. Such a pall of dust and smoke wreathed over the field that no objects were visible at a distance of over a hundred yards from any angle to the men in the British trenches.

These oncoming shells centered from so many angles on the heavily reinforced German line that often two of them would strike together in midair before reaching the bombarded trenches. When this occurred there would come a deafening concussion that would set the eardrums to ringing for many seconds afterward; for the moment mercifully closed to sound other than a dull, distant murmuring, in the depths of the stunned brain.

At such moments it would seem to the man in the trench, waiting and enduring, as if Nature herself were trying to close her ears for his protection.

Then the torpor would pass in a renewed sense of hearing; a painful sense, preternaturally sharpened. Would well again the roar, as if a thousand thunderbolts were mingling their wrath a few feet over the man's head.

Again, the dissonance of a furious "whoof " – and the soil opening in craters before the horrified gaze, as if the mouths of the earth were opening feebly hungrily to swallow the warring human atoms who sprang from it, and whom it had sustained. Thus, through minutes of waiting that were as hours, while before the dilated eyes of the men there changed the face of the world.

It was such an upheaval as must occur when, through a convulsion of nature, new lands, vomited from the deeps, are thrown upward above raging waters.

The terrain changed continually, like the scenery of a swiftly moving film. The effect after a time, upon the consciousness was grisly. For the mind refused to grasp the terrific significance of what the eyes revealed.

It was all too horrible for the mentality to dwell upon. Here, among these reverberating and uproarious surroundings, was applied one of war's sternest tests.

Was there a weakness, a lack of balance and coordination between the nerves and the brain? Here, in such diabolical infernos, did such poor devils fall victims to the chaos known as "shell shock." Only one man among the Pats so suffered that day. The consciousness wavered and shattered before this spectacle of visible death; swooping, waiting, thundering.

Surely, here was applied the acid test. The principle of "the survival of the fittest" applied to the shuddering brain as well as to the body of blood and bone.

Here, against the sight of livid death, and with the waves of black fear beating like billows against the soul, only one power could prevail. And that was the power of will.

So the stronger minds closed themselves, in these hours of hell, to all else than one consideration. And this was the consideration that makes possible a victory in a battle of blood or a battle of life.

They remembered only that there was a fight on. And they held to that thought alone!

If it were possible, the din increased. Because of the smoke it was dim roundabout, as if the veil of twilight were o'erspreading the sky. If a Patricia wished to speak to his neighbor, though their elbows touched in the trench, he was forced to place his lips at the eardrum and bawl with all the power in his lungs. Even then, the man listening would catch the sound faintly in a thin shriek, as if it were borne by the wind from a great distance.

Tumbled and roared and warred over their heads swirling Niagaras of noise, bellowed the steel spawn of Krupp's, seeking to blast the road to Calais.

Now to the men, desperately waiting, came a nerve-probing phenomenon.

Out of the crashing wrack, that was as of crags tumbling into moaning seas, it came, this mysterious note; this shred of imagined sound that dominated all that uproar. Stealthily, furtively, sneeringly, as if the lips of the god Mars himself had whispered it from his lookout in illimitable space, came the words of warning, of menace, to the ear of the brain:

"They're coming!"

Now, amid the wail of the shells, the whine of projectiles rising in crescendo, the thrumming of monsters coursing the heavens, the booming groan of death, it came again, the warning, but from another source. It was shrieked now; a faint, thread-like shriek as if a voice – or perhaps the echo of many voices – cried from another world. Again seemed to volley the words:

"They're coming!"

Piercing paralyzing dissonance of incredible volume, came the words, pitched in *timbre* that overrode this riot; a clear, faint, dominant call. It drifted by the front line trench where had been stationed Nos. 1 and 2 Companies of the Patricias, now a welter of dead and wounded. It came to the support trenches wherein crouched the members of Nos. 3 and 4 Companies, fighting like mad.

It was as if the phantoms of gallant dead who had fought for truth in ages of world battling had shouted the warning from No Man's Land of the beyond, mingling their voices in this faint far cry of warning, of anticipation, of questioning. As if the glorious dead inquired of the beleaguered living:

"Will you hold?"

I have said that the ghostly words drifted by the front line trench to the consciousness of the men in the supports. It was so. The front line trench had been wholly demolished by the shell fire. Where it had been was filled with dead and wounded men. Such as it was, it lay ready for Hun occupancy – if the Germans could cross No Man's Land when came their order to charge.

Every Patricia gun, and every gunner left to use one, had worked to the last. Time after time the machine guns had been buried under showers of dirt and debris. Time after time the men had dug them out and set them showering bullets again toward the German trenches.

Gradually, gun after gun was put permanently out of commission. The gunners died, or fell writhing at their posts, many times dropping in the open where a bursting shell had torn the parapet clean away.

Broken down and blown in by high-explosive heavy howitzer shells, enfiladed by shrapnel and Maxim fire, where the front trench had been showed now only a broken and uneven hollow. It was strewn with bodies. Some moved in ghastly suffering. More were still.

The support trenches, where repaired – to continue fighting – the few survivors from the front line, many with wounds, after their position became untenable, also suffered severely. But being farther back, the destruction was not so savage – and the men in the supports were not destined to be dislodged. Whipping their rifle bullets over the parapet, with deadly marksmanship for which they were famed, for them was to be reserved the final triumph of the day.

The bombardment from the German batteries had lasted for four hours.

The Patricias could tell from the flashes of their rifles and the recoil that the pieces were working. But, in the din, they could not hear the

Princess Patricia's Light Infantry beating off a German attack, May 8th, 1915.

explosions of their own guns at their shoulders!

It was ten o'clock of the morning. Again, piercing the inferno, sounded that ghostly voice:

"They're coming!"

At last!

Dimly through the smoke clouds the Patricias in the support trenches saw the gray-clad figures of the Huns springing out from behind hedge fences, perhaps two hundred yards away. They came running across No Man's Land in skirmish formation. Their bayonets were fixed, but the deadly work of the Patricias' rifle fire had apparently caused them to change their usual method of mass attack.

They never used the bayonets; not that day.

Unreal they looked and ghostly, appearing in the rolling smoke and sulphuric fumes like emissaries from the pit itself. Some of them, in front, were now near enough to be revealed to the vision of the foremost Patricias in ludicrous guise. Their eyes were glaring; their mouths were open, showing that they were yelling like bloodthirsty madmen in the din; they bent low and leaped like apes along the ground.

They bounded toward the remnants of the front line trench, only to drop in waves.

Even had they been destined to occupy it in force, it would have been a hollow victory. For now, of its defenders remained not an able man. Dead and wounded were now its only tenants.

Every vestige of anything above the ground had been swept away. Even the mounds of earth, left after the earlier stages of the bombardment, had been blown to atoms.

But behind were the support trenches, from seventy-five to a hundred yards back. And from them spat death at the oncoming waves of Germans.

Beneath that terrible concerted rifle fire, from the picked dead shots of many nations, the gray line wavered, broke and retreated in disorder when still fifty yards from the remnants of the front line trench.

The repulse was by rifle fire alone. The machine guns, and the batteries behind the Pats, had all been put out of commission.

A few of the Huns reached the broken trench. They did not do it by traveling the remaining distance across the open. They crawled there, on their bellies, through craters and shell holes. They sought a vantage ground to shoot at the support trenches. But most of them died there.

Ensued assault after assault on the support trenches, for now the

Huns knew where the trouble was coming from.

The attention of their machine guns and batteries was diverted to the support trenches. Sallied across No Man's Land repeated waves of gray-clad infantry, with fixed bayonets, only to break and run back. They never reached the support trenches, though they attacked time and again as the hours wore on.

Gas and tear shells were now released to overcome the regiment that the "might" of the "supermen" could not legitimately subdue. Thanks to the masks that John Bull had been so prompt in dispensing, after the first attack, the attempt was futile. However, some of the men, who were not prompt enough in adjusting their masks, suffered for it; particularly through the tear shells, as it happened on this occasion. These shells, upon bursting, would bring a sharp pain to the eyes, and immediately afterward the vision would become seriously obscured and tears would rain down the cheeks, making it impossible for the soldier to shoot.

The artillery was raising havoc with the defenders of the support trenches. It was at this point that the Huns were centering their effort to break through into Ypres. After Ypres; Calais; the domination of the Channel; the investing of England; finally, Canada, the United States, the world.

The Huns had first to take those support trenches. It was a matter of a few yards to the support trenches. Ypres lay about a mile beyond.

Those support trenches constituted the particular stone wall against which the Huns dashed their heads in vain in that decisive phase of the war.

It didn't look much like a stone wall; this ditch, lined with fighters in strange gas masks, with men toppling on every side as shells, shrapnel and machine gun bullets rained into it. But there they crouched, those who remained; firing like automatons; some swearing, some silent, but every man intent on his job.

His job was to wound or kill – preferably to kill – every Hun he could wing in those waves of infantry that came successively surging across No Man's Land, only to falter, turn and hurry back.

The job was done in a workmanlike manner. No Man's Land was thickly carpeted with gray, presenting a weird appearance through the smoke veils of many colors that billowed and wreathed above the field.

The intensity of the Hun bombardment is indicated by the fact that, of the hedge fence under which the support trench was located, not a sliver was left after the battle!

How was it possible for a handful of infantry, with rifle fire alone, to repulse infantry attacks backed by artillery fire in such frightful profusion?

If you had seen my good friend, Sergeant Christie, at work that memorable morning and afternoon, you would readily understand the seeming miracle.

Sergeant Christie – to my mind the greatest fighter among the Pats, which contained so many fighters, – was the famous Canadian bear killer, guide and hunter. He stood six feet tall, weighed 180 pounds of bone and muscle and was one of those blond fellows with steady, keen blue eyes. He hailed from British Columbia.

Christie's job that day was to kill Germans – and it was all in the day's work. Moreover, if every man in the world liked his job as well as Christie did that one, there would be no grouches left to discourage the sunshine.

At last accounts he was still on the job, and if he had been in the habit of cutting notches for the Hun mortality he created, he would have needed an Indian totem pole to preserve the full record.

Hour after hour Christie maintained his position, firing like an automaton. He set a pace that his comrades couldn't keep up with. He was with the snipers, and throughout the battle he kept two men busy loading rifles for him, while the Germans fell like flies!

There you have the whole story of the Pats' victory that day, especially when you recall that the regiment had many other men who were as sure shots as Christie, – men like Foster, Nelson and McDonald. There were others; too numerous to mention.

One Christie is worth about fifty Heinies, which is why the Kaiser's back is going to be broken in this war. The deluded Fatherland, in its colossal vanity, selected der place and "Der Tag," but it hasn't got der men!

But the day was to prove that of the Patricias' supreme sacrifice. And among the men who answered roll call in "the far country" with the ensuing calm was my Fred.

My Fred, of the Soldiers Three who had struck hands in the forest that summer day at Nighthawk Lake, only a few short months before! Whose voice had sounded with the two others'; pledging grimly in the voice of Canada:

"We're on!"

First, Rob, the poet, had gone, while he visioned Canada of the snows, the land he loved. Now Fred, the nature lover, the pathfinder, the adventurer; sunny, bonny, friendly Fred, his soul filled with the zest for life!

And for him had been reserved the most terrible of war's tragic fates: "Missing."

When is known to the loved ones the final resting place of a soldier, in that fact is a certain sad, reassurance. The mound is marked; it is known; it is remembered. The living may plant blooms of memory thereon, and water them with their tears.

But – "missing"! To be here; then to be gone; nobody knows where!

It happened in the thick of the maelstrom of the afternoon. Fred, who had fought the Germans to a standstill from cover to cover, was last seen with another man shooting from a peephole and leveling Germans with every shot, for Fred never missed. Thereafter, no survivor of the battalion could remember seeing him. They knew only that when night came, and they were finally relieved, he was not with them, nor did he answer at another earthly roll call.

His friends asked themselves many questions.

"Was he perchance torn to pieces by a stray shell? It may be! But it is more likely that he ventured into a communication trench and sought No Man's Land 'on his own.' His restless spirit was always seeking some such hazard."

He may have seen a German hiding in a crater or shell hole, firing at the Patricias. He may have gone there to try conclusions with him. He may have been killed, either in combat or by a German shell, and been buried later in an unmarked grave by the enemy."

None of his friends knew of the manner of his fate. But, in my shelter in the rear of the lines, I knew that he was dead, and moaned while the despair of these black days gripped my spirit afresh.

It had been Soldiers Three. Now Soldiers Two had found eternal bivouac.

Editor's Notes to Chapter XXV:

1) The PPCLI suffered 392 casualties, including 175 killed out of a force of 550 men. From the beginning of the Second Battle of Ypres until relieved May 9th, 1915 they lost 700 men, killed, wounded and missing.

2) James M. Christie, #1576, was awarded the Distinguished Conduct Medal for this action. Later in the war he was commissioned and won a Military Cross. During the war he was wounded twice; April 22nd, 1916 and July 16th, 1916. Christie was a legendary figure in the Patricias. He was 40 when he enlisted, and was a noted hunter. He died in 1939.

3) #209 James Foster; born Ireland 1886; commissioned into British Army, 1915; #126 Harry Nelson, DCM; born England 1877; wounded November 1916 and struck off strength; #860 Sergeant John MacDonald, DCM; born Scotland 1881; served 7 years with Cameron Highlanders; died of wounds September 15th, 1916.

4) Who is Fred? Munroe has disguised the true identity of Fred (he could be a fictitious character), but only one miner, who enlisted in No.4 Company, was killed May 7th/8th, 1915. He was #1754 John Spanswick; born England 1875; served 8 years in the West Yorkshire Regiment; commemorated on the Menin Gate Memorial, Belgium.

Chapter XXVI

ECHOES

Toward evening of that awful day of May 8th my Patricias – or the remnant of them – were in desperate plight, but hung on. They fought as only men of their breed can fight.

Colonel Buller sustained a frightful wound, losing an eye. Major Gault was also severely wounded. Both men remained on duty.

During the afternoon a message was sent from headquarters asking "how long the Patricias could hold out." It came to Major Gault, who had already received his wound.

He sent this reply:

"Till the last gun is fired and the last man is gone."

No other messages were sent – or received.

There were not more than two or three batteries supporting the Pats. They were all removed as factors, by the enemy fire, during the first hour of the bombardment.

The sadly needed relief come near dawn of the next day. Arrived the Third K.R.R.'s to take over the Patricias' trenches.

The German attack, the fiercest thus far recorded by history, had spent its force. The regiment of Patricias, undergoing an epochal hammering, had held the Huns outside the support trenches.

And right there the Hun was held for two years! Finally to retire sullenly in "strategic retreat."

The Second Battle of Ypres was pivotal. The Germans had the men, the machinery, the initiative. Since then, it has become evident that they then possessed the power to have pushed on to Calais, had they continued to have hurled the full measure of their strength into the effort. For then the Allies were nowhere near so strong, in men, machinery and munitions, as they are now. Moreover, the Huns lacked the big essential of the fighting man, the sporting spirit to take a chance.

Just one thing impelled the Huns to relax their efforts on the road to Calais after the Third Battle of Ypres, which was soon to follow. It was too costly. And Russia, then a power to be reckoned with, was threatening the east. The overrated star of Von Hindenburg was to rise there; Destiny, with her tongue in her cheek, was shaping the plan for a wooden statue which idolatrous Germans were to drive full of nails of precious metals – and pay stiffly for that precious privilege. A Von Hindenburg was to be "made" through the treachery of complacent Russian generals who could be bribed.

The Hun realized that he could lash his hordes forward on the road to Calais; inch by inch; yard by yard; mile by mile. He could have done it. But he underestimated his attrition. His losses thus far in the fighting, culminating in the Second Battle of Ypres, and destined to grow with the Third, had been stupendous. As the attacking force, he paid a heavier penalty in casualties than did the defenders.

Against his infantry attacks, supported by a stunning tempest of artillery, the rifle fire poured into his gray-clad masses did such terrible execution that he faltered on May 8th. Afterward he sullenly lay down, and then gave his major attention to the Eastern Front. In his estimation Russia afforded an easier nut to crack!

Fortune eventually favored him, but not before the Slavs had fought gallantly against the odds of treachery in their own camps, and amazed the men who, by this time, had the self-styled prefix of "super" pretty nearly knocked off by the battlers of every nation engaged against them.

Man for man, what nation among all these contending against Germany, has failed to surpass her in sportsmanlike fighting? Two elements have worked for Germany; or make it one: organized ruthlessness. Could the Allies have achieved the coordination the Kaiser's crowd has shown, the "inner ring" would have been smashed before now. But, at the present writing, the Allies seem to be learning.

Thus far, the Kulturhounds had been sniffing, trying to find a weak place in the line of the Western Front. After the battles of Ypres their disappointed gaze turned eastward.

The Western Front has decided dynasties. It established that of the Hohenzollerns, through the victories there of Frederick the Great. It first established Napoleon; then, after he had lost his way in Russia, as Germany seems now likely to do, it broke him. It will break Wilhelm. Like the little ex-Czarovitch, son of Mr. Romanoff of Siberia, the Crown Prince of Prussia will weep because he will never be an Emperor.

All these issues were bound up in the capital target shooting, at moving targets, of the Princess Patricias on that spring day in front of Ypres! The Patricias had blocked the road and saved the day.

But what a terrible penalty had been exacted from them by the god of war!

But even while paying it, they had managed to prevail, against the most tremendous odds, by super-human efforts.

For instance, there came the time, late in the afternoon, when it seemed that the Huns were destined, after all the sacrifices, to prevail. A number of them had gamed temporary lodgment in the remnants of the front line trench. From that post they were firing at the support trenches.

They had reached there only for one reason, and that a grave one to the defenders. The Patricias were almost out of shells for their rifles!

It was then that Major Adamson, though wounded in an arm and shoulder, saved the situation. Acting upon a swift inspiration, he went here and there among the dead bodies of the Patricias which strewed the narrow floor of the trench and secured a bandolier here, an equipment there. He rushed to the soldiers who were out of ammunition and distributed the scanty supply with his own hand.

Then the Pats fired with especial care. They waited till they had a full bead on each Hun figure. They did not miss.

In the evening came a full supply of ammunition. Shortly afterward the remnant of the front line trench was wholly rid of Huns. Most of them were dead. A few contrived to get back across No Man's Land in the gathering darkness.

One despairs of even touching upon all the elements of human nature that entered into that great battle. But there should be mentioned one, of peculiar inspiration.

It was the revealment of the bond that in this fight united all the elements of Canada against the common foe; a bond like that which is today similarly uniting elements in the United States, in the same exigency.

No survivor of that storied remnant of Patricias will forget how, throughout that afternoon, Lieutenant Papineau, then the only unwounded officer of the battalion, rushed up and down the trench, rallying the men, encouraging them, rendering every aid in the supreme and successful effort to hold the Germans.

Papineau was a descendant of the famous "fighting Papineau" family, originally foes of the "Union Jack" and active participants in the Riel Rebellion.

But in the world's war was presented a situation like that of the North and South of the United States, once embattled, now reconciled and fighting together against the modern Attila.

No man fought more bravely before Ypres on May 8th, to repel the invader, than did Lieutenant Papineau. There was no more inspiring picture presented of a reunited Canada than these efforts of the son of a house that had once been against the flag.

Papineau established a splendid record that momentous day, and he worthily followed it in a brilliant military career on the Western Front. For gallantry he was successively promoted till made a major, and was finally killed in action, fighting for the Canada he loved.

The toll taken of the Pats on May 8th was terrific.

At the roll call on the night of May 7th, No.4 Company, which held the support trenches, numbered 155 men. When relieved, all that remained were 47 N.C.O.'s and privates. There were no officers. In fact, there were but two officers of the entire battalion unhurt.

No. 3 Company, which also held support trenches, came out with 49 men out of about the same original number. The ill-fated Nos. 1 and 2 Companies had been stationed in the front line trench, where the enemy's fire was so terribly destructive in the first hour of bombardment. No. 1 Company had only 15 effectives and No. 2 had but 22!

This small remnant had no rifles nor bullets left. If they had they would have died fighting.

These figures are eloquent of the havoc created in this racked battalion, which previous to the battle numbered nearly 700 effectives. The attrition is also eloquent of the high risks then prevalent on the Western Front, before was organized the splendid artillery system of the Allies to protect the men. Consider that, when the Princess Pats crossed to France in December, the battalion contained well over a thousand men! After this they had received several drafts, amounting to about 800 men.

After the Second Battle of Ypres, 133 men and a few stretcher bearers were all that were left out of as fine a body of fighting men as ever donned uniforms.

Grim figures, these. Figures which on that memorable day, when their valor brought the Huns' plans to naught, placed the name of the Princess Patricia's Canadian Light Infantry in the highest of proved instances of sacrifice and lion spirit in the annals of the world's war.

Just this handful of men had interposed between the Germans' boast of "Ypres in three days" and the realization of the dream! "Ypres in three days; Calais in a fortnight." That was the programme which came to grief right there.

Had the Huns gained those support trenches, they might as well have walked into Ypres. This observation is made advisedly. For they did not gain the support trenches.

The full story of that magnificent stand will never be told. The men fought like Bengal tigers, never flinching an inch during the entire bombardment and ensuing infantry rushes.

Not one man, or a few men, but all the men; men o' the line and officers, wounded and dying, one and all showed the same indomitable courage and spirit. The losses among the N.C.O.'s alone were terrific. Of the sergeants and corporals only six remained.

The decimated battalion was removed to Ypres and remained there recuperating for several days. Already echoes of that splendid stand were in circulation through the army; echoes that will never die. For the inspiration of truest heroism is imperishable.

After this they were comfortably settled in a field some five miles farther back. There was a general official disposition to allow this hard-worked regiment – what was left of it – a brief rest from the rigors to which the men had grown accustomed.

On May 14th the battalion received orders to proceed to support trenches, where they enjoyed themselves as enjoyment goes on a battlefield. That they should be depressed by the loss of so many of their comrades was inevitable. But they were sustained by the spirit expressed in that grand phrase of the British army; the phrase that expresses the most worthwhile requirement of life; to "carry on." And they knew that is what their comrades who were gone would have them do.

They remained in the support trenches till May 18th. The next day they were sent to billets on a farm. They received a visit from Sir John French on the 20th, who inspected the brigade.

He made a speech, informing the men that Italy was that day declaring war on the side of the Allies. He deplored the losses before Ypres of the Patricias and the 80th Brigade. He praised their great work in the trenches. He said that the memory of their exploits would endure for all time.

In speaking to the English regiments he said that their badges showed no honors of the past, glorious as they were, that exceeded those won that day.

The Patricias enjoyed some beautiful days, basked in the sun and gratefully welcomed opportunities afforded for much needed baths.

On May 24th they were again ordered back to the firing line. The fighting lasted all night, with very heavy gun fire, but the Pats only did reserve duty at that time. They took their lunch on the road and heard many wild rumors regarding why they were there.

They soon heard that the Germans had managed to take another trench, and that the remnant of the "Stone Wall Brigade" was going to support a counter-attack to retake it. Then they heard that the British had retaken the trench, and captured other German trenches with it.

After remaining on the road in front of the firing line all night, with shells and bullets crashing and spattering everywhere amid an awful din, the Pats were ordered to retire to support trenches and dugouts. They were then told that there was not going to be an attack; that it was "a false alarm."

The Patricias had just received recruits of some fifteen new officers, to replace those killed and wounded before Ypres, and a small number of volunteer recruit privates. This was the first experience in actual warfare for both officers and men, but it was marvelous to note how quickly the attitude of the cool fighting veterans of the command steadied these newcomers. The effect was especially noticeable upon their new superior officers.

It didn't take long. For those Canadians had come there to *fight*, and they were looking for it that night. It was just a matter of leading them to the fracas. They had joined for that purpose; they wanted to come to grips with the enemy, just as the first Pats had done these past weary months.

From where they were they could see nothing, and there is nothing which tries the nerves so much as to be fired at in the open without being able to see the enemy to retaliate. This was the plight of these new officers and recruits of the Pats. They bore themselves well under it; a little nervous, only they hated to have Heinie enjoying all the fun!

Heavy winds and very cold weather for this season of the year now prevailed. It was poor weather for crops. But what did the Patricias care for crops, even though some of them had been interested in such matters at home? They were soldiers now, engaged in a struggle of life and death.

They spent the 27th and 28th of May trying to make themselves as comfortable as circumstance would permit. Here they proved the power of philosophy. Most of them told themselves firmly that they were comfortable – whereupon they *were*!

They were now in Ypres, the latest order having taken them there. Notwithstanding the reduced size of the battalion they had for the past few days had their usual work to perform. They had long, tiresome marches in the dark, loaded down with ammunition, equipment and rations. The gait was slow with the usual jerky stops.

Often these abrupt stops would be accompanied by the rifle of a man in front colliding with the head of the man behind, or perhaps in the chest. Maybe, in such case, the weapon would even cut the face of the rear man. At such moments mental words of sulphur, with no molasses, would flit through the brain of the man assailed.

The men in khaki are nothing if not philosophical. But these marches amid necessary quiet in the dark, with their short spurts and jerky stops, with the thuds of rifles colliding with the anatomy of the man behind, are hard on the temper. A soldier's troubles are not wholly confined to the trenches!

"Hole to the right," or "Hole to the left," is passed along the line. Then is passed the word, "No talking!" even though a rifle has just caught you in the face. A little more jerky progress and a stop; this repeated time and time again; the programme going from dark till 10 or 11 P.M. Then the mud of the trenches; a hole here; a bridge there.

Then – most grievous injury of all! – back comes the word along the line: "No smoking!"

Whereupon, deeply disgusted with army life, the boy his mother raised to be a soldier, registers a silent protest, deep in his soul. It takes this form against imperious discipline that will even bar fags, though the precaution be necessary:

"Aw, go to hell!"

I pass to a scene in Ypres on May 26th.

A section of one of the companies was passing through a ruined city. They chanced upon the body of a dead Irish soldier lying in the street. He had belonged to the Fifth Lancers. His number was 4281.

The Pats held a brief council. They decided to bury the soldier where he fell.

They procured a shovel and pick and dug a grave there. Perhaps two and a half feet of earth and stone covered the body, which they wrapped in a blanket.

"Say the Lord's Prayer, Jack" was suggested by Pipe Major Colville. He complied, while a half-dozen Canadian privates waited about the rude mound with bared heads.

Could the dead man's friends in Ireland have witnessed this rite performed by brothers from across the sea, it would have accomplished more toward cementing the bond between the peoples of the British Empire than would all the propaganda of a hundred years!

Editor's Notes to Chapter XXVI:

1) Agar Adamson went on the command the Patricias. He recorded in great detail the life of the Regiment in Letters of Agar Adamson, CEF BOOKS, 1997.

2) Talbot Papineau was killed at Passchendaele on October 30th, 1917.

Chapter XXVII

SOLDIERS – THREE ?

On May 28th General Allenby visited the temporary headquarters of the battalion. He was accompanied by General Snow and a few other staff officers.

The effect of their visit was soon felt. The battalion was ordered to pack all blankets and equipment and to prepare for a short march.

At 3 P.M. the order was carried out. All blankets were wrapped in rolls of ten and piled on transport wagons. The battalion, now of small numbers, was marched about six miles to tents already erected and quite comfortable.

Then, with extra suddenness this time, came another order, and by the 1st of June my Pats found themselves marching away from the Ypres Salient, in which they had won enduring laurels.

For the first time since arriving on the fighting front they were now in the French portion of Belgium, and frankly, they appreciated the transfer to the Armentieres salient.

In reaching the new stand the P.P.C.L.I.'s passed through Renninghelst, Dranoutre, Locre, Bailleul, Steenwerck and other small towns. The march took two days and covered some twenty-five miles.

The difference from the vicinity they had left was marked. The country was beautiful, caressed by the breath and smile of approaching summer. The farms were larger – and much cleaner than those upon which they had in recent months been quartered during rest periods. The farmers were much more prosperous.

Also, they were French, and the Belgians suffered by contrast, in the estimation of the boys. The Belgians had always been surly, distant and unfriendly, but these French people were sociable and given to entertainment.

This part of the line was very quiet, it appeared. It was reported to the Pats that a whole brigade had just occupied this trench for a week, and during that time it had suffered only four casualties.

Whereupon the Pats, now only 250 strong, proceeded, on taking over that trench, to boost the proportion of casualties, to be suffered by themselves! Of course, however, they saw to it that plenty of reprisals were exacted.

The Patricias succeeded immediately in their lively intention. During the first four days they suffered four casualties; one a day. This was certainly doing better, from their standpoint, than the brigade which had preceded them! But it certainly fell far short of the pace to which they had been accustomed. For, even before the slaughter of May 8th, the battalion's casualties had reached as high as forty a day.

A word of explanation is required here, regarding the method of "Pat's Pets," whenever they reached new trenches. If those trenches had the reputation of being quiet ones, the situation always changed directly after the Pats entered them. Within a few days they were certain to become uproarious.

In fact, it was the same with the entire 27th Division, which was one of the most aggressive organizations that ever butted into the Western Front, looking for trouble – and finding it. Canadians and English alike; both were over there for no tea party, but to fight. And their idea of a fight was to fight all the time.

This irritated the more stolid Fritz. He saw no reason why he should not be allowed to rest between fights, and dream of the Rhine, and sauerkraut, and beer, and the yard-and-a-half of German dog that he left behind him.

However, the members of the 27th Division saw no reason why Fritz should be allowed to dream. They had a method of disturbing these excursions of fancy to a pretzeled Beulah Land. This method always produced, and speedily, glorious fighting all up and down the line. Witness the Pats' immediate jump of the casualty record, instanced above. But be sure that they inflicted more than they sustained!

When the Pats, or any other unit of the 27th Division entered trenches that had been reported quiet – and they were always being sent to these, it was never long before there was noise unbounded, with the maddened Heinies keeping up their end.

It was only at St. Eloi, in fact, that the Pats had entered trenches that were otherwise than quiet at the first. They seemed to like that first riot, and thereafter they worked eagerly to produce imitations of St. Eloi.

They started in at these new trenches in the same manner. Instead of taking things easy, the whole battalion set themselves to stinging, piquing, angering Heinie Fritz.

An incessant pecking with the rifles was kept up from the hour the Pats entered the trench. The atmosphere, which had been serene, was now rent with constant cracks. Whenever you caught sight of anything gray and moving, fire at it. That was the unwritten rule, and it was followed to the letter.

The result was that, before nightfall, Fritzie Attila Hun was frothing with rage and trying to get even. All up and down the lines of rival trenches, which at this point were several hundred yards apart, there was now a constant exchange of rifle shots.

Most of the Canadians believed that you get all your hell right on earth. They had been receiving a lot of it lately, and they yearned to pass it on.

Moreover, as will be seen shortly, the old adage "If you're looking for trouble you generally find it," still holds good!

Ask my boys!

The days passed by; pleasant days, drifting toward summer. On this sector, which had been quiet till the new troops came, considerable hell was now exchanged between balmy morns and dewy eves.

The morning of June 5th, 1915, was especially lovely. Throughout the brush the birds were singing. All about were fertile farms and buildings far more pretentious than those in the desolate portion of Flanders the Canucks had just left.

It was a day for gods and men. One to inspire the well-doing with the inspiration to shoot, with renewed zeal, at Huns!

Which my Pats were doing.

They were up at dawn, looking toward the German trenches, eight hundred yards away. Every peephole had its watchers. They were not looking at the sky, though it was tinged with the rosy blush of morn.

The universal hope was that it would prove a busy day. To somewhat paraphrase the poet Longfellow, when he dealt with the village blacksmith:

"Something attempted: kill a Hun –
And earn a night's repose!"

The Pats' snipers had selected a spot in the rear of their trench, overlooking it by some twelve feet. The eminence, which afforded a fine view of the German line, was covered with brush in which the snipers were wont to secrete themselves.

From this observation point a very alert watch was constantly maintained for German heads, or any other wooden obstruction that chanced to be moving around the Hun ditch.

At daylight the lookout reported some men moving on a hill behind the German lines, a thousand yards away. It was thought perhaps they constituted a ration party, advancing to the German lines.

Spoke Private Nelson, one of the best snipers in the battalion, to

Private Pendy.

"Jack, let's get out over here and try to cop one or two of those boys on their way back."

So, with two well-oiled rifles and with two field glasses, the pair went back from the front trench to the snipers' elevation.

They sprawled on their stomachs on the ground, feeling sure that they could not be seen. With the glasses at their eyes they lay there perhaps a half hour while the sun still hid in the eastern sky. Nature was preparing to give the Western Front a perfect summer day.

Their eyes strained through the glasses, pointing at the hill, while they hoped for the return of that party. Still nothing could be seen.

Finally a sharp crack sounded. A bullet landed near them. They remained quiet, shrouded by the high grass, their rifles lying close to their hands.

In five seconds there came another crack, also close at hand.

"Nelse," asked my Pendy, "do you think these are meant for us, or are they overshooting from the Heinie trenches?"

"Oh, overshooting, Jack," answered Nelson. "I don't think they're meant for us. We were here all day yesterday and were all right. Nobody can see us here."

Nothing more was said. Not more than three seconds passed, hardly a breath after Nelson's last word. Then:

Bang!

The sound was more than an ordinary crack. It was the signal that a bullet had torn into some object, close at hand.

Remember, that bullet had whizzed from the muzzle of a rifle from 800 to 1,000 yards away. It was the third to lodge around the pair within a minute.

Now it was to be learned that the shots had been intended for the two snipers, and that again the marvelous telescopic sight rifle of the Germans had made good.

Nelson and Pendy still lay on their stomachs, each leaning on an elbow, field glasses at eyes turned toward the hill.

With this especially loud crack, like the sound produced by the breaking of an electric light bulb, only louder and sharper, Nelson dropped his glass. His startled gaze turned.

"Jack!" he cried. *"You're hit!"*

Pendy did not answer. He rose quickly and stepped down into the trench.

Blood was spurting through a hole in the khaki over his breast.

Comrades sprang toward him as Nelson yelled for assistance. The hands of veterans of the trenches have, through grim experience, grown swift and deft. In a flash they stripped away his coat and shirt and clutched for emergency bandages, which are always in the kit of the soldier.

It was high time. From a wound in the right breast pulsing jets of blood were leaping, like miniature intermittent fountains. These jets shot fully four inches from the skin before they wavered and fell earthward.

The bullet had entered the right breast and passed through the body, emerging at the lower end of the shoulder blade and thence on through the cloth that covered it. There was only a slight hemorrhage at the back, however.

In passing, the bullet had cut a portion of the auxiliary artery and then coursed through the top of the lung. Also, for good measure, it went through the brachial plexus, producing an ultimate paralysis of the right arm that lasted for some time. In finally emerging, it went dangerously close to the spinal column, and then hustled on looking for another victim!

Certainly, the unknown sniper did a workmanlike job. From his standpoint, after such painstaking effort it is regrettable that the victim of that shot was not wholly annihilated, but still lives to interpret for me the story I would tell in words of my own if the Great Arbiter had given me the gift of speech!

However, had it not been for the quick thought of Sniper Jim Foster, the job would have been probably completed right then and there.

As they stripped away his clothing, Jim noted the jets of blood, spurting as if a water hose pipe had been cut. In a flash he had thrust a finger into the wound.

"Quick!" he yelled. "The bandages!"

Comrades of the trenches are rude and primitive in methods, perhaps, but when it comes to "first aid," they are *there!*

Swiftly the bandages were applied and the hemorrhage was stopped. Then the good boys and brave Corporal MacIntyre, of the stretchers, came rushing to extend aid.

Pendy shook his head and started to walk toward the end of the trench, beyond which was the dressing station.

A half-dozen comrades followed him, carrying the stretcher, imploring him to let them help him out of the trench. Then they would put him on the stretcher and carry him to the dressing station.

He shook his head and walked on. He was too weak, too numbed with the shock, to talk. But he remembered that, if he could walk the half-mile to the end of the trench, they could then gain the open and be partly out of range of the German rifle fire.

Otherwise, if they left the trench before they came to the end, they would be still within rifle range, and the snipers of the Huns would have another excellent chance. The trench was too narrow to admit of his being carried through it on the stretcher. So there was nothing else to do than to walk.

He reached the end of the trench. The others helped him out. They put him on the stretcher. He could not have walked any further. They carried him to the dressing station.

The M.O., a bright, keen, capable young fellow, stripped off the clothing that the boys had gathered about him. He lay on the stretcher, bare to the waist.

The M.O. looked at the wound, swiftly attending it. Then he looked at my Pendy.

"Man!" he said, "your life depends on your keeping absolutely quiet. You are not to move at all!"

Pendy lay silent. The M.O. continued:

"Remember! Absolutely quiet! If you move at all, the hemorrhage will likely start again and you will bleed to death in a few minutes."

Again he shook his head. "I don't know how you ever got here?" he said.

Dreaming it all, from my shelter far back of the front lines, I next saw my Pendy upon a cot. His face was white; his eyes closed; he did not stir.

I woke, whining, tensed, shaking all over. The vision faded; the vision I knew for truth.

Was it to be, after all, Soldiers Three in the fields of death?

Chapter XXVIII

" CARRY ON ! "

From this time on my active interest was transferred from the front. It was centered in the fate of the man who had been taken to the rear. It followed him back to England across the Channel; it remained with him through the weeks and months of his battle for life, the issue of which was at first dubious. It lay with him during his long and weary period of convalescence.

My spirit turned sadly from its constant following of the Patricias, both in my waking and sleeping hours. The man I loved above all was no longer with them; never again would he battle in the trenches. His shattered arm would prevent that.

But, aside from this, was the consideration of the breath of death, the breath which congealed my soul.

Like Bob and Fred, the gallant pair of the Soldiers Three, so many of my friends of the regiment had left this world forever! New faces had succeeded most of those I had known and loved. Visioned with my weird power, these new faces were those of strangers. Had I met them in the flesh, they would not have known me.

So dumbly, humbly, forlornly, I turned to my world, now peopled with the heroic wraiths of the past. Wraiths of the fields beyond, that seemed calling to my Pendragon to come!

So, before telling you the remainder of my tale, and of the further fortunes of Pendy and myself which ultimately brought us back to the Northland we both love so dearly, I will relate very briefly the subsequent history of the Patricias up to the time Colonel Buller was killed.

It was a gallant history. The successors to those who had fallen in the spring campaign of 1915, rallying around the few veterans who were left, nobly maintained the honor of Canada's premier regiment.

They "carried on"!

The P.P.C.L.I.'s remained in the trenches at Armentieres for a week. Then they retired to houses in the rear of the trenches.

While there they received reinforcements of 500 McGill students.

These were divided into three groups and they were fine athletic fellows.

Ensued for a month the humdrum of trench life. Then the 27th Division received orders to march south. They entrained near Albert and proceeded by short comfortable marches through a beautiful farming country. They went to a place called Bray.

They were relieved by French at Cappy and Eclusier. Here there were many marshes and chalk hills. Rations had to be brought up in barges on the Somme Canal. In this work the Canucks revealed the training of their native land. They handled scows, barges, and boats like deep-sea sailors.

Here, too, the Canadians received their first trench mortars. These were used to throw large tins, filled with high explosives, into the German trenches.

During this period the battalion had better times in the trenches than at any previous period since the arrival in France.

After several months of this life the 27th Division received orders to proceed to Salonica.

However, the Patricias did not accompany them there. On November 8th, 1915, the Pats, which Regiment had been affiliated with the 80th Brigade of the 27th Division of the British Expeditionary Force, was formally transferred to the Canadian Contingent by the British military authorities.

This was done to facilitate the reinforcing of the depleted ranks of the Pats from Canadian forces by volunteers at home, it being long before Canada resorted to conscription.

It must be understood that the reason why the Princess Patricias were first detached from Canadian forces at the outbreak of the war was because it was a selected battalion composed of men who were trained fighters of different nationalities. They were the pick of the Anglo-Saxon race, and of other races throughout the world. The ranks were not filled exclusively by Canadians. For instance, there were 35 or 40 Americans.

Besides these, there were several Boers from South Africa, some Australians, a few Russians, one Rumanian, two or three Germans, two Hollanders; some Swedes, English, Irish and Scotch; and last but not least, the grittiest bunch of Canucks that ever left Canada for a hell-roaring fight.

In all, there had been 1,200 men in that first splendid bunch that sailed from Canadian shores, and nearly all of them found death or grievous wounds.

Besides these there had been three drafts, of 200, 300 and 500 men respectively, up to May, 1915.

The general order transferring the Princess Patricias to the Canadian Contingent, issued by Sir John French, General Officer Commanding the British Expeditionary Force, contained a fine tribute to the Patricias.

It read as follows:

BATTALION DAILY ORDERS

By LIEUTENANT COLONEL PELLEY

8th November, 1915.

APPENDIX "A"

The following extract from the Brigade Routine orders, 11th Infantry Brigade, B.E.F. France, is herewith appended for information:—

I. Transfer of P.P.C.L.I.

On the departure of the Princess Patricia's Canadian Light Infantry, the G.O.C. takes this opportunity of placing on record his keen appreciation of the splendid services rendered by this Battalion to the 80th Brigade.

This Battalion joined this Brigade on its formation at Winchester, in November, 1914, and has remained with it ever since.

The gallantry of the P.P.C.L.I. during the fighting of ST. ELOI, and later during the second battle of YPRES, when the Battalion hung on to their trenches with unparalleled tenacity and lost over 75 per cent of their effectives, has won for them not only the admiration of their comrades, but when the history of the war is written, will earn for the Regiment a reputation which will stand amongst the highest in the record of the exploits of the British Army.

The G.O.C. in bidding them farewell and expressing the deepest regret at their departure knows that he is not only voicing the sentiments of himself and his staff, but also those of the whole of their comrades of the 80th Brigade.

They proceeded from Amiens to Flixecourt, and there they were used as an instructional battalion for the British O.T.C. They proved of great value to the British in this capacity, as they were particularly familiar with all the intricacies of trench war fare, and no battalion was better fitted to teach men for this work than the veteran P.P.C.L.I.

It was only one day's ride from Flixecourt to the Ypres Salient, and they left the train within a day's march of their destination, Northern France, and proceeded to billets where they remained for a few days.

There they met their first Canadian comrades, a band of the Lord

Strathcona's Horse.

As the boys were leaving the train, the band played, with a touch of whimsical humor, "Hold Your Hand Out, Naughty Boy."

General Alderson inspected the battalion here. He pronounced them the steadiest men he had seen. They were brigaded with the Canadian Seventh Brigade, consisting of the Royal Canadian Regiment, the 49th and the 42nd Battalion.

They occupied trenches in Wulverghem and Messines. They also had several trips into the trenches at Zillebeke and Hooge. This was their old fighting ground, and those who were left from former engagements appeared quite at home in this district.

Fighting was very heavy at Sanctuary Wood. It began in earnest on June 2nd, 1916 by the Germans blowing up the trenches of the C.M.R.'s. They broke through and almost surrounded the Pats in Sanctuary Wood. Although every devilish instrument of war was brought to bear on this wood, and the Pats' effectives were reduced to 87 N.C.O.'s and men, they refused to yield an inch of ground. All the attacking by the Germans failed to dislodge them.

Major Gault, while lying on a stretcher with one leg shattered by a shell a few minutes previously, heard one of the officers ask a sergeant "if there was any way to retire from the wood in case the few remaining men were overpowered and had to retire."

The Major raised himself upon his remaining leg and said to the officer:

"There is no such thing as retiring for Patricias! We must fight to the last!"

And so they fought, till reinforcements arrived.

At this writing Major Gault, with one leg, is still on duty.

The Pats held on for three days and nights; held like grim death, while their wounded were lying in hundreds about them, deprived of rations and water. The men who were left preserved their scanty ammunition as best they could, using it only when attacked.

Colonel Buller was killed while leading his men in a counter-attack. He jumped out of the trench to allow a group near him room enough to make a good start. The last words from his lips were: "Forward, Patricias!"

The only remaining commissioned officers after the fight were Captain MacKenzie, and Lieutenants MacPherson and Currie.

The Regimental Sergeant Major Anderson, was severely wounded in the leg, which was later amputated.

During the battle the 42nd and 49th Battalions made several gallant attempts to rescue the Pats and drive the Germans back, but without success. It was finally accomplished, after eleven days' fighting, by a concerted attack with reinforcements of artillery.

The wounded were taken first to the dressing station, where everything possible was done for them. There they remained usually till night, when they were removed by field ambulances to the first field hospital. There they received further treatment, and amputations were performed if required. There, too, they were labeled for the various hospitals throughout France and Belgium – and "Blighty."

It was to dear old Blighty that they all longed to go. This was the Mecca to which all wounded Canadians wished fervently to be consigned, their haven of cure and rest.

Editor's Notes to Chapter XXIX:

1) Herbert Buller commanded the PPCLI until June 2nd, 1916, when he was killed in Sanctuary Wood during the Battle of Mount Sorrel. His body was brought back to Voormezeele where he was buried beside Lieutenant-Colonel Farquhar.

3) Adjutant P. MacKenzie, MC, was struck off strength July 1916; Lieutenant J.R. MacPherson, DSO, was killed in action August 26th, 1918; Lieutenant G.S. Currie DSO, MC, left the Regiment in August 1916, and 1186 RSM J. Anderson MC, was wounded twice, March 18th, 1915 and June 2nd, 1916. He was struck off strength June 20th, 1916.

Chapter XXIX

MOPPING UP !

After the terrible sacrifice at Sanctuary Wood my Patricias were idle for a time, not having forces of sufficient experience to "carry on." But the recruits who joined the regiment showed the same eagerness to learn and get into the actual fighting that their predecessors had displayed. They felt that the burden rested solely on service, and forthwith they took up the cudgels to render the lions subsequent history of the organization, that all the world now knew, as glorious as had been its beginnings.

For this determined spirit, which has been maintained from the first, the magnificent prestige of the battalion has been responsible, of course. Those who reinforced it from time to time have seen the need of maintaining its high standards, and they have done it. They are doing it now, while I approach the end of my story.

I wish to speak briefly of a matter which is vital to every reader, of any free nation, who peruses these pages.

You have often heard, from the written word or perhaps from speakers, that the Allies are in this war to protect or to avenge other nations.

Right here I wish to draw a distinction; to put the matter in a little clearer light, as I see it.

To put it concretely, we will take the United States, the last great world's power to join the other free nations in the struggle against German ruthlessness. The United States of America is not fighting for France; she is not fighting for Belgium; she is not fighting for Rumania.

She is fighting for one nation, and that – herself. Just as Britain, France, Belgium; each for herself.

But no selfish object of conquest is contained in the war which these nations, together with Italy and the others engaged against the Central Powers, are waging. For it is a defensive warfare, carried on against unparalleled aggression and a cynical ambition to yoke the world with

Teutonic thought and shackles of bondage.

In this war, altruistic purpose emphatically be longs at home! Each of the Allied nations fights for the right to maintain its integrity.

This deadly need, quite naturally, was sensed by the soldiers in the field long before the people at home wholly realized the situation. The people of the United States required full time to learn the German purpose before they massed solidly behind President Wilson at the call to arms. It is not strange that this required an interval. It had not been thought possible that modern times, amid civilization theoretically enlightened, could produce anything so monstrous as the German idea. But the episode of the *Lusitania* started a revulsion of feeling in America which resulted in that great country entering the conflict for the reason that every other Allied contender had entered it, and that reason was self-preservation.

So, from the start, the men from Canada who were engaged in the struggle knew that they were not fighting for the motherland. They were fighting for themselves, for the very soul of Canada.

It was early in the fight that the Allied soldiers perceived the stealthy idea behind the Teutonic programme of efforts. It required no keen detective acumen to read this. Remembrance supplied the knowledge; the proper piecing together of the acts of Germany for over forty years, since the Franco-Prussian war.

Now the main issue was to be decided on the Western Front; upon the old battlefields where Frederick the Great established the house of the Hohenzollerns; where Napoleon at first triumphed, then fell; where Wilhelm was to attempt world domination, and fail.

It was well understood by Canadians how the Land of the Maple Leaf was to have fallen a victim to Prussian aggression. Germany planned to take her foes one at a time. The interruption of her programme, at the very outset, explains the rage which possessed her when Britain entered the lists.

The peculiar German mind had not taken into account that the civilized world would be at no trouble to grasp the fact that the Hun intended to clutch it, piecemeal, at his leisure.

There is ample evidence that these objects constituted the German programme:

France would be speedily conquered, the attempt helped by the illegal invasion of Belgium. England would not interfere. After a few weeks, more territory would be wrested from France. There would then be peace; or rather, an armed truce; say for ten years.

Then Britain, lulled and unready as the Teutons would hope, would be attacked. Victory, of course, would speedily come to the German supermen. Without reference to the fate of colonies, Canada should be yielded up to Germany.

That Teutons cherished this vain dream is well known. The former American ambassador to Wilhelmstrasse, James Gerard, reveals the interesting plan in his book on German intrigue. It had been gravely decided that, after the transfer of Canada to Germany, the provinces should be re-christened with guttural, outlandish, unpronounceable Hunish names!

Then would come another truce, say for ten years more. Meanwhile, the German joss would squat behind the southern border of his new provinces, a line three thousand miles wide, and leer southward at the United States of America. When the time came the Teuton hordes would pour into America from the north and attack by sea from the east.

It was surely a fantastic dream, one worthy of the descendants of Attila, made formidable as Attila never thought of being, through the exercise of the devilish arts of modern destructive science.

It was not many months – no, weeks – after the Germans had started in to realize the dream that they found they had made one fatal error in reckoning.

They had not counted on the other fellows.

Had the Junkers believed Britain would enter the conflict the attack on the world's peace would have been deferred. With the violation of international agreement in the case of Belgium, Britain looked ahead, saw the danger to the world and to herself; and declared war. Every other Allied nation has the same reason.

So the Canadians went to Europe to fight for Canada. They had no more desire to accept a future order to substitute the English tongue for one that sounds like a gargle, than had the Americans later, when the issue was put to them.

They rather liked the idea of continuing to speak the English tongue, that which gave Magna Carta to the world.

Canada, nor any other single nation, relished the prospect of waiting supine till Germany was ready to attack and steal her. In such event Canadians were ready to fight till the last drop of blood was shed and the last gun was silenced. But they well knew that bravery and muscle alone could not prevail against the devilish machinery of conquest that Germany had been massing through the years.

Canadians' realization of the true core of affairs was shown by their ready response to Britain's call. Their firm adherence to the principle for which they fight has been shown in recent months. After tasting of the very dregs of bitterness, of sacrifice, of desolation in this war, they affirmed the policy of conscription by an overwhelming vote. They were grimly ready to carry on to the death, in order that future liberty might be assured.

The clearness of Anglo-Saxon perception, spreading through Britain and the United States, is what has nullified the German plan in its inception and prevented a series of future murderous holocausts for the next few decades, in the interest of Prussianizing the world.

The determination to crush this spirit grows with the Allies' sufferings. The modern Lucifer, with his slogan of ruthlessness, shall fall as did his mythological predecessor.

This unrelenting spirit to do and die, which the Hun had not reckoned on, is what impelled the filling up of the gaps in the ranks of the Princess Pats as fast as they were depleted. Time and again almost wiped out in those earlier murderous days was the battalion. But the Huns found that, following the old myth, they had sown dragons' teeth, from which sprang further numbers of armed men to oppose them. For the honor of the regiment toiled and strove and suffered these recruits, and they added to its glories.

Now I come to an explanation of the term that gives this volume its title.

The Canadians crossed the seas prepared to treat the Hun chivalrously. They did not then know him for a Hun. They regarded him as a mistaken brother.

One out of innumerable incidents proving his Hunship, for the purpose of this chapter stands out in my memory.

It was during our attack on Courcelette. Our first wave had passed and had taken the front line of German trenches. In them were many Germans. They raised the cry of "Merci, Kamerad!"

The tolerant Canadians listened. It was in their blood to extend chivalrous treatment. They directed the prisoners back to the counting stations and swept on toward the second line of trenches.

Now occurred a fragrant instance of the treachery that is inbred in the Hun.

Those Germans rushed to machine guns left in the trenches. Many Canadians who were running toward the second line of trenches fell dead, riddled from the rear by the men whose lives they had spared.

It was incidents like that at Courcelette that bred in the Canucks, as the war developed, a spirit of ruthlessness that was in some respects equal to Fritz's own.

There was just one difference. In the Canadian brand of ruthlessness there is no treachery and no dissimulation. Candidly, he is out to kill Fritz, and Fritz knows it.

It is from such incidents as Courcelette that the business of "the trenches" is religiously pursued by the Allied armies.

When the first line of trenches is taken nothing but meek and unconditional surrender goes. The man who has whined, "Merci, Kamerad!" is carefully searched for weapons, and he goes back with his fellows to the counting stations under a strong guard. The wounded are also carried back, if they are not able to walk. All machine guns and other weapons found in the trench are removed.

This part of the work goes on while the main force is sweeping on toward the second line of trenches, or the third, perhaps. The section of the force which "house-cleans" the trench just taken is called the "moppers."

The name is graphic, and means just what it implies. When the moppers leave that trench there is no opportunity for evil left in it.

All those who refused to surrender have been killed or desperately wounded and taken away.

In the earlier days of the war large parties of Germans used to remain behind, hiding in trench saps and dugouts and in camouflaged machine gun emplacements, ready to loose the spew of death at the Canucks' backs as they hurried on toward more trenches.

Now, instead of large parties of Huns remaining for this pastime, the pleasure is indulged in by only a few extra venturesome souls.

The moppers are expert bomb throwers. And they are handy at every form of destruction.

Every spot, every dugout, every shell hole that may hide a German receives immediate and deadly attention. No mere wounds are administered in this work. There is only death.

The Huns said they wanted war waged ruthlessly. They are so waging it – and getting it back, with interest.

Chapter XXX

IN BLIGHTY

So now I leave the detailed record of the exploits of my Patricias. Their deeds at Sanctuary Wood – ironic name for a theatre of such sanguinary events – show how nobly were maintained the traditions of Ypres.

They had carried on. They are carrying on to this day, fighting with historic gallantry and deathless courage against the enemies of world liberty and justice.

Of this regiment, whose fame will be immortal, I, its first Mascot, am proud indeed!

I pass to Pendragon, reverting to the late spring and summer of 1915.

In retrospect, those weeks I spent after he was wounded, the vision of which casually I had seen in a dream, seem interminable.

I was gripped with a strange unrest, a great fear, a despair which throbbed in reactions that left me weak and trembling. My appetite failed; I slept but fitfully and lay for hours brooding; I shrank and trembled the more at the constant thundering of the guns, the savage detonations that I had hated so thoroughly since coming to the scene of terrors.

I remained where I had been since following the Pats across the Channel; with the transport, back of the front lines. I would have liked now to leave and try to find Pendragon. But he had told me solemnly that I must remain there, and I had there remained for months. I could not leave till he came for me, or sent for me.

So I remained in constant worriment. I felt my strength dwindling. I grew thin, languid, feverish. I waited, wondered and hoped, despaired.

Said one of my friends one morning: "That dog is as thin as a rail! He is worrying. He will surely die if he doesn't see Jack."

I rose, trembling. A great wave of gladness swept through my spirit. The black Thing of which I had not dared to think had passed.

At last I was assured, in these blessed words. He was alive!

My friend continued:

"We had better write Jack about it, and see what he says."

So the letter was sent. An answer quickly came.

The next few days I spent in great excitement. The month was August. But so exalted was my mood that the black shadows which usually beset me during that month, so hateful to all dogs, were beaten back. I thought only of one thing; that I was to see him again and soon.

Came the preparations, the farewells of my kind friends, the trip across the Channel to Blighty. Then I found myself on a train, speeding in the direction of London.

I was offered food, but I could not eat; I was too excited. I only drank, for I was feverish.

Finally the train stopped at Paddington Station. I was tied among trunks.

Shortly, at some distance I heard a voice, which I had heard so often in my dreams during these wretched months of uncertainty. It was the voice for which I had longed; which held for my ears the sweetest music in the world.

It was the voice of Pendragon.

With the joy of it I stood for a moment as if carved in stone; my ears cocked, my eyes wistful, trembling inside as he walked toward me. It seemed *unreal*, this flood of joy welling within me; as if the fact were too good to be true. Would I wake, again to realize the bitterness of separation?

"Bobbie!" I would have scarcely known the gaunt figure in khaki, with the pale drawn face and with the right arm in a sling, as he bent over me. But the voice!

The last vestige of bewildered doubt was swept away. I realized my happiness.

The power of expression is an inestimable gift. I am told that there are poor creatures congenitally unable to express their joy. I am sorry for them; they miss the very cream of life. But as for me; when I am glad, everybody within sight or hearing knows it!

After the jubilant reunion, the leash that had held me for days was removed. I was again with the one man in the world I was fairly living for. My spirits were now as unleashed as my body.

The boys at the front, past and present, now receded into the background of my memory. I was back in the world that had been made for two; Pendragon and myself. First he took me to a large building where there were many eatables and we partook of what was for me, following the gastronomic custom of an English day, a bite in bed, breakfast, a midmorning bit, luncheon, afternoon tea, dinner, and supper after the show; all in one. For I ate as I had not eaten in months.

I saw my companion concernedly watching my thin sides as I ate on and on and on. But I fawned up at him, trying to tell him not to worry; that soon now, that I was again with him, those sides should be sleek and round. Which they soon were!

It seemed that, following our old custom, we were now to be "on the go." For Pendy informed me we must now be moving, as he had a leave of some days and we were to visit that famous town of which I had often heard children singing at play, while they circled round holding one another's hands:

"London bridge is falling down."

Those children must be mistaken, however. For I have been there, and I can assure them that the bridge is still standing.

Not only once, but several subsequent times during our long stay in Netley Hospital did we visit London, and I will now tell briefly of our grouped experiences, not only there but throughout the British Isles.

At various times we were invited to visit some of the best known families in the Isles, and always did we receive the finest courtesies, which British people are noted for extending.

We attended dinners given for wounded soldiers, and many other functions, where the guests in khaki were made to feel how deeply sensible was England of the efforts of the men who were defending the cause of world liberty on the Continent.

One of our most enjoyable visits was to Hampton Court at Richmond-on-the-Thames. We motored to Hampton Court and entered the former home of kings and queens by the west front, bordered on both sides by short stone pillars. We went into the court through a large stone archway; proceeded through the clock court; thence through a colonnade into the Dutch gardens where grew many beautiful flowers.

We saw the Lion's Gate, and also the corridor where the ghost of the beautiful Jane Seymour is reputed to walk of nights; also the private stairway leading to her apartments.

Next we visited Cardinal Wolsey's kitchen. There still stands the table he used, set as he left it with the plate and service he employed. The iron grate and fire pokers employed in his lifetime are still there. About the table were four chairs, carved by the deft hands of those days. On the walls are the horns of deer shot by the Cardinal.

We passed out of Hampton Court through the Three Avenues; and beautiful thoroughfares they were, running straight as arrows for miles and flanked by evergreen trees.

We motored back to London and visited Westminster Abbey,

wherein stand lifelike wax figures of England's kings and queens garbed in the clothing they wore in life.

I am glad to have been one of the soldiers privileged to meet Lord Hardwicke and friends in the House of Lords. On that occasion one of the Canadian soldiers sat on the "woolsack," the seat of the Chancellor, and remarked to his Lordship:

"This is a very comfortable seat. Where do *you* sit?"

Everybody, including Lord Hardwicke, laughed.

His Lordship explained that the King and Queen sat in iron seats back of the Chancellor's chair, these seats being enclosed with iron bars. I wondered at this, as we went away. Why did they enclose those seats with iron bars? I had heard that King George and Queen Mary were very kindly. However, perhaps these bars had been erected a long time before, when royalty was more savage and like Kaiser Wilhelm, I reasoned.

During Queen Victoria's reign only one of these iron seats was occupied, even in the earlier years before she was widowed, as the King-Consort was not permitted to sit.

In the outer room of the House of Lords were shelves filled with thousands of volumes. It constituted one of the most elaborate libraries on earth.

From there we went to the House of Commons and heard a debate between Asquith and Redmond.

On the way out of the Parliament Buildings Lord Hardwicke pointed out the spot where stood Charles I when he received his death sentence.

From time to time we visited many places of interest in London. One that I enjoyed visiting especially was London Tower, where for centuries were confined many noted criminals – and others. For more or less of injustice has been dealt out in London Tower.

The names of many past inmates of the Tower are to be seen, carved on the walls.

We also visited Windsor Castle, and the famous church connected with it. Services were being held there at the time, and the choir was singing beautiful hymns.

These are only a few of the places visited by me with sundry of wounded Canadian soldiers. Wherever we went people received us with open arms and hearts. No words could adequately express the kindness we encountered everywhere. War is the oddest of necromancers. While it makes wills cold and rigid, it touches hearts till from them gush warm springs of sympathy.

By word and deed the people evidenced deep appreciation of the service of the Canadian soldiers. It is safe to say that no folk on earth could extend more cordial welcomes to wounded and convalescing soldiers, unless it be the Irish, where was encountered the very soul of hospitality.

We had an excellent chance to attest this, for before we came home we paid extended visits through the British Isles.

As I looked back and remember, no other people, of course, can approach the Irish in the spirit of hospitality. Every house is welcome to the colonial soldier. No matter what may be the feeling toward the English people, the appearance of a Canadian carries the *open sesame*. Canada's glorious record at the front has deepened this feeling among the Irish. For no people admire heroism more than the honest, hospitable, warm-hearted folk of the Emerald Isle.

Nor must I forget to mention the glorious Highlands, that gave so freely of their sons to repel the foe that unchecked would have invaded the land immortalized by the genius of Sir Walter Scott.

From every family one or more of the menfolk were in the trenches. The region of enthralling scenery had been stripped of much of its noble stock of heroic traditions; big, splendid, fearless fellows gone to do their share in crushing the menace of the world. About every table were vacant chairs.

Every day brought its memories of the absent, and too often came news that a loved one would return to the Highlands and home no more.

Under these circumstances the colonial soldier was doubly welcome to occupy the absent one's chair, if only for a cup of tea.

And it was the same in Wales. In time of the test, the bond which held the British together, for justice and the glory of the Empire, was found unbreakable by the Hun, who in his folly had hoped otherwise.

And under the lash of suffering the bond cemented by the blood of centuries had strengthened.

Through the clouds of anguish streamed the sunshine of brave smiles. Through the pall gleamed the spirit undying, the will and the courage to endure till God's will was accomplished, and the world came forth from its Gethsemane with Liberty, that the Hun sought to load with chains, forever free to lead the hosts of men.

Chapter XXXI

NETLEY HOSPITAL

We were in Blighty for a year and a half. But not all our time was occupied with jaunts such as I have briefly described. Rather, only a little of it. Most of the time my Pendragon was in the hospital; suffering cruelly, the recipient of constant and most careful attention from the best of surgeons, and slowly but surely mending.

Netley Hospital, distant seventy miles from London, was the most famous hospital in the world in peace time, it being the British army and navy hospital. Since the outbreak of the war, through the admirable efficiency of its ministrations its fame has spread.

It is a remarkable building, a quarter-mile long, three stories high and built of brick and stone. Within the giant structure are three-quarters of a mile of hallways. On either side of these corridors are hundreds of wards, each ward accommodating from twenty to forty patients.

The floors are of oilcloth, and are polished every morning, so that they glitter like glass. Every cot is immaculately covered, and shows not a wrinkle when its occupant is convalescent and out of it. The care taken of every detail within the institution is beyond praise, and all concerned with the interior arrangements are held to rigid account.

Behind this great building is located the British Red Cross Hospital, consisting of fifty huts, each hut containing twenty beds.

Just a little instance to illustrate the difference between the methods of the Hun and of civilization.

In one of the wings of the Netley Hospital were, during the time we were there, a hundred or more wounded German prisoners. These men received the same careful attention, the same food, the same treatment in every way as did the British wounded.

The reports brought of the treatment of British wounded by the Huns differ materially from this!

Allow me, too, to mention a matter which gives me considerable satisfaction to this day.

In admitting me within the precincts of the hospital a precedent was broken. For dogs had never been allowed to enter there.

The exception that was made in my case I owe to the courtesy of the Commandant, Sir Warren Crooke-Lawles, a fine Irish gentleman. Realizing the honor conferred upon me, I was always very careful not to abuse the confidence reposed in me, and I behaved at all times like a gentleman. No; not *like* a gentleman; *as* a gentleman. I am a four-footed gentleman.

What a difference one little word does make, to be sure! If the Kaiser had said "Wait!" instead of "Start!" the Hun would have postponed his disillusionment regarding his own powers.

The grounds surrounding the hospital were magnificent. Well-kept lawns were shaded with large evergreen trees beneath which the convalescent soldiers loved to rest.

Adjoining the hospital was the estate of Mrs. Elliot Yorke, a benevolent lady who entertained the wounded soldiers at tea twice weekly. The estate was called Hamble Cliff.

A fine driveway connected the hospital grounds with this estate. On entering the grounds of the estate the sweet odor of innumerable roses growing on the terraced lawn extended to the callers the most subtle and enticing of welcomes.

The patients enjoyed to the full the hours spent in this hospitable house and in the adjoining gardens. Sometimes tea would be served on the lawns under the sweeping branches of great evergreen trees.

It was the same on the hospital grounds. Every effort was made to entertain the soldiers. Two, or sometimes three, weekly concerts would be given either by amateur or professional entertainers. It was the steady custom of entertainers at the theatres of Southampton, four miles away, to arrange programmes for the amusement of the soldiers.

Reverting to the Yorke estate, the house was built by Admiral Sir Joseph Yorke with prize money received from the Dutch wars of that period. A gun which had been captured from the foc'sle of one of the Dutch frigates stands now on a bank of the estate overlooking the waters of Southampton Bay. The date inscribed upon this gun is 1788.

From the grounds runs a road which leads to the village of Hamble, a thoroughfare whereon the soldiers loved to stroll. In Hamble is a church which dates from the Norman conquest in the eleventh century. The name of the village is taken from the French. At one time the church was a monastery.

On the road from Netley to Southampton, about two miles out and halfway between the two places, is located Netley Abbey, a picturesque ruin said to have been built in the days of Henry I. It was destroyed during the reign of Henry VIII, when occurred the Reformation.

I suppose the Reformation was a good thing. From what I have heard told of Henry VIII, I should imagine that he *needed* reforming!

I looked with much interest upon this abbey. I heard that cannon balls that were shot from the river during that trouble of so long ago are sometimes dug up in the neighborhood of the ruined cathedral. But now the old walls are covered with ivy and time has crumbled the stone which the builders evidently believed, judging from the solidity of the structure, would permanently endure.

Now the abbey holds the aspect of peace. Still endure in the world, however, wars and rumors of wars as the generations live and die!

The Canadian soldiers loved to roam among these ruins – and be glad that they were still alive! The beauty of their present surroundings deepened the love and the instinctive hold upon life, just as the miserable experiences in the trenches conspired to make them reckless, feeling that life was not so precious a gift after all; and thus making them more willing to risk it in battle.

So, I think, the psychology of the military powers, while grim, is particularly effective! For war is a game of life – and death.

Many benevolent families of the surrounding countryside, one of the most beautiful in England, entertained the soldiers at tea.

The year and a half spent in this hospital, in the very prime and flower of my life, holds in retrospect the deepened impression of having been one of my happiest intervals. I was petted by everybody, from the kind Commandant and the sweet Sisters of War to the most distinguished visiting men and women.

Many princesses, countesses, duchesses, and other "esses" I cannot remember, stooped to stroke my sable coat, to pat my "apple" head, and to say to me many complimentary things.

Yes, and finally the throne, the Dowager Queen herself!

I recall the excitement which rose upon a summer day when it became known that Alexandra, the widow of the genial King Edward, would visit us.

Needless to say, in the time intervening before her visit there was much preparation and bunting. I suppose the coolest head in or about the hospital was my own.

All the wounded soldiers were in line on the grounds as Alexandra, whose face still held distinct traces of her early remarkable beauty, approached us. They were drawn up in the order of their commands.

So it chanced that, in turn, she passed before the English, the Canadians, the Irish, the Scotch, the Welsh, the Australians and the New Zealanders; this array well representing the extent of the Empire

Wounded Canadians in Netley Hospital, England. Jack Munroe, left arm in white sling, sitting behind Bobbie Burns, Mascot of the Princess Pats.

upon which the sun never sets.

She shook hands with many of them, but I may be pardoned a natural satisfaction in the recollection that she paid more attention to me than to almost any other soldier in the line.

When she came to me she stopped and looked down intently at me. I looked up at her with my engaging open smile.

She turned to those who were with her, called me something that sounded like a "noble fellow" – I did not quite catch it, because my attention was absorbed by a bird fluttering in a nearby tree – and asked who I was.

"He is Bobbie Burns, the Mascot of the Princess Patricias, Your Majesty," answered the Commandant.

Then she bent down, as the princesses and other noble ladies had done, and stroked my coat and said kind words to me.

You think I was overpowered by the condescension of the great lady? That I fairly trembled with incredulous ecstasy deep inside of me?

You are quite wrong if you think that. I was pleased; I do not dislike attention. But I took it wholly as a matter of course.

Why not? My blood was as royal as her own.

I was pleased at receiving her gracious attention, of course. But I am pleased at receiving the gracious attention of everybody. I am a democratic dog, you see. I speak to everybody and everybody speaks to me.

It is as it should be. Isn't that what King George and all of us are fighting for? To make this a democratic world – or keep it so? A world of and for the people, "that liberty shall not perish from the earth"?

Finally we left Netley for Ramsgate Hospital. This is located on the east coast. We did not remain there for so long, thank God! How I hated it there!

For, when we first approached it, I fell to trembling, and I was ill at ease while we remained there. Why?

Because from Ramsgate you can hear the rumbling of the guns in Flanders.

Finally we moved again, this time to Liverpool. We boarded the steamer *Scandinavian*. Around me was green, undulating, sobbing water, I remembered.

I was overjoyed. We were upon the Atlantic, steaming toward the land I loved best of all.

Canada!

We landed at St. Johns, New Brunswick, in nine days. In three days

Troup of show girls, visiting Netley Hospital. Man sitting at right was blinded and deafened by shell shock at Ypres. Jack Munroe standing at rear.

more we were in Toronto.

There I was presented with a medal by the Humane Society of Toronto. I was much pleased, for I sat in a chair, while Pendragon told about me, and I was admired by an audience of over a thousand people.

I confess, I am never tired of attention!

But within my spirit there burned a hot impatience. Often my gaze turned to the north.

I yearned for Porcupine, set among the northern spaces, hedged by the clean white mantle of the snows. I yearned for my chickens that were, by this time of the year, mostly hens. I wanted my rabbits.

Most of all, I wanted Rex!

And when, soon after arriving in Toronto, my Pendy told me that we were immediately going north, I was glad.

Chapter XXXII

" A TOUCH OF NATURE "

It was three months later.

Still the white mantle of snow, of which my Rob of the Soldiers Three had dreamed when he lay dying, covered the rugged Northland that I loved.

It rested, dazzling, upon the flat reaches. It climbed the ridges and lingered at their crests, as if anxious to meet and mingle with the white cloud vapors that were like moving icebergs in the blue sea of the sky. It settled in the sombre plumes of the evergreens and weighed them down.

On this afternoon that waned toward evening, though the air was keen and the icicles which hung pendent from the giant rocks were still unmelted, there was a thrill of coming spring.

In a wild freshness, in a resined fragrance it stole through the Northland. Stirred in the crowns of the deciduous trees a southwesterly wind. It breathed of long, languorous, sun-drenched days to come; of fantastic shadows stealing over the rippling waters of winding lakes; of Canada, fairest of forest dryads, dreaming in the vapors of incense rising from the brown urn of the soil.

Through the day I had followed my Pendragon in the bush. He strode ahead, the crackle of breaking sticks and twigs mingling with the soft scuff of his snowshoes. I padded along without trouble, as the snow was firm enough to bear my forty pounds.

The sun was low in the west now. I knew that soon we would be stopping to camp for the night.

The shadows deepened below; above us the arch of steel-blue sky darkened to purple.

Here in the bush I could not see it, but I knew that from a rocky hill crest I could be watching the red coals of the sunset cooling to gray ashes on the hearth of the west.

Suddenly Pendragon stopped. I anticipated supper. I wagged my tail.

Soon came the ringing of his woodman's ax. With the speed that only those can understand who have fared through the wilds, wresting from

Jack Munroe and Bobbie Burns, Toronto, 1917.

them their living as they went, he prepared for the night.

The rude shelter was built. His blankets were unrolled. From over the crackling fire stole the odors of savory bacon frying, and of steaming coffee. Soon we fared like two kings.

After he had gone to sleep I lay by the dying fire. My nose between my forepaws, I watched wistfully. For what? I did not know.

I was oddly restless; apprehensive; fearful. The strange sense which had aforetime warned me of trouble was again disturbing my spirit.

The purple of the twilight had long since been swallowed in the maw of the dark. The hint of spring had been buried with the sunset. In the air was now a wintry chill. Enfolding us was the menace of the night.

No; it was not the night itself. How many hours of dreamless slumber had I passed in the dark security of the forest, where no police are necessary to guard, as in lighted cities!

No; it was something alien, sinister, intrusive, this menace that the night held.

I sensed it and lay trembling, alert, with wistful gaze that was not sharp enough, however, to pierce the gloom outside the wavering arc of radiance cast by the dying fire.

Roundabout was silence, that usually I found so soothing in these wilds. But now it was a thing of terror, a brooding strain that would presently snap and release an appalling climax which it was now breeding.

I stole a fearful glance at the shelter of boughs. A flame leaped up from an embered log in the fire. I dimly beheld Pendragon stretched in his blankets, sleeping soundly. The ax that he had carried in the trenches, as in the forest, lay by his side.

In that moment came a sound which set me trembling. It summoned an ugly memory. Even in my present trips throughout the forest with Pendragon I flinched whenever he fired his rifle, because of the memories of those evil days overseas.

Now I heard the sound again. Startlingly close there rumbled the thunders of the guns that, for so long during my stay on the Western Front, set me cringing and disturbed my rest.

The cannon fire I had heard in embattled Europe now split the silence of Canadian forests in the night!

Had those stealthy enemies followed us home across the seas?

Then I saw something else, that froze my blood.

Out of the shadows of the bush, into the wavering circle of radiance cast by the dying fire, leaped several crouching, savage, gray-clad figures.

Bent like uncouth apes, as had been their fore-runners leaping to their death in No Man's Land at the Second Battle of Ypres, they came bounding toward the shelter under which slept my Pendragon. In the hands of these ghostly Huns were fixed bayonets.

I wriggled in an effort to rise and defend Pendragon, but a paralysis of horror held me. My snarling mouth loosed a strange sound, the mingling of a growl of rage and a whine of fear.

Like mad I struggled to rise, but the net of my fears held me helpless, threshing, raging.

"What's the matter, Bobbie? Dreaming again?"

My eyes open; at first bewildered, incredulous; then sparkling with joy.

In wild relief my glance flashed about my *real* environment.

We were in the living room of the cabin on the edge of the forest at Porcupine. There were the moose heads upon the log walls. Pendragon's rifle and ax lay extended on rests next them. Rugs of soft skins covered the rude floor. Charred logs popped and roared and crackled in the fireplace. A soft wind of April crooned in the still white outer spaces.

"Snow sliding off the roof wake you, Bobbie?" asked the beloved voice again.

Snow sliding from the roof! So *that* was the sound which had suggested to my drowsing brain the thunders of the guns!

I stood at his right side, fawning up at him, awaiting a caress. Then – I remembered.

Again o'erswept my spirit a wave of passioned revolt. For his right arm hung stiffly at his side. What had Fate given him, who had sought the great adventure?

But, after all, he had returned. He alone of the Soldiers Three, still lived, and health was returning to him, a glorious flood. While Rob lay in Flanders, in a grave marked with a wooden cross – and Fred – where lay he?

Yes; he was back with me in our beloved Northland. But I knew that it would never be quite the same again. The dream just broken, of ranging the wilds with him as we had done for years before Canada called her sons; it was a dream of the past.

For a woodsman needs *both* his hands. We would never fare far afield again.

With my heart suddenly bursting with sorrow for him, I rose, a little stiffly, and walked around to his left side; walked humbly, with my eyes upraised in love to his own.

His gaze followed my progress, which may have been a little slower than in the past. His left hand descended to softly rub my head. He looked down at me seriously, as he had looked in the memorable moment when, before the great adventure, I begged him and he told me: "You shall go!"

"Dreaming of the old hikes, Bobbie? Were you? Oh, well, all things must end; and you know, you're growing old."

Growing *old*? And all things must end?

How can such things be, when there is immortality?

I looked up at him and tried to tell him that he was wrong. I spoke with the only speech I know; soft mutterings, deep in my throat.

But he was not looking at me. He glanced down at his right arm, that hung stiffened and useless at his side.

"Ah, well, Bobbie," he said, a little absently, "I guess it was worth it!"

Then passed the last vestige of my melancholy mood. Came one in its stead of fierce exaltation. Because of his arm; because of the countless sacrifices of myriads, on the battlefields and in the support trenches of the homes; because of the lives laid down and the inspirations which flow from the souls that wrong has sent across the border, God's will was accomplished.

Never should the Hun set his bestial foot upon the sacred soil of Canada. Never should his touch stain the Flag of the Crosses of freedom. Never should he invade the storied land of Canada's great neighbor to the south. Nor upon that of the land below it, now torn with internal strife. Nor, finally upon the ground of the great sun-bathed continent that lies below the Gulf.

Herein, as through the world, the fate of oppression was sealed and the hour of deliverance for Liberty was at hand.

So, being wise, I knew that it was right that he had been maimed. We would do as best we could, and then, again whole, each of us revived in endless youth, we would range together the fields of the Beyond.

Pendragon was speaking again. I knew the tone; and loved it best of all. It was a little teasing.

"Anyway, you should learn to stay at home, old fellow. A rolling stone must stop some day. And now you have responsibilities. You are a family man, remember!"

I wagged my tail as my look, now proudly possessive, followed his own.

It was for this; the bond supreme, the life tryst with eternity which requires the peopling of the ages, that I had hurried home in odd restlessness ; eager, thrilling, wistful, like:

"A hunter home from the hill."

There by the glowing fireplace lay Myrex; my proud, shy, beautiful Myrex, snugging her six wee children; hers and mine.

Myrex?

Her name seems familiar to you? Why not?

I have told you of her, earlier in these pages. I call her Rex, for short.

She is Myrex; my love, my pal, my wife. She is mine, and I am hers; her soldier, home from the wars.

THE END

John Alexander Munroe
(1873-1942)

Jack Munroe was born on the family farm near Boularderie, Cape Breton on June 26th, 1873. At 12 years old he left Nova Scotia with two elder brothers to find work in the Montana mines. He attended school in Montana where he was an excellent athlete, excelling at football and boxing. By 18 Jack was prospecting in the American West, and experiencing the rugged life of the tough mining towns. In 1900 using his athletic skills and an extraordinary strength he first boxed in the public arena and by 1901 had won three fights before losing his first, a 20 round bout, with the experienced professional, Hank Griffin.

In 1902 the Heavyweight Champion, J. Jeffries was touring the mid-west offering a $250 purse to any fighter that could stick four rounds with him. On December 19th, 1902 Munroe faced Jeffries in Butte, Montana, managing not only to last the four rounds, but knocking down the Champ and winning the $250. This launched Munroe's professional boxing career. Over the next two years Jack would climb up the boxing rankings. On August 26th, 1904 he was the first Canadian to challenge for the World Heavyweight Championship when he met Jeffries in San Francisco. It was a terrible outing for Munroe who was knocked out in the Second Round.

Munroe continued to box, having five more bouts, including a 'No Decision' with the famous Jack Johnson on June 26th, 1905. In April of that year he found Bobbie Burns in Mexico City. The immediate heart-felt bond between the two would last 14 years.

By 1906 Jack had returned to his true love, mining, prospecting, and staking claims in Northern Ontario. He founded the town of Elk City (later Elk Lake) and became it's first Mayor in 1909. Munroe moved to Porcupine in 1910 and became part of the great mining boom staking claims around South Porcupine and Golden City.

He added to his already significant reputation during the great fire of July 1911 when during a great fire he controlled the evacuation and coordinated the bucket brigade of 150 men. They doused the buildings with water preventing the fire from spreading and saved Golden City.

With the outbreak of war in August 1914 Jack and Bobbie made their way to Ottawa to join the Princess Patricia's Canadian Light Infantry.

Jack Munroe, the boxer, circa 1904.

His Attestation Papers list Munroe as 5 foot, 11 3/4 inches with an expanded chest measurement of 44 inches. Interestingly under "Are you prepared to be inoculated," was written, "not wishing to be inoculated." The rest of his war story is told dramatically in *"Mopping Up!"*

One important fact he does not emphasize in his book is how severely he was wounded. The bullet entered his right shoulder and entered into his chest; it is described, "bullet entered 1" below middle third of right clavicle and emerged back through scapula near inner margin... He spat blood for an hour or two after he was wounded. The subclavian artery was injured and formed an aneurism. Also complete paralysis of muscles of shoulder and upper limb. Operation for ligature and cure of aneurism was performed October 12th, 1915. Suture of brachial nerve trunks performed December 8th, 1915."

It was clear Jack would never regain use of his right arm. Another doctor wrote, "...paralysis of right arm caused by GSW through chest severing nerves of the brachial plexus. Can abduct arm 45 degrees and can flex elbow fully. Complete loss of power right hand which is red and cold. Sensation has returned but is now hypersensitive." There was also clubbing of his fingers.

In December 1916 Jack Munroe returned to Canada for further treatment, accompanied by his ever-faithful Bobbie. On arrival in Toronto Bobbie was greeted like a home-town hero and was honoured by the Toronto Humane Society in January, 1917. The event was attended by 1,000 people. Jack and Bobbie toured Northern Ontario, giving patriotic messages. Jack became a regional recruiting officer for the C.E.F., being commissioned in the Canadian Forestry Corps for his new job. It was during this period he finished writing *"Mopping Up!"*. It was published in February 1918 by The H.K.Fly Company in New York. It sold well and Jack received $1,000 in Royalties.

Munroe was discharged in December 1918 and tried his hand at a few occupations before returning to Northern Ontario. He set up near Kirkland Lake and founded the Jack Munroe Mining Company.

In was in the fall of 1919 when Jack, returning from a trip, did not find his little collie faithfully waiting for him at the train station. Bobbie was 16 years old and his time had come. Jack never found his old pup and it appeared he had gone off into the woods to die. Their great relationship, which had lasted 14 years and many adventures, was over. Jack later said, "I felt that I lost something that could never be replaced." He never owned another pet.

In 1923 Jack Munroe married a concert singer, Lina Craine and the

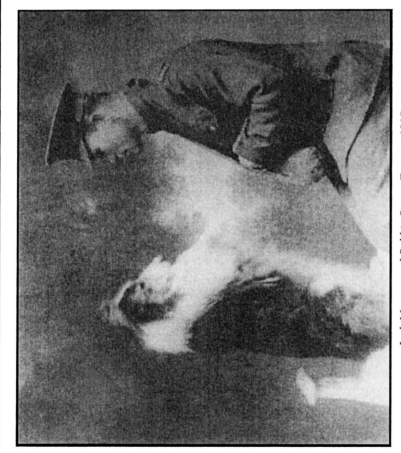

Jack Munroe and Bobbie Burns, Toronto, 1917.

couple settled in Northern Ontario, living in Red Lake in the summers and Kirkland Lake in the winters. In 1937 Jack was diagnosed with cancer and the couple moved to Toronto. On February 13th, 1942, Jack Munroe died. His obit read: "Suddenly at his home, 12 Laws Street, on Friday February 13th, 1942. John A. Munroe, beloved husband of Lina Craine Munroe. Resting at the above address. Funeral service Monday, February 16th at 1:30 pm. Internment Fairview Cemetery, Acton on arrival at about 4 pm." That was all. The legendary Jack Munroe had passed almost unnoticed. He was an exceptional man and his great adventures should have received much more acclaim than the few lines written in an obituary. Lina passed away in July 1962.

The legendary Jack Munroe is buried in Section G, Plot 2 of the Fairview Cemetery, Acton, Ontario. He was a great Canadian.

Editor's Note:

The life of Jack Munroe would have vanished if not for an exceptional book on his life published in 1994 by Black Moss Press. The Editor is indebted to Dorothy Farmiloe's "The Legend of Jack Munroe".